WITH
MORTAL
VOICE

WITH
MORTAL
VOICE

The Creation of
PARADISE
LOST

John T. Shawcross

THE UNIVERSITY PRESS OF KENTUCKY

ACKNOWLEDGMENTS

University of Pittsburgh Press for permission to reprint "The Rhetor as Creator" from *Milton Studies* 8 (1975) 209-219, ed. James D. Simmonds, in revised form as Chapter 1, and "*Paradise Lost* and the Theme of Exodus" from *Milton Studies* 2 (1970) 3-26, ed. James D. Simmonds, in revised form as Chapter 11. Duquesne University Press for permission to reprint "The Metaphor of Inspiration" from *Th'Upright Heart and Pure*, ed. Amadeus P. Fiore (Pittsburgh, 1967), pp. 75-85, in revised form as Chapter 2. University of Washington Press for permission to reprint "The Son in His Ascendance: A Reading of *Paradise Lost*" from *Modern Language Quarterly* 27 (1966) 388-401, in revised form as Chapter 3 and in part in Chapter 8. University of Wisconsin Press for permission to reprint "The Hero of *Paradise Lost* One More Time" from *Milton and the Art of Sacred Song*, ed. J. Max Patrick and Roger Sundell (Madison, 1979), pp. 137-147, in revised form as Chapter 4. University of North Carolina Press for permission to reprint "The Balanced Structure of *Paradise Lost*" from *Studies in Philology* 62 (1965) 696-718, in revised form as Chapters 5 and 6 and as sections in Chapters 3, 8, and 9. Rowman and Littlefield for permission to reprint sections from *Paradise Lost* (Philadelphia, 1966) in revised form in Chapters 3, 8, and 9. University of California Press for permission to reprint "The Style and Genre of *Paradise Lost*" from *New Essays on Paradise Lost*, ed. Thomas Kranidas (Berkeley, 1970), pp. 15-33, in revised form in Chapters 8 and 9. Eastern Michigan University for permission to reprint "*Paradise Lost* and 'Novelistic' Technique" from *Journal of Narrative Technique* 5 (1975) 1-15, in revised form as Chapter 12.

Library of Congress Cataloging in Publication Data

Shawcross, John T.
   With mortal voice.

   Includes bibliographical references and index.
   1. Milton, John, 1608-1674. Paradise lost.
I. Title.
PR3562.S48   821'.4   80-51944
ISBN 0-8131-1450-0   AACR2

Contents

Preface

RECENTLY a friend observed that studies of literature and literary figures have generally been distasteful to readers, including him, because they have so often not been concerned with literature. And he specifically instanced John Milton and his works, citing a number of highly regarded and influential scholarly books. Though I am strongly convinced that Milton and his works must be given historical treatment for us to be confident of the context in which he wrote, I certainly have long agreed with the major thrust of the observation that Milton has not always been treated as a literary artist. Most frequently he is treated as poetic theologian or polemicist or exemplar of Renaissance man. And what literary propensities the less recent past has found in his poems have usually centered on narrative and character or traditions only. The aim of the present book is to examine some literary approaches to *Paradise Lost* and to analyze the poem in these several ways to determine its literary achievement. Such approaches to the poem, seemingly disparate but ultimately interacting, allow a more complete picture of the poem as an artistic creation. The poem is more than the sum of its parts, but only by exposing those parts will we receive a more valid understanding of Milton's literary achievement.

A literary work comes into being through what I call its pre-text and its execution. Those elements which constitute its pre-text are its structure, its theme(s), its underlying beliefs or formative concepts (its thesis), and its genre. Those elements which constitute the literary work's execution include the writing process itself; the language (including imagery and sources); style (a function of both pre-text and the elements of execution); and subject, theme, narrative, or character development. The form of the work, in Burkian terms, is created by the elements of the pre-text and by the results of the execution. As any creative artist knows, the writing process for *Paradise Lost*, like any other work of art, was not a beginning at the first line, a continuous putting down of successive parcels of lines, and an ending at the last. Nor, indeed, do such elements of the pre-text as structure allow that misconception to persist. Allan H. Gilbert, among others, has shown that the poem was developed over a number of years by employment of various sections revised and rearranged or newly written for changing intent, genre, and structure— see *On the Composition of Paradise Lost* (Chapel Hill, N.C., 1947). But the completed work is an entity, unified by repetitions, echoes, developments in later sections of materials appearing earlier, and the like. Additionally, *Paradise Lost* is unified by recurrent metaphor which takes on full, or at least fuller, meaning through its repeated and various use. This is not identical with saying that there are repetitions of language, for example, the well-known symbol of Adam and Eve hand in hand, which help chart recurrent or varying forms of action or characterization. Metaphoric meaning, as I use the term, implies the meaning imbued in a word or phrase and determined by its usage and particularly its continued usage. It becomes a key to the unity of the poem and its craftsmanship, and to such matters as structure, thesis and theme, style, and rhetorical stance. A study of metaphoric meaning shows *Paradise Lost* to be an integrated poem in a literary way that has been insufficiently investigated, and it adds a significant depth to characterization, to the narrative voice, to the message, to the process of writing itself, and to style. Citations of repetitions or echoes or developments of larger narrative elements or symbols do not supply this texture. Besides, metaphoric meaning proclaims the constant conscious control that Milton exerted over his lengthy poem.

More than any other literary work outside the Bible, John Milton's *Paradise Lost* continues to be read as religious document, with attendant questions as to the acceptability of its thought and philosophy. Of significance in answering such questions is the way the poem is read, and for the most part, it seems to me, the poem has run afoul of some critics because it has been read superficially and not really as literature. It has been most frequently pursued by scholars as a storehouse of knowledge, allusion, influence, and the humanistic world of the classics and the Renaissance. And the reputation thus denounced

upon it has often been that of a dusty old classic read in school because it looms large in western culture.

What one means by literature, of course, hovers about any study.
In broad terms, literature may certainly include gesture and plastic
commodity, and the meaning or relevance of a work may be of almost total significance for the modern reader. But this demands
comprehension of literature as something which is created by a writer
to achieve some communication of idea, effect, emotion, aesthetic
reaction. The writer takes raw material and does something with it;
he does not simply present it. The communication of idea, effect,
emotion, aesthetic reaction is dependent upon both the writer and
the reader. If either fails, the communication fails. But I hasten to
warn loudly that one should condemn without extensive analysis
neither the writer (as, say, Ezra Pound has been in *The Cantos*) nor
the reader (as, say, those who find in Lawrence Durrell's *Alexan-
drian Quartet* a meaningless contrivance only) when communication
seems to fail. The writer may simply be misunderstood or he may
evoke unrelated prejudices, as in Pound's case, or the reader may
simply be too astute to be taken in by technique alone. At least there
is some communication in both these examples, and insofar as there
is communication, the work is successful at some level. Unordered
presentation of material is possible, but this elicits reader action, and
in this (as in some of the attempts of recent dramatic troupes) comes
what communication there is: a self-communication, although one
can argue that selection of material and any kind of timed presentation (even if changed each time it is presented) creates an ordering
and thus author action. The point is, literature is the product of a
mind and what is communicated is the product of two minds. It is
the responsibility of the student of literature to describe what that
mind has attempted, and how, and what the response of at least one
person has been. Whether the product communicated is meaningful
depends not only on substance but on time, place, and audience.

Poetry is an art, and the following comments will indicate why I
read poetry and what I may derive from it. The communication we
receive in reading poetry is not at all what we receive from perusing a
history book. I have not learned from Milton that out of evil may
come good, but he has made the idea more meaningful to me; he has
caused me to realize it anew, to articulate it for myself, and to see its
application in more ways than those presented in his poem; and he

has given me aesthetic pleasure in recognizing the various means by which he has presented the concept. I have not learned from Milton the ways of evil in this world or the human frailties that allow it success, but he has made such matters memorable and enduringly so for me. The occasion today, or yesterday, or tomorrow, recalls the "truth" that he has seen, the view of life's situation with its sometimes joyous, sometimes oppressive reality. *Paradise Lost* has the nearly unique position of being criticized as meaning only, meaning which the most vociferous critics have deplored (read "misunderstood"); in contrast to such readings, this book attempts to present the poem as literary work while trying to prune away some of the bases for misreading or misunderstanding. Its subject is Milton's achievement in *Paradise Lost* as a creative artist, and its thesis is that the evaluation of the epic as one of the truly great masterpieces of artistic creation should depend upon the viability of its literary approaches. The expansiveness of subject and thesis permits unity of its parts only through perspective and a tracing of approaches as they impinge on its several parts. Although sections of this book have been published previously in different form, it is not, I hope, a mere collection of essays but, rather, a total view of the poem that will more sharply focus its parts for the reader who finds these literary approaches to be useful critical tools.

· ONE ·

The Rhetor as Creator

UNDERLYING this study of *Paradise Lost* is the belief that literature is a consciously contrived product of an author's mind, attitude, talents, planning, and execution. I deplore the attitude that seems to exist among some scholars that nothing much happens between the thought or emotion of the author and its presentation as art form. Obvious though this notion is, failure to recognize it lies at the base of the antagonism one finds in criticism (particularly in Miltonic criticism) toward structural, numerological, and psychological studies.

The author is a creator and Milton associates himself with the archetypal creator, God. The poem we read is Milton's creation, a similitude of God's creation; because of its subject matter he functions as a surrogate of God for man to "repair the ruins of our first parents by regaining to know God aright." The function describes the teacher, the minister, the prophet-priest. In *The Reason of Church-Government*, Milton had equated the writer and minister. "These abilities, wheresoever they be found, are the inspired guift of God rarely bestow'd . . . and are of power beside the office of a pulpit, to imbreed and cherish in a great people the seeds of vertu, and publick civility. . . . Whether this may not be not only in Pulpits, but after another persuasive method, at set and solemn Paneguries, in Theaters, porches, or what other place, or way may win most upon the people to receiv at once both recreation, & instruction, let them in autority consult."[1] The imagery of the ear as the entrance of God's Word to his earthly ministry is a commonplace, and one might compare the mutilation of the "false" minister's ears as symbol of his inability to communicate God's Word. *Paradise Lost* is the work of a Milton who still conceived his function in life as that for which he had been schooled, the true minister he had epitomized in 1627 as one of those "whom provident God himself has sent to you [England] / and who brings joyous messages from heaven, and who / teach the way which leads beyond the grave to the stars" (*Elegia quarta*, ll. 92–94).[2] His creation becomes the surrogate Word of God, and like God he has had to accommodate his message to the comprehension of his readers. Some of that accommodation we shall examine in this study. It is not always an obvious accommodation, but then God's creation is not an easily graphed or formulated product either. Indeed, the work of Sir Isaac Newton was not only to reduce God's creation to laws and formulas but also to reassert, for the people, the reality of the God who had created so complex a world.

Like God's, Milton's creation is complex, built on structural principles and numerical organization; it is unified by elements ("ideas" accommodated as words) that are capable of adaptation and agglomeration, of destructive misuse and catalysis; it is a range of all manner of absolutes and aggregates from any one extreme to its opposite. It *is* a similitude of God's creation. The world of man created by God is presented as if through a kaleidoscope, yielding a sense of its substance and its essence. The poem depicts "actual" events of man's history and the implied action which each man in his life will undergo; it renders the thoughts of the past and present and the potentials of the future. The accumulated knowledge of the world is delineated in the poem through simile and suggestion (thus keeping time perspectives intact), and one can read what he wants, changing as twists of the instrument refocus the constituent parts or the angle of vision. The twists may predicate man's hopes and fears or man's psychological state, but throughout, the presence of the creator of the bits of glass can be discerned—whether he is the God whom Milton is trying to portray aright or the poet who has constructed the instrument. The prophet (or true minister) sees the world beyond toward which he leads his community, pointing out the paths that will end there and the paths that will detour, retrace, or pervert. The poet renders the vision, or accommodates it, by whatever means he can. The aims of the divine *vates,* or prophet-poet, are those of minister of God, and few have denied Milton that post in *Paradise Lost.*

Yet such didactic aims demand three important considerations: the specific aim or intention of the *vates,* the means of achieving that aim, and the human medium through which such intention will be channeled. It is, of course, impossible to state with exact coincidence what anyone's intention is under any particular set of circumstances. Not only can the observer not make such statement, but neither can the person himself. He can give what seems to him to be his intention—the conscious aim—and he may later recognize unconscious influences and drives, but his statement will still be subject to error, of emphasis if nothing else. And the observer can only approximate another's intention—whether conscious or unconscious—from authorial statement, from pragmatic evidence, from reader response, and from inferred signification through psychological symbolization and analysis. But the fact remains that an author does write with a conscious intention and at the same time out of his individual being, coloring that conscious intention as well as the execution. The rather recent hue and cry against the intentional fallacy has done a disservice to literary criticism by making it reprobatory to talk of authorial intention. Intention does exist and it is the literary critic's duty to try to determine the contexts of that intention. Inevitably, such analysis places the critic in a complex of experience and knowledge, and his own psychological being. That this is so can be seen, as example, in the world of humor. The basis of humor is encased in the foregoing remarks, for the comic plays upon what he believes to be his audience's experience and knowledge (most obvious is the topical joke) and attitudes. The audience will not recognize, say, an obscene joke unless they previously have understood the meanings and application of the language implied. But this in turn says that the comic knew these meanings and this substance, and he assumed at least that some of his audience did too. A fit audience is always sought by the public commentator; he will adapt to his expected hearers or try to manipulate them (the "warm-up") to become receptive. The poet is not different. Of course, there are unconscious jokes, ones in which the speaker has not realized what he has said. Sometimes he becomes aware of what he has said; sometimes he must be told. And sometimes these unconscious jokes—like psychological slips of the tongue—are the result of the unconscious. "Intention," therefore, includes authorial statement and unconscious meaning; it can be approached by analysis of pragmatic evidence, by the reader's response (although at times this may say more about the reader than about the writer), and by psychological analysis of the author.

Milton's artistic intention as an emulation of God's creation will be discussed in Chapter Two, his philosophic intention as thesis and theme in Chapter Three. The intentions are twins, and the poem they produce offers up Psyche's confused seeds for man to cull out and sort asunder with incessant labor. In orthodox terms, God's creation of the universe and man was intended to replenish Heaven with true, faithful, and loving spirits after the fall and expulsion of the rebellious third of the original angelic host. Milton's creation is to aid that replenishment positively by asserting God's great love seen in his eternal providence and negatively by countering the antiheroic element that sees God as unjust and tyrannic. The didactic aim of the prophet-poet is to teach how one knows which seed is which. Direct statement will do it (God the Father's, God the Son's, Raphael's) but few will ever heed direct statement. Accommodated words will do it, but one must listen and read, compare and contrast, and remember and evaluate. Few do. The oneness of the intention throughout the poem is scored by awareness of these elements of Milton's creation — by themselves, agglomerated, adapted. The minister must repeat himself, must give strong hints (not "tell," because the conceit of man makes only that which he "independently" determines acceptable to him), must offer the abstract by the tangible. In the sermon which is the epic *Paradise Lost,* the minister Milton gives such hints as when Belial argues that not making war will require "Hard liberty" whereas war will bring defeat and then "the easie yoke / Of servile Pomp" (II, 256-257). It is clear that Belial has exactly reversed the circumstances, for their liberty will be easy because they will "live to our selves, though in this vast recess, / Free, and to none accountable" (II, 254-255). The first hint Milton provides for his reader in this instance is that such concepts as "hard" and "easy" (and "good / evil," "life / death," "love / hate," "obedience / disobedience") depend upon one's personal drives and id, not necessarily upon some inherent truth. And the second hint lies in the allusion to Matt. 11:30, "For my yoke is easy, and my burden is light," where God's truth is that only man's yoking of himself is hard. The dialectic and reversal of image and meaning is, as we shall see throughout this study, a major device used by Milton to establish his message. The fit audience will realize the mirror image of argument, the twisting of truth, the paradox of the antidivine. Further, the minister of the poem repeatedly offers the abstract through a concrete image, as typically in these lines:

> which having pass'd
> At length into the limits of the North
> They came, and *Satan* to his Royal seat
> High on a Hill, far blazing, as a Mount
> Rais'd on a Mount, with Pyramids and Towrs
> From Diamond Quarries hew'n, and Rocks of Gold,
> The Palace of great *Lucifer*. . . .
>
> (V, 754–760)

We recognize this description just before the opening of the War in Heaven as the first version of Pandemonium and Satan's throne as drawn in Book II, and the self-aggrandizement and psychological import are likewise clear. But the dialectic point is being made which similar iconographic representations yield: the ornate, resplendent, multifarious world is evil, and the contrasting "sacred Hill" of God is simple, unadorned, and only a kind of "flaming Mount" because the "Brightness" of God has made it "invisible" (V, 598–599). Unfortunately, man is often given to material and tinsel values, and the plea of the psalmist, "Teach me thy way, O Lord, and lead me in a plain path, because of mine enemies" (27:11), or the admonition of Paul, "But I fear, lest by any means, as the serpent beguiled Eve through his subtilty, so your minds should be corrupted from the simplicity that is in Christ" (2 Cor. 11:3), is little heeded.

Pragmatic evidence of Milton's philosophic and artistic intention will emerge as we proceed, the philosophic intention being achieved through the artistic execution. If nothing else, the structure and numerological relationships indicate the complexity of creation; if nothing else, they evidence the existence of the creator behind the creation. Such examples of the pre-text manifest the nature of artistic work that lies between the thought of the author and the presentation in artistic form. In general, the overall device is a philosophic one expressed in literary terms: the world of opposites, each of which moves from one extreme to the other and, for the most part, which together create the vagueness of distinction characteristic of man's thought. That is, right reason and wrong reason, expressed in dialectic terms, are difficult for man to distinguish, who needs guidance in separating the essence of one from the essence of the other; the poem is itself structured to equate the potential confusion, although Milton points the way to truth by various means, and it is built with materials that man can confuse. This study indicates the signposts Milton has erected to point out the correct path to right reason. The ideological (and hence artistic) arguments over *Paradise Lost* that have repeatedly emerged since Dryden are a result of wrong reading that has not been aware of such pragmatic evidence. Milton's perspective, concern for man in his everyday life, both within his individual world and within his communal world, has been missed. But is the fault in Milton and his poem or in the reader (for example, the reader who sees only Sin and Death as allegoric figures)? Whether we view the poem as falling into the tragic mode or the comic mode really depends upon our angle of vision as we turn the kaleidoscope. Are the pieces of glass that constitute any view of life the right pieces of glass? Is a specific arrangement *only* a step toward a new — and better or more desirable — vision? Or is there a beauty in each specific arrangement, each to be cherished of itself and each change to be equally cherished without regret for the past and desire for further change in the future? Life is tragic, Milton says, if, like Satan, we lament the present because it is not the past, or if, like Eve, we lament the present because it is not what some future seems to hold. Adam, thus, partakes of the satanic tragedy of life by an act which will purportedly maintain at least one aspect of the past as it was since he cannot accept what appears to be the new present, and he knows that his act will bring a changed and unknown future. While the comic mode suggests a kind of hope of the future through the maintenance of the present, it also understands that the present is not exactly maintainable. Change is thus desirable, and the final lines of the epic clarify this paradox of a moving present. The comic lies in acceptance of the present, but it is a present ever changing.

The myths of return and of exodus exist together as complements, and Milton's intertwining of these mythic foundations makes that cogent. While the present moves to the future and becomes the past, so too it moves in a directed line forward. Milton as Christian poet sees the end of that line as a reunification with the substance of God. But the line is composed of each individual generation (or rather, each individual life of each individual generation), each undergoing the cyclic movement of life. The tragic lies in the attempt to deter either of these movements. In the poem we see this in Satan who wishes to return to a past that really did not exist, for the Son is and always was God; in Adam, who wishes to maintain a part of the present as if it were the whole; and in Eve, who wishes to change the present into a future that will never be a reality. Milton the creator has given us a similitude of God's creation by offering up many views of the kaleidoscope. His urging for man is ultimately the moral one, to accept the paradox that the present is to be cherished though it changes with each moment of time. It is James Joyce's message as well.

The technique by which the author evokes awareness of the ever-changing present takes many forms: time is compounded and seemingly confused, though it moves in a straight line; the reader is "harassed" (in Stanley Fish's expression) to alter his way of thinking throughout the poem, and indeed again and again as he rereads and newly sees on the basis of the past readings; the language is manipulated to take on the force of meaning of its current context and then to alter as it is reused and remetaphored; the poem itself emerges as a structure, but one that appears differently in different lights or from different vantage points or through altered emphases. As example of the present ever-changing, the poem is a shadow of God's creation. But what is to be especially remarked—and the various aspects of style underscore this—is the persistence of a germ of truth that is unchanging throughout the poem and that is so because it is unchanging in Milton's view of God.

Concepts of change—time: past, present, future; movement forward or back, as well as seeming nonmovement; hope and fear—are in man's mind, not God's, whose omnipotence, omnipresence, and omniscience are unadorned, always the same, unaccommodated. The poem demonstrates the paradox in various ways by time representation, by story lines, by characterizations, by the underlying myths, by language usage, by style, and by a contrast of the allegoric and unrealistic. The most obvious example in the poem of this contrast is the role of Satan, an allegoric figure usually discussed as a realistic view of man. It is perhaps through Satan that Milton's great achievement in *Paradise Lost* as a creation emulating God's and as a rhetorical argument with a threefold basis can most easily be seen. For while praise (employing the epideictic stance of the rhetor) of God's providence is dependent upon recognition of the negativity of the satanic which exists in life because of the existence of free will, and while defense (employing the forensic stance of the rhetor) of God's way toward men is dependent upon the factor of the satanic in man, the primary intention of the poem to guide man in this life (the deliberative stance of the rhetor) will be achieved only if man is able to discharge the speciousness of the satanic appeals. Such specious appeals operate within concepts of time, of meaning of life and action, and of the self, both alone and in community.[3]

The romantic view of Satan has been that of the quester after value and the rebel against a tyrannic God. He is a Steppenwolf, in the terms that Hans Mayer discusses Hermann Hesse's novel,[4] by being an outsider to the establishment and a troublemaker. Satan wishes to replace the establishment against which he rebels, but he replaces it with an imitation. With the ascendancy of Satan in the world of men, the norm is replaced by the antinorm, which in turn becomes the new norm. Whatever is eternal truth, such as God equates for Milton, is missing in such envisionable sallying backward and forward of political and social life. Without Adam's asides, one can read Books XI and XII as this kind of oscillation. For Milton, the eternal truth—the paradise within—will be realized only through Adam and Eve's (mankind's) acceptance of life as it is, as a present ever-changing. It has been detrimental for an appreciation of *Paradise Lost* that literature has generally offered the outsider as some kind of hero against the abuses of society, largely, I suppose, because authors (and most politically radical thinkers) have taken the path of individual subjectivity (such as a Byron or a Paul Goodman) or the path of elitism (the Bloomsbury group). Apposed to the outsider is Everyman, who has too often been cast aside as bourgeois, and Adam and Eve both allegorically and intellectually can be so viewed. To reject Adam and Eve politically and socially is to superimpose a different kind of tyranny. The outsider may become part of the proletariat (Steppenwolf may become Everyman), but he has not balanced the rational and irrational in a given social system by doing so—although one must seriously question whether, say, a Friedrich Engels ever truly was absorbed into this middle-class world. As Mayer brilliantly demonstrates, our problems today are in great part a result of Everyman's becoming Steppenwolf—the defiance of establishment principles and values for the sake of defiance, with a resultant noncommunity and wallowing in individual subjectivity. Satan proposes becoming Everyman, and Adam and Eve presume in their fall to becoming Steppenwolfs. Milton resoundingly rebuffs both courses of action. For Milton, the revolutionist against the tyranny of monarchy, the answer lay in recognition that revolution is Everyman's concern, not just an intellectual elite's, not just his in some kind of ivory tower. He may not have quite rejected a disgust with the rabble because of their selfish predilections, but he did join in working toward a goal through functions contrary in various ways to his own personal ambitions and denying an acknowledgment of his individual superiority. In his epic — and my reader, I trust, will come to agree — he shows the way in which authentic values are pursued by Everyman and of what those authentic values consist. Sympathy for the oppressed and wronged is certainly maintained, but this depends upon definitions of oppression and injustice. And hate for the establishment depends upon the establishment. "As therefore the state of man now is," man must "sally out and see his adversary" (to paraphrase *Areopagitica*) or remain duped as to oppression, injustice, and establishment. The way to regain an unoppressed, just, nonestablished world is to achieve within men a change in themselves, and it is through the re-creation and instruction of his poem that Milton hopes his reader will be as Adam in Books XI and XII. One does not change man's social conditions or political institutions of and by themselves.[5] These will change with man's education in good and truth and become lastingly changed only through such education. Nor does one simply cure man's immediate ills, or, as Milton wrote in Sonnet 15, "For what can Warrs but endless warr still breed, / Till Truth, and Right from Violence be freed."

The path that the artist who is an outsider may take to aid in bringing about a successful world order is, Mayer writes, "a combination of artistic individualism in the traditional bourgeois sense and a decision not for subjectivism but for revolution" (p. 319) — a true fusion of Steppenwolf and Everyman. *Paradise Lost,* built upon traditional forms and genre, employing Latinate language and sublime style, dealing with material from which "any writer" would not have failed "to shrink back deterred" (these are A.J.A. Waldock's words), breaks all the rules and gives us a new form *sui generis,* employs a greater proportion of native language and syntax than any other comparable English work, and refashions the seemingly nonmalleable biblical legend into an excitingly unpredictable and iridescent poem, whose challenges lie in every line and image. What Milton has done is use a mold, as it were, which he has fractured into ostensible nonunities. While the narrator emerges as Milton the poem's creator, he often becomes the voice of collective conscience as well, offsetting material drives by moral behavior for a socially ethical world. Though much impels the reader to consider that death can become the Gate of Life, Milton, unlike his predecessors who stressed that life would not be fulfilled in life, leads us to discern that experience is fulfilled in living, not after death, if we accept life as it is. Not, I hasten to add, with a stoical attitude that things should be—must be—changed, but an acceptance of life as meaningful and wonderful, albeit imperfect. The poem in this light becomes one of the earliest statements of a political ethic common to the twentieth century: it is in daily life and in Everyman's being a hero (rather than through the heroics rejected in the proem to Book IX) that life has any true meaning and the worth of man can be meaningfully evaluated. The poem fuses the established values of man—artistic, human, ideological—with revolutionary values to forge a creation reasserting God's wisdom and presence. It is as much a political poem as a philosophic one, for its concern is man.

Whether we wish to stress what we have "learned" from the poem or its artistic being is an individual preference. In a masterpiece like *Paradise Lost* these go hand in hand: the intention of the author—or his message—dictates the artistic work which has been created to make the instruction palatable, and the artifact itself illustrates and reduplicates the message. In this study I shall stress such approaches to a fuller apprehension of that literary artifact as metaphoric language; the structure afforded by language, sources, balances, parallelism, varying organizational principles, and mythic patterns; genre and generic mode; style; and "novelistic" technique. Such artistic tectonics lead to consideration of the message in terms of thesis and theme; inspiration and meaning; psychological, philosophical, ethical, and political concepts; and mythic foundations. My view of literature is that the more we know (however we come to know anything), the more will we believe we have learned from a specific work. Perhaps some do learn "the reward / Of disobedience . . . and fear to transgress" (VI, 910-912), though I doubt it. More likely, the words cause the reader to think of the concept it encases and from his experience to acknowledge a truth—or does one cynically see it as the source of the born loser's difficulties? Probably this is what learning from literature is: reminders, reconsiderations, individual truths molded from experience resulting from the catalyst of the literature we read. The significance of literature may lie in what it causes us to think about, but its worth lies in its artistic achievement.

I see lines VI, 909–912,

> let it profit thee t' have heard
> By terrible Example the reward
> Of disobedience; firm they might have stood,
> Yet fell; remember, and fear to transgress

as contributory to the high evaluation of the poem because of their artistic placement, their description of Raphael through their style, and their psychological truth about man who only listens but does not learn to do until experience has passed. These lines summarize the first half of the poem and imply what the second half, as reversal, will be. They illustrate so well what *Paradise Lost* achieves as literature and what the reader learns. The interrelations of language, structure, and meaning here examined should lead to awareness of further interrelationships as the poem is reread. For the reader too is a creator — and the hints of this study should bring him closer to the poem's creator and maybe its only begetter too.

TWO

Inspiration & Meaning

IN *Paradise Lost,* Milton displays his artistic intention to emulate God's creation, and his ability to achieve that intention is a function of God's presence within him. "All is, if he has grace to use it so, as ever in his great Taskmaster's eye." Inspiration is literally a breathing into, and for Milton as Christian poet it is the breathing of the *spiritus* of God into him as mortal. Such "inspiration" supplies the life-giving force which will bring about creation. For the poet, the result is his poem. Theologically, inspiration implies divine action which will enlighten the mortal mind to receive divine truth. The poet's creation thus inspired will present the truth which is God: it will be an emblem of God's own creation. So viewed, *Paradise Lost* becomes the creation of God and Milton, its subject matter offering comparison and contrast between God's creation of Heaven and the universe and Hell, and what man can make of his world if he is inspired by God or if he is perverted by Satan. Should man receive the inspiration of God, his world will reflect Heaven and there will be a paradise within; a form of unity will ensue. Should he succumb to the perversions of Satan, his world will reflect Hell and he will be a hell himself; a form of nonunity will ensue. The present chapter looks at the ambiguous division between pre-text and execution. For the author's inspiration to write his poem, his intentions in writing the poem, and the revelations of his work lie within the execution itself. To understand the pre-text we must understand authorial drives, and to evaluate the execution we must recognize authorial intent.

The need for joint action between God and man is explicit in Sonnet 7 as well as other early poems. But the basic equation which underlies this inspiration is the mystic union of God and man in terms of sexual intercourse. One need remember only Donne's famous

sonnet "Batter my heart, three person'd God" to realize the preval-
ence of this metaphor. The metaphor figures the spirit (*spiritus* or
anima) of God as the dynamic, creative, fiery male force and the re-
ceiver of God's spirit as the passive, dormant, cold female factor.
Union, as in intercourse, will create, the opposites being fused into
that which partakes of both: a poem dominated by mortal action but
imbued with divine truth. Such metaphor derives from natural observation, from alchemical experiment with sulphur and mercury,
from the age-old paradigm of earth-fire-air-water, even from the
mystic properties of bread and wine. It is common to mystic expression such as that of St. Teresa of Avila. In *Paradise Lost,* Milton employs this metaphor, as we shall see, with a complexity of meaning
and application that encompasses all areas of man's life. The epic is
itself a creation which discusses on various levels creation as it occurred in orthodox belief, as it occurs each day in man and to man,
both bodily and conceptually, and as it will occur in the ultimate
union at the end of time. With the War on Earth at an end, so that
God will be All in All (III, 339-341; VI, 730-732; 1 Cor. 15:28),
worthy man will be "reduced" to God by Michael (who is related to
Hermes as guide of the dead) just as he led back the faithful angels
"Under thir Head imbodied all in one" (VI, 779) at the end of the
War in Heaven. In this apocalyptic vision, the embodiment of all in
God, the One, is necessary for full return from *ex deo* creation, and it
implies in the context of the metaphor we are examining an unend-
ing coition.[1] Here the colloquial meaning of the word "die" as sexual
intercourse becomes significant, for "to the faithful Death [shall be]
the Gate of Life" (XII, 571).

We should note the infernal parody that is implied throughout.
The unfaithful couple with Sin, Satan's "perfect image," through her
enticing them "with attractive graces," and they beget monstrous
things, like the hell hounds which kennel themselves in her womb (II,
653-659). This return-to-the-womb parody of the return of God has
not previously been remarked. Whereas God inspires, Sin entices
bodily and, it is implied, through such narcissism as that by which
Satan had fallen. This is the reason behind Raphael's perturbation in
VIII, 561ff., when Adam, in a preview of what will cause his fall in
IX, says that all higher knowledge falls degraded in Eve's presence;
she is flesh of his flesh, bone of his bone, his image before him. A sexual note is also struck by Sin's description as "a Serpent arm'd with

mortal sting," for not only is a serpent a phallic symbol, here trans-
ferred to the woman because she is the aggressor and the entire context suggests perversion, but the words "arm'd" and "mortal" and
"sting" all involve sexual puns. For "arm'd" implies a gun which will
fire bullets; "mortal," the engendering of life; and "sting," piercing
and inoculation by something like a bee's stinger. (Of course, serpents are frequently positive symbols, think of Donne's natal serpents
in *To Mr. George Herbert, With One of My Seals,* or Aaron's rod,
which dashed to the ground before Pharaoh becomes a serpent,
Exod. 7:9. As one of God's *signa,* the serpent [phallus] figures a mystery of life and of God's greatness in creation: for faithful man, the
means of generation of the good; for those enamored of Sin, the
means of generation of evil.) The nonunity, or rather annihilation of
being, that unfaithfulness will yield appears not only in the image of
the hell hounds, gnawing their mother's bowels (in contrast with
everlasting life in unity with God), but in the resplendent throne of
pearl and gold on which Satan sits in Pandemonium; Freud showed
that gold was considered the excrement of hell, that gold and treasure were equated with defecation, and that defecation dreams, with
feces piled high, represented the death wish. The irony of Satan's
wishing for death, which this throne as psychological symbol implies
(though death wish is also clear from his soliloquy in IV, 71–78,
86–102), lies in his begetting Death with Sin, in his abhorrence of
Death, in the Son's redemption of man to make death the Gate of
Life, and thus in the ambivalent metaphoric meaning of the word
"die." Satan, as antihero, would of course show death wish and uncreation, as opposed to the heroism of the Son, through whom comes
life, eternal and blissful. Through Satan's concept of life comes
death; through the Son's concept of death comes life.

The proem to Book I of *Paradise Lost* (ll. 1–26) addresses first the
"Heav'nly Muse" who inspired Moses on Horeb or Sinai. Who is addressed has been under discussion for a number of years.[2] In this
chapter, I propose that the spirit of God, at least, is invoked, regardless of which specific person of the Trinity is intended. The Holy
Spirit is explained by the love of the Father and the Son, however,
which has thus created the third person of the Trinity. The Spirit of
God (his *virtus*) is therefore an aspect of God while implying the presence of the other two aspects. The Holy Spirit does not otherwise specifically enter Milton's poem, but his presence is never really missing,

and as purveyor of justice (in the trinal concept of truth, mercy, and justice), he is of great importance to a poem hoping to justify God's ways to men. It would be man's love of God that would create his spirit of holiness, and this as theme of the poem (see Chapter Three) asserts the justice of God.

Moses was typologically identified with the Son in his role as prophet (here expressed as shepherd, a role the poet plays for his readers), and the first chapter of Deuteronomy tells of how God spoke to him on Mt. Horeb, and Exodus 19, how God spoke to him on Mt. Sinai. First, God inspires Moses, who has protested that he is not eloquent but slow of speech and tongue (4:10), by being with his mouth and teaching him what to say (4:12).[3] Moses is to lead the chosen people forth from bondage as, we deduce, Milton hopes to lead forth his fellow men from the bondage of sin through his poem. Later, on Mt. Sinai, God speaks the words of the laws (including the ten commandments) which will keep his covenant and make the Israelites his peculiar treasure above all people. Milton, too, elaborates the law of God throughout and specifically by reference to the Son's example.

> The Law of God exact he shall fulfill
> Both by obedience and by love, though love
> Alone fulfill the Law. . . .
>
> > (XII, 402-404)[4]

Next, the "Heav'nly Muse" is invoked by virtue of her inspiration at Zion (2 Sam. 7). David, ancestor of Jesus, king of the Israelites and thus typologically identified with the Son in his role as king, wished to build a temple for God's ark of covenant. The word of the Lord came to Nathan, the prophet, that David's act would be rewarded by his seed's establishment of a kingdom to last forever: "I will be his father, and he shall be my son" (7:14). The importance of the Son and the Son as Man to the whole of *Paradise Lost* has only in recent years been recognized, but here there is another allusion (following soon after the "one greater Man" in l. 4) not only to the Son but to the Apocalypse. Milton's poem becomes his temple for God's covenant. Or contrasting with "Sion Hill," the Muses's aid is invoked by her presence at the brook of Siloam, which flowed by the temple of Jerusalem, identified with David's temple on Zion. Here the reference is to John 9, in which Jesus heals the blind man by anointing his eyes with clay (a symbol of mortality) and having him wash in the pool of Siloam. The role of priest—Jesus said, "I must work the works of him that sent me, while it is day: the night cometh, when no man can work" (9:4)—underlines the reference and again points to Apocalypse. Clay as a symbol of mortality shows the biblical message that we are all blind until we have experienced the trials of being mortal and have then bathed ourselves in the spirituality of God's Logos ("the Oracle of God"). For Milton, the blind man, the allusion had special significance, as seen when he asks the Spirit to illumine that which is dark within him (I, 22-23) and when we remember that the blind man is blind, not because he has sinned or because his parents have sinned, but in order that the works of God should be made manifest in him (9:3). The concept of knowing good by knowing evil, of the development of a paradise fairer far after the Fall, is hinted at in this allusion to Siloam.

We see in these few lines an appeal to the Heavenly Muse to inspire the poet so that he can function as prophet, king, and priest of God's Word in order that he may manifest the works of God in his poem. Should he be so inspired, he will have asserted Eternal Providence and thereby have justified to men the ways of God toward men. Like Moses, he hopes to teach how order comes out of chaos, light out of darkness, good out of evil, through his imagery in his poem, and even through himself as the enlightened blind man. The suggestion in the reference to the blind man healed, that one must first be mortal—that is, fallen—before God's truth can be meaningful, is underscored first by the appeal that the spirit raise and support that which is low within him, for Milton himself is fallen man; second, by his beginning in the darkness and evil of Hell (for man is born depraved according to Calvin); third, by Michael's words and Adam's realizations in Book XII; and fourth, by the sexual imagery of supine Man awaiting God's inspiration.

Milton calls on the Spirit of God, who seems to be another aspect of the Heavenly Muse, by the continued and unspecified use of the polite second person into lines 27ff. The temple of Zion, cited just before, has led to invocation of the Spirit, for God prefers "th' upright heart and pure" before temples: "Know ye not that ye are the temple of God, and that the Spirit of God dwelleth in you" (1 Cor. 3:16); "know ye not that your body is the temple of the Holy Ghost which is in you, which ye have of God, and ye are not your own?" (1 Cor. 6:19); "Lord, who shall abide in thy tabernacle? who shall dwell in thy holy hill? / He that walketh uprightly, and worketh righteousness, and speaketh the truth in his heart" (Ps. 15:1-2); "The way of the just is uprightness; thou, most upright, dost weigh the path of the just" (Isa. 26:7). Through the probable allusion to Isaiah, we see the relationship between the upright heart and justification of God's ways. The Spirit is seen as a dovelike creature which stretches out its wings and sits on the vast abyss (Chaos) and impregnates it. In summary, we have the main motif of the poem: out of chaos will be created the universe (in VII), out of evil will come good, out of darkness will come light (throughout the poem and especially as we move from II to III, and in the illumination of the blind poet and his blind readers), out of disordered elements will come dovelike creatures (men who have been engendered by the Spirit of God). Perhaps we should also note that the dove was a symbol of the Holy Spirit, and of course white creatures will emerge from black elements. The infusion of God as male force on the dormant and womblike abyss is the cosmic parallel of the besought infusion of God on the receptive poet, as the colon after "pregnant" indicates. The poet is paralleled with the abyss, and the sexual imagery of the latter appertains to the poet. Milton's poem will, it is hoped, also produce dovelike creatures— will, that is, if he can assert Eternal Providence to man's understanding. Justification of God's ways will ensue if Milton can demonstrate God's love for man and if he can help bring man to love God (with its implications of faith in God and therefore obedience to God). Since love is, I believe, the theme of the poem, it is natural that a basic image pattern derive from the nature of love and that the perversion of love of God derive from the nature of sexual perversion shown in the satanic parodies.[5]

The lines referring to the dovelike creature are drawn from the Gospels' discussion of Jesus' baptism (Matt. 3:16; Mark 1:10; Luke 3:22; John 1:32), and we should note that each declares Jesus as Son of God.[6] Those who are thus generated, we deduce, will be sons of God and thus worthy of return to God at the end of mortal time. But Milton as hopeful poet also thought of the descent of the dove to the apostles, who then "began to speak with other tongues, as the Spirit gave them utterance" (Acts 2:4), and probably of the psalmist's wish for "wings like a dove" to "fly away, and be at rest" (55:6). Only the dovelike creature will be able to soar to Heaven and find his eternal rest. The narrator is portrayed as a bird throughout the poem, and he must therefore be a dovelike being, created by God's inspirational infusion of his dark and blind self.[7]

We should recall that in dream psychology a bird and flying have sensual significance; flying dreams are erection dreams, hovering signifying erotic experience, and falling, erotic temptation accompanied by anxiety. That Milton's work is a "dream"—not only in the sense of a divine vision with apocalyptic revelation—is emphasized by his frequent citation of nightly inspiration. "Nightly I visit . . . as the wakeful Bird / Sings darkling, and in shadiest Covert hid / Tunes her nocturnal Note" (III, 32, 38–40);[8] "yet not alone, while thou / Visit'st my slumbers Nightly, or when Morn / Purples the East" (VII, 28–30); "my Celestial Patroness, who deignes / Her nightly visitation unimplor'd, / And dictates to me slumbring, or inspires / Easie my unpremeditated Verse . . . who brings it nightly to my Ear" (IX, 21–24, 47).[9] Of course, part of his night is his blindness, as the proem to Book III shows. But the psychological implications of his "dream-poem," if we may call it that,[10] are consonant with the sexual imagery used in the bird image of the first proem and thus are worthy of citation. There are sections in which the poet's ascent, flight, and descent are explicit. The creational relationship between the Spirit of God (as male force but presented as female inspirer) and the poet (as female factor but presented in terms of dream psychology as male) is conveyed by the flight of the bird-narrator through the auspices of the Spirit from the depths of Hell through Chaos and Ancient Night to the heights of Heaven to the reality of Earth, followed by fluctuations of flight though based on Earth and extended in Books XI and XII beyond the world of Books IX and X. In Books XI and XII, we have the birth that will ensue from Adam and Eve's seduction, and in the total poem we have the birth that will ensue from the divine rapture of the poet by the Spirit of God. As the bird-narrator descends in Book IV, we have statements of anxiety, although the earthly fall is only foreseen in that book; they are stronger in the proem to Book IX, in which the earthly fall will actually take place. The anxiety of the proem of the seventh book is for the poet himself, lest he not be inspired further by the Spirit. The implication in his calling Calliope, muse of heroic poetry, but an empty dream[11] is that his dream-poem, inspired by God, is worthwhile and will not prove sterile. Continued inspiration only will bring birth, and so the ensuing birth, out of the watery abyss, is that of the created universe itself, then of man, then of woman. When we reach Book IX, anxiety for self again arises, for decay or cold or age may depress the narrator's wing, should the Spirit of God desert him. Such depression of flight implies the denial of erotic experience and the impossibility of creation at this point of climax. Without relation of the climactic point of the stated subject of the poem, man's disobedience, the insemination of the poet's "message" by inspiration of the Spirit would not take place.

The "message" is finally delivered in Book X (originally and significantly, Book IX in the first edition): The Son's judgment looking forward to the Incarnation and ultimately to the Last Judgment preceding the return to God makes clear what God's providence is—His Son—and why His ways are just. The remaining two books (a single book in 1667) delineate resolution for the poem and the poet with the conclusion that death can be the Gate of Life and with the desiccating imagery of the final lines of the poem. At the same time, these books depict the cyclic generation which Adam and Eve's disobedience has begot. Also, it is hoped that there will be some dovelike creatures born of Milton's poem.

The nightly visitation of Milton's inspiring Muse brings to mind contrastive references in the poem. Such references encase for Milton the poet the question whether his inspiration truly comes from God or from some nefarious source. First, one thinks of the contrast to Asmodai in Tobit, "the fleshliest Incubus," who killed Tobias's wife's first seven husbands, referred to at IV, 167-171; V, 221-223; and VI, 362-368. Asmodai was a fallen angel, infamous as a demonic nightly visitor, who seduced his victims by taking the guise of the true husband (the bridegroom). Only Raphael, "the medicine of God," as the name means in Hebrew, is able to vanquish him. Here is an obverse example of the poet's nightly visitation, one that emphasizes sexuality and lustfulness. It becomes another instance of distorted mirror surfaces in the poem (compare also note 16 in Chapter Eleven, below). The difference between the love-making of Adam and Eve in Books IV and IX indicates the potential difference that the dreamer would encounter were his visitor an inspiring muse or were his visitor not what she seems. Secondly, the nature of these opposing nightly visits—by Asmodai and by the Muse—is echoed in

Satan's visit to Eve as she sleeps in Book IV (related in Book V) and in God's presence in Eve's dream in Book XII. In the latter case, the visitation to Eve takes place during the day, thus suggesting that Milton's constant night may even be others' day. The positions of these allusions in terms of structure (see Chapter Five) makes Milton's evaluation of his inspiration clear to us, for it depends on the product of his dream—the poem we are reading. It will beget dovelike creatures for the fit audience, though few; for others it may hatch vain empires. But the fault is not the inspiring muse's or the poet's; the fault lies in the potential perversity of man. Essentially the mythic pattern here involves the archetype of twins ("doubles"), those two sides of man's nature suggested by the words "supine" or "rebellious" (or "meek" or "bold"). The archetype of twins formulizes the seeds of opposites within man (for example, Castor and Pollux, or Klytemnestra and Helen).

We can not help being struck by the sexual overtones of the metaphor of inspiration: the poem itself is the creation of God and the poet; it simulates an act of generation through psychological motif, subject matter, strategically placed proems, and rhythm; it deals with creation which is bodily, conceptual, and physical; and it suggests constant generation through impregnation of its readers with its "message." Milton has written a poem which makes meaningful Isaiah's words: "With my soul have I desired thee in the night; yea, with my spirit within me will seek thee early: for when thy judgments are in the earth, the inhabitants of the world will learn righteousness" (26:9). Just as some of Adam's progeny fall, so some readers will not receive the inspiration of the work—which like God's created universe holds all (then) available knowledge, all that one needs for "life"; but some will be fit audience though few. "God is also in sleep, and Dreams advise" (XII, 611), says Eve, and so now awake with God's judgment of restoration before them, she and Adam accept Providence as their guide (as should each reader). As they wipe the few natural tears from their eyes (compare note 6), the final resurrection of soul is suggested, for "God shall wipe away all tears from their eyes, and there shall be no more death, neither sorrow, nor crying, neither shall there be any more pain: for the former things are passed away" (Rev. 21:4).

THREE

The Thesis & the Theme

THE philosophic intention of *Paradise Lost* predicates its thesis and its theme, and the concepts of love, providence, and the Son, which have been mentioned in the last chapter, are their foundations. In its simplest terms, the thesis of *Paradise Lost* is that "Eternal Providence" (I, 25) can be asserted for man, thereby justifying God's ways.[1] Milton begins with this as argument and ends with its realization as Adam and Eve leave Eden with Providence as their only guide (XII, 647). The circle is complete. The disorder of time, plot, and action throughout the poem represents the seeming lack of order in life and the seeming lack of reason behind the forces which alter man's life and world. But the organization that can be seen unifying the poem asserts graphically the order that God brings out of Chaos, the good He brings out of evil, and the wisdom He exhibits in making us contemplate and judge rather than merely accept. Man — and the reader — must labor to see whole, and the more he scrutinizes, the more he sees. God has provided, just as the epic provides,[2] all we need for understanding, but man has not always had the insight to realize that the ways of God are purposeful or the faith to yield himself up to God's providence.

The structure of *Paradise Lost* leads us to considerations of the thesis in terms of disorder-order, imperfection-perfection, proportion, and thought leading to reason in turn leading to faith. The seeming imperfections — such as the Fall, the future seen by Adam — which disturb the circle (even the placement of time and action, which seem not to allow continuity) disappear when our perspective encompasses the whole. The imperfections emphasize man's limited, mundane, temporal, egocentric view of himself and his world. (The Ptolemaic system of the universe that Milton employed as *schema* for his epic accentuates such egocentricity.) These are not imperfections; they are part of a bigger and more complex perfection. Proportion is observed in a kind of symmetry and in balance. Disproportion would result from total seeming perfection, that not offset by disorder and imperfection. Rather, the underlying numerological relationships imply, as Pythagorean thought, the presence of the Godhead and their provision by Him. The center of the poem at the end of Book VI, the keystone of the poem's geometries, indicates, as Mother M. Christopher Pecheux has observed,[3] the "defeat of Satan by the Son —at the beginning of time, during his mortal life, and at the end of time." It embraces all providence.

Providence is the opposite of Chance, the attribute of Chaos. What God provides is the Son, first, to defeat Satan, who will rebel as God has foreseen, in Heaven. Secondly, because man, whom God has created to replace the fallen angels, will choose to disobey through the deceit of Satan, who will thus think himself avenged of God, God provides the Son to show mercy to man and effect his redemption by defeating Satan, Sin, and Death, on Earth. Finally, God provides the Son to defeat Satan again at the end of mortal time when He judges those who will regain the blissful seat of Paradise. The justification of God's ways lies in the demonstration that man can learn the nature of good by knowing the nature of evil, that he can rise after first having descended, and that obedience is the natural consequence of love.

The theme of a literary work is a concept made concrete through its representation in character, action, and imagery. The stated subject of *Paradise Lost* is man's disobedience, and therefore the climax of the poem has been considered man's fall in Book IX, when Eve disobeys and Adam out of love settles his fate, and ours. The employment of this subject and climax to substantiate the above thesis, however, would suggest that the Fall has been part of eternal providence, a dangerous conclusion in view of Milton's frequent discussions of the role of free will. Although God foresees, he does not foreordain man's actions. Provision does not include man's actions, which are, rather, the results of his exercise of his free will. The injunction against partaking of the tree of good and evil has been part of God's way; the judgment in Book X, the result of man's breaking of obedience, is part of God's way; and both will be justified by Milton in the poem. But the disobedience and the Fall, lying between these two examples of God's way, have resulted from man's own free will—perverted,

yes, but still man's exercise of free will. Nor can Milton hope to justify disobedience and its attendant fall. The Fall becomes fortunate, it
is true, for only by falling does man learn how to rise; this lesson is
achieved through man's act and God's providence. First, God has
provided man with free will, but man has chosen to fall, and God,
foreknowing this, has provided the means to rise again. The lesson is
demonstrated throughout the poem as light comes out of darkness,
creation out of chaos, illumination of the poet out of his blindness,
even, as Don Cameron Allen has pointed out,[4] the Heaven of Book
III only after the descent to Hell. God has provided the positive
values, but for prelapsarian man the negative values had not existed.
Rhetorically as *a* climax, the Fall represents a high point of the
poem's action. But it can not be *the* climax of the poem because of
the structural patterns and its incongruity with the thesis.

  The climax of Book IX is the high point of Satan's activity. From
the point of lowest ebb on the burning lake in Book I, Satan moves
constantly upward in his plan of subversion to the point where he
succeeds in urging Eve to disobey, Adam following. His former glory,
related in Books V and VI, contrasts sharply with his action in the
"present" action of the poem. His real stature existed before his rebellion when he was a faithful archangel, but he prefers to believe
that he had attained it when he challenged the most high, that is,
just before his defeat by the Son in Book VI. At that point, he
mocked the inability of the faithful angels to defeat him, saying in
derision, "O Friends, why come not on these Victors proud?" (VI,
609).[5] The position of Satan described in Books V and VI comes as a
kind of continuous heightening from Book I, but this shows the speciousness of Satan's sense of his own glory, for the situation described
existed before the beginning of Book I. In the course of the narrative,
Satan attempts, through harassment of God and his creation, to
reach again what he mistakenly believes to have been his former
height. As he reaches this false height and gloats of success to his cohorts in Book X, he again falls, now to a "monstrous Serpent on his
Belly prone" (X, 514). Nor can the fallen angels ever again reach
their true former height, for they "by thir own suggestion fell, / Self-
tempted, self-deprav'd" (III, 129–130). The remainder of the poem,
that is, history as speculated through Michael, is a constant fluctua-
tion of Satan's metaphoric height as some men are seduced to the
devils' party while some—Noah, Elijah, the types of the

Son—resist temptation and depravity, until the Son himself conquers death to make it the Gate of Life.

Since the Fall has not been part of God's providence, the climax created by that Fall can not be considered God's climax. It is Satan's climax; it has been brought about by Satan's deception of man. Only God can discern deception when it is hypocrisy (as it is in Satan's disguise and his feigning of virtue and wisdom). It is for this reason that in Book III, after He has ordained that the fallen angels will not find grace but that man will because he has been deceived, we have Uriel, the regent of the Sun itself, deceived by Satan; Milton underscores the means by which man will fall and the reason for granting grace. For God's providence, the climax of Book IX is thus a false climax. In balance, the climax in Book III does involve God's providence and may thus be considered God's, or rather the Son's, climax.

Although he assigned the crisis of the poem to the general area surrounding the Fall, E.M.W. Tillyard remarked the intertwining of the theme of regeneration, surely a part of God's providence.[6] This theme exists throughout the poem, but God's providence of man's opportunity to rise though fallen is first set forth explicitly in Book III. Man shall find grace, God says, but some mortal must pay the rigid satisfaction of death for death "to redeem / Mans mortal crime" (III, 214-215). As Harris F. Fletcher has documented, "All this is carefully worked out in *Paradise Lost* which opens with the idea fully formed . . . the situation involving man's obedience is repeatedly woven into the main theme, or becomes the main theme of the poem."[7] This, of course, is not a climax resulting from a structural development, but it is a point of high interest and great emotional response. It is, therefore, a climax, not the climax of the poem, nullifying Satan's climax. The climax of Book IX evolves from the crisis between Satan and man in the narrative present; that of Book III, from the crisis between the Son's action for the future and what man's action will be in the future.

As we shall see in Chapter Five, Book IX of the second edition is balanced by Book III. What I suggest for these two climaxes is thus another element in the contrasting plan, built on disorder or creating disorder. Whereas Satan subverts man to bring in Sin and Death, God grants grace to allow that man will be "sav'd who will." Whereas Satan out of hate and envy shows the way to what can be eternal death, the Son out of love and charity gives himself to show the way to eternal life. Whereas Satan's deceitful arguments will lead to a judgment of travail and expulsion from Eden for man, and possibly eternity in Hell with Satan, the Son's future action, God proclaims in Book III, will lead to a New Heaven and Earth for the just, for then "God shall be All in All" (l. 341). Note Satan's inability to effect an absolute and unchangeable result for man, but the Son's achievement of return and constancy. Whereas Satan's climax in the narrative present, appearing about three-quarters of the way through the poem, moves us to the beginning of man's journey through the world, God's climax in the future world of man, appearing about a quarter of the way through the poem, moves us toward the completion of that world. God's climax is set forth before the first appearance of man, and it is as if that climax always existed (as Milton believed it did in God's great providence, for God foresaw its need) even though it is concerned really with the end of time. The Son's action on Earth is strongly contrasted with Satan's action on Earth. God's climax is not a rhetorical climax, developing from a structural crescendo of successively forceful elements, for it exists before any of the elements leading to it are put forth. Thus seen, can there be any more meaningful statement of God's providence? What God provides exists before any use for it exists, even literally in the poem. But here, too, the climax is dependent upon man's will, for had man not chosen unwisely, there would have been no need for provision of the Son as Man.

If we reject the climax in Book IX as the focal point for the assertion of God's providence, we should reject the fall of Adam and Eve as primary theme of the poem. I differentiate "subject" and "theme" as "material used" and "unifying idea," the former being that through which the latter is exhibited in order to establish the thesis. The subject of man's disobedience, which entails the theme of the Fall, does not establish the thesis, because subject and theme are dependent on man's action. The climax of Book III telescopes God's providence of the Son as regenerative agent. In contrast with the later climax in Book IX, this one is preceded by the fallen angels' exercise of free will and followed by man's exercise of free will. The subject of man's disobedience has in Book III led to another theme, that of regeneration, but the requirement that man exercise free will to make regeneration necessary removes this climax and theme as primary for the substantiation of Milton's thesis. Besides, the climax does not culminate any structural development. No more than that in Book IX can it be the climax of the poem.

In balance with the contrasting plan of the poem, which emphasizes disorder, Milton employed a structural scheme of similarities, which emphasizes order and unity. The center of this scheme lies in Book VI, as the Son, noting the saints who will circle God's holy mount, ascends from the right hand of Glory to defeat Satan with the three-bolted thunder of God. Just before his ascent, the Son had mentioned the end of time when even he shall be subject under God so that God may be All in All, for all others whom God loves who love God will come to God through the Son. (At this time there would be no further need for the providence of the Son.) Just after his ascent in the chariot of God, his Sign in Heaven, the Ensign of Messiah, blazes aloft: "And then shall appear the sign of the Son of man in heaven," reads Matt. 24:30, "and then shall all the tribes of the earth mourn, and they shall see the Son of man coming in the clouds of heaven with power and great glory." This is clearly the beginning of man's time, but the language is that of the Apocalypse, thus scanning all time for man.

God has provided the Son to defeat evil at all stages of man's life, to guide man and to judge man. This is Milton's concept of eternal providence, and this justifies God's ways to man since all things are provided to save man. What we have are the Son's roles as prophet (conqueror of evil), king (earthly guide), and priest (agent of afterlife). The climax of Book VI is structurally the highest point of the poem; it deserves the highest emotional response as theological drama; and it is the turning point of the action, even though temporally it has occurred before the poem began—again a statement of providence. Without the defeat of Satan there would be no poem as we know it, for there would probably have been no Creation (to occur in Books VII and VIII), no resolve on the devils' part to harass that "new Race call'd *Man*" (presented in Books I and II), no assay of the "Organs of Fancy" (in Book IV) and its application and results (in Book IX), no judgment (in Book X) and its anticipatory counter-offer of mercy (in Book III), and no need to recite the past (in Books V and VI) and at least that particular future in Books XI and XII. This climax in Book VI is the turning point of the action, too, as the final statement of the cause of man's first disobedience. The Fall has not been "causeless," as H.S.V. Ogden supposed;[8] it has been the "thing," to use Milton's Ramistic vocabulary, which has come to exist from the "cause" explored in the first half of the poem. In the second half of the poem, we turn from cause to effect and its recurrences. In the climax of Book III, conflict is implied in Satan's bout on Earth with the Son as man; the Son exhibits love of man and faith in God the Father. In the climax of Book IX, there is conflict in Satan's assault on Eve and her now sinful exhortation of Adam; but Adam, though he too exhibits love of a different sort, rejects faith in God. In the climax of Book VI, the conflict arises between Satan and the Son, who, out of love for God the Father and faith in Him, obeys God's word to "Pursue these sons of Darkness" (l. 715). The conflict in Book VI is therefore the most basic, since it is the conflict between good and evil, light and darkness, order and disorder, creation and chaos. As the location of the most basic conflict in the poem, the end of Book VI must encompass the major crisis of the poem, also, for crisis is that point at which opposing forces interlock in the decisive action on which the plot will turn. As we have seen, without this crisis we would have no poem.

The subject of man's disobedience has been used to exhibit the theme of God's love, for it is God's love for man which best illustrates his providence and justifies His ways to man. The Son as Man, in his love for man, will fulfill

> The Law of God exact . . .
> Both by obedience and by love, though love
> Alone fulfill the Law. . . .
>> (XII, 402-404)

And thus will the great "Comforter" (the Holy Spirit) write on men's hearts

>> the Law of Faith
> Working through love . . .
> To guide them in all truth, and also arm
> With spiritual Armour, able to resist
> *Satans* assaults, and quench his fierie darts.
>> (XII, 488-492)

In the War in Heaven, the Son has put on the terrors of God, for "at his right hand Victorie / Sate Eagle-wing'd" (VI, 762–763), showing the wrath of God against the disobedient, the unloving; but on Earth the Son will put on God's mildness to make the vast abyss pregnant with dovelike creatures. All that Satan can hatch are vain empires.

The climax in Book VI is not dependent upon man's free will; in asserting eternal providence to man, Milton is not hampered by the incongruity of the other two climaxes. The War in Heaven came about through the envy of Satan and his followers when God begot his Son, and they fall through their own false judgment and choice. But the justification of what has been provided for man and the ways that God has moved toward him are not dependent upon this exercise of free will. The War on Earth, recounted in Books XI and XII, contrasts with the War in Heaven most strikingly through this basic difference.

Recognition of the end of Book VI rather than the Fall of Book IX as the focal point of the poem leads to the realization that Milton is really concerned with man in the Christian world, a world which will end with Judgment Day and the resurrection of the dead. Although all time is implied in *Paradise Lost* and allusions project us into the Christian era, narrative elements conclude with the Son's defeat of Satan, Sin, and Death as foreseen through Michael. Yet, it is man's action in the contemporary world that worries Milton. The apocalyptic view is everywhere in the poem, and we remember the belief that the millennium would come to pass in the mid-seventeenth century. As God the Father announces in Book III, the Son will judge the living and the dead in the "general Doom":

> Then thou thy regal Scepter shalt lay by,
> For regal Scepter then no more shall need,
> God shall be All in All.
>
> (III, 339–341)

In the midst of the climax of Book VI, the quotation from 1 Cor. 15:28 again appears (VI, 730–733), yielding awareness of the presence of the judgment throughout the conclusion to that book. The frequency of allusions to 1 Cor. 15, which details the certainty and manner of the resurrection, can not be coincidental; there are at least eighteen more references in *Paradise Lost*. Most pertinent to the present discussion is verse 26, "The last enemy that shall be destroyed is death," which appears at III, 258-259 ("While by thee rais'd I ruin all my Foes, / Death last, and with his Carcass glut the Grave"). The Son's ascendance and man's resurrection are constantly in Milton's mind. And the many antitheses of narrative, imagery, characterizations, and structure within the poem may owe something to verses 42-43 of this same biblical text: "So also is the resurrection of the dead. It is sown in corruption; it is raised in incorruption: It is sown in dishonour; it is raised in glory: it is sown in weakness; it is raised in power."

The concept of the return to God which the previous discussion develops is of course enhanced by a pyramidic structure within the poem, both in its relation with Hesiod's Hill of Virtue and the holy hill of Zion and the rough upward path to the Plains of Heaven, higher than which one can not go, and in its emphasis upon order and unity.

These qualities — order and unity — are achieved when God is All in All, when we reach the climax of Book VI (fully understood), and when we reach the symbol of completeness and perfection as we proceed through Book XII. But the poem itself represents this order and unity brought out of disorder and disunity. Whatever seems disordered is proved not to be when rightly understood and arranged, and whatever seems disunified is seen not to be when man accepts providence as his guide through love of God and by recognition of God's love of man.

The balancing of Books III and X, with their different judgments, underscores the Son's role on Earth and toward man. In both, the multitude sings of the New Heaven and Earth that those who "shall receive no stain" will enjoy; we hear them declare, "Just are thy ways, / Righteous are thy Decrees on all thy Works" (X, 643-644). This is the Song of Moses (see Exod. 15:1-19; Rev. 15:3 and 19:1-2),

> That Shepherd, who first taught the chosen Seed
> In the Beginning how the Heav'ns and Earth
> Rose out of *Chaos*. . . .
>
> (I,8-10)

We note too that lines 4-5 of Book I also look toward the Judgment when the "one greater Man / [will] Restore us, and regain the blissful Seat," and that in Book XII Michael foretells the dissolution of Satan and his perverted world, and the rise of the

> purg'd and refin'd
> New Heavens, new Earth, Ages of endless date
> Founded in righteousness and peace and love,
> To bring forth fruits Joy and eternal Bliss.
>
> (XII, 548–551)

A contrast between these fruits of the Tree of Life and the "Fruit / Of that Forbidden Tree" is also intended, but the disunity which this contrast implies is dispelled when man accepts God's providence and makes death the Gate of Life.

Just as the poem begins with the fallen angels expelled from the heavenly paradise, it ends with fallen man, Adam and Eve, expelled from the earthly paradise. The fallen angels have had to act to escape their Hell, but all they do is revenge themselves upon God by harassment and traverse Sin's bridge over the abyss intercepting the stairs to Heaven. The fallen Adam and Eve will have to act to escape their world, torrid now with heat, and parched; whether they ultimately rest in Heaven or Hell is for them to choose. They wander, solitary, but with Providence as guide. It is hoped they will be able to bring light out of their darkness, not simply escape darkness, not simply superimpose a means of avoiding evil. Milton wishes to inculcate in his readers, his fit audience, the acceptance of Providence as guide, so that the Son as Man will be example. "Redeemer ever blest," and so that the Son as Judge will provide "respiration to the just, / And vengeance to the wicked" (XII, 540–541). The action of the poem is certainly centered on man, for Milton's didacticism is discernible everywhere. But God is the metaphysical and physical center, as Harry Robins has indicated in his discussion of direction,[9] and it is to this center that faithful man will return, through the Son, so that God will be All in All.

The question of the hero has, therefore, been wrongly attacked. Satan is an antihero in his perverse and specious fortitude; the Son, a kind of hero in his just and honest deeds. And Adam and Eve as mankind come close to constituting the "hero," but they are such as Everyman was, buffeted by the antitheses of Satan and the Son. The question will be taken up in the next chapter. At this point, we may remark that the foregoing is seen in narrative elements, in imagery such as Albert Cirillo has so brilliantly demonstrated,[10] and in simile; but can we really talk of a hero in a morality play? I suppose that if we see the work as composed only of Books I, II, and IX, as it would seem so many do who read it in fragmentary form, the drama is one making Adam and Eve the hero and Satan the antagonist. But this is hardly Milton's poem. God's mercy and the Son's ascendance within the poem—actual or implied—remove any real suspense or plotting in heroic terms. Rather, it seems to me, the suspense lies in the composition, the rhetorical parries, the expression of the resounding truths that we know we will hear.

Paradise Lost is about the losing of paradise, but the *theme* in the simplest terms is love. We see it in the providence of God which the poem asserts, in the love of the Son for God the Father and thus for man, and in the realization of Adam in Book XII, which thus justifies God's ways. By contrast, we see the hate of Satan and its generation of revolt, revenge, and deceit. Love leads to eternal life; hate, to eternal death. The love of Adam and Eve at first is commendable, wedded love being most praiseworthy, but it is also clear that self-love and external love can be dangerous and lead to false reason. The recognition of thesis and theme puts less stress upon the fall of Adam and Eve than has often been suggested; rather, the central episode of Satan's revolt against God and his defeat by the Son is illuminated as the origin for the difficulties man will experience and as continuous admonition of Satan's defeat before, during, and at the end of time.

What I have suggested has two points of significance—structure, theme—to which will be added a third later—mode—that require a somewhat new view of *Paradise Lost,* although others have recorded the importance of Book VI. Dick Taylor, for example, wrote that Milton "closely integrated the battle into the plot, structure, and thought of *Paradise Lost* so as to relate it to almost all the themes and narrative threads with which he supported his great purpose"; he concluded, "Set in the center of *Paradise Lost* and closely interrelated with the preceding and subsequent books, the battle constitutes a structural point of balance which maintains a dynamic equilibrium in a complex of far-reaching ideas and powerful action."[11] Douglas Knight, to whom Book VI is the point at which we first recognize Satan fully, proposes that we see the poem "in the form of a cross, the arms two separable dramatic positions which Satan occupies in the poem and Book VI the point where they meet."[12] Seen structurally, the poem can not be read primarily as I assume it usually is: a drama of human failing culminating in the Fall. It is a story about the way man is deceived into temptation, an allegory of the forces of good and evil, and a didactic statement of the means to conquer evil—yes; but it is also a statement of the Christian myth of Christ. Milton has not used myth as, say, William Faulkner does in *The Sound and the Fury* or Nathanael West does in *Miss Lonelyhearts*; that is, he does not use the monomyth to expound a contemporary analogy. Rather, he presents that which he believes to be central myth from which myth is derived; his poem itself becomes that myth, but only when we recognize the structure and theme which I have been urging. (See the discussion of the myth of return in Chapter Ten.) Such myth is, of course, of the comic mode, as it moves through and past the potentially tragic.

The theme of the poem is accordingly different from what the literary histories tell us. Knight defines it as "the discovery of individual responsibility simultaneously with the opposed discovery of a baffling and inscrutable divine order" (p. 56). It is, as I have tried to show, in simpler and more Miltonic terms, love. Once we understand God's love of man, we understand Providence; once we understand Providence, we see God's justice; once we see God's justice, we should love God with all the attendant responsibilities of that love. The wrath of God is provoked only by nonlove. The subject of man's disobedience is most appropriate, for it implies a lapse of love of God and is countered by the Son's obedience in Book VI (and later on Earth), which arises from his love of God the Father. The subject underscores the theme, and the theme achieves the thesis.

· FOUR ·

The Hero

SO MUCH has been written about the hero of *Paradise Lost* that separate consideration must be given here to the subject. Milton's execution of this staple of the epic depends, of course, on the thesis, theme, and genre. The question concerning the hero is really various questions: is there a hero in the poem? if there is, who is the hero? if there is no hero, how does one view Satan? and the basic question, what does one mean by "hero"? The existence of a hero in *Paradise Lost* has always been assumed, it seems, although Addison at one point states there is no hero, contradicting Dryden's candidacy of Satan, but then he argues that the Son would be more likely if a hero must be advanced. Probably, the classification of the poem as epic has led many to make the assumption, and certainly its being viewed as tragic has. If the poem does fall under the comic mode, as I shall contend, then the concept of hero must be different from the heroic stature assumed; the hero would not necessarily be one of noble rank, fighting to overcome injustice and succumbing in the process, and his action and achievement need not be exemplary.

In a concept of tragedy, Satan is hero only if one believes that God has been and is wrong in his treatment of the angels and particularly Satan, and perhaps in His ways toward man. The "heroic" Satan, who, it is argued, undergoes change from glorious figure in Books I and II to despicable devil with his soliloquy in Book IV, still blights Milton criticism, as a recent article illustrates.[1] First, Satan hardly seems heroic in Books I and II when one reads carefully; he lies, deceives himself and others, boasts without foundation, aggrandizes himself, sets up situations to promote himself like any con man of the daily tabloids. His exciting speeches and rhetorical arts have won over readers as well as the imaginary auditors. But second, and even more important because we are immediately thrust back in time to the condition leading to the War in Heaven, and, of course, forward in the poem itself although we do not then realize it, is Satan's doing that which he accuses God of doing: assuming superiority and leadership over others, who thereby become inferiors and followers. There is hierarchy in Heaven and Satan acknowledges that hierarchy approvingly, according to the earlier parts of Raphael's account in Book V. But the "begetting" of a being to whom Satan is ranked "inferior" and "follower," not very logically but with great psychological validity, causes him to rebel against God. First, he objects to that which he himself asserts and in Books I and II demands of his cohorts. Second, he acts out of pride and envy, without allowing others (God or his followers) to exercise their own unconditional or unconditioned decisions. And third, like too many critics, Satan forgets that the Son is God[2] and that the "begetting" of the Son is not suddenly introducing someone new who is superior to Satan, but rather establishing an administration in Heaven. (The Son is, rather, part of the great providence of God who has total prescience.) The Son is still God, and Satan's reaction is the result of an awakening that he has as high a position as he will ever have in Heaven.

One of the paradoxes of life that *Paradise Lost* adumbrates is that nonchange involving the present is an unacceptable concept to most minds, who nonetheless strive to achieve nonchangingness for themselves and their associates in the future. While Satan can not accept the status quo of his life in Heaven any more than Adam and Eve through deception can accept the status quo of their Edenic life, he still seeks a world of stasis after his fall: "A mind not to be chang'd by Place or Time" (I, 253), a "Divided Empire with Heav'ns King" (IV, 111). This is the fascistic lure of all Republics or Utopias or New Harmonys or conforming nonconformists. The fullest literary answer to this paradox is Joyce's in *Ulysses* or more obviously in *Finnegans Wake*: all of you who have fallen, wake up; accept life as it is in all its goodness and all its evil and all its being. Surely, Bloom and Earwicker are the prime examples of the opposite of the antihero in literature.

Satan is willing to accept, it seems, position under God and over other angels, along with, apparently, Michael and others, until such time that God's generation into Father and Son underscores Satan's lesser position to God. This aspect of Satan's being is just as evident in Books I and II as it is in Books V and VI; why else advancement of "revenge," "immortal hate" (a static condition), "courage [!] *never* to submit or yield," "A mind not to be chang'd by Place or Time," the emphasis on *reigning* even though in Hell, the opening of Book II with Satan splendiferously set on a throne with the other fallen angels below him, looking up? Milton has not given us two different Satans in *Paradise Lost,* one in Books I and II and another from Book IV on; what he has done is make emphatically clear that such matters are in the eye of the beholder. Milton has not really tried to mislead, either, for the simile of the bees is clearly intended to manifest that these superheroic statures of Book I are but swarms of buzzing little drones, superheroic only in their own eyes. The simile of the "Pigmean Race" or "Faerie Elves" repeats the message, the narrative voice remarking, "they but now who seemd / In bigness to surpass Earths Giant Sons / Now less than smallest Dwarfs" (I, 777–779).

Probably, Milton thought that his epic showed that God had not been wrong in his ways toward Satan and, of course, it was his aim to justify the ways of God toward men. He did not anticipate rejection of God, though he recognized the need to make the rules of God's world acceptable to man. If God has not been wrong in his ways toward Satan, then Satan can not be a hero driving out injustice. If Milton succeeds in justifying God's ways toward men, as I have attempted to prove that he does, then man (Adam and Eve, or mankind) does not function as hero in the usual sense of the word for a piece of literature controlled by the tragic mode. And Adam shows none of the qualities of the epic hero that we have come to expect from works like the *Aeneid.* Adam is progenitor, but further likenesses to an Aeneas lie in material not included in the poem. In the story of Adam and Eve we have the potentialities of one of two common heroic figures: either one who falls through some *hamartia,* which he must overcome to achieve a new balance in his world, previously unbalanced through evil or injustice or his own excess or misjudgment, or, one who founds a new world to reject the past and develop a glorious future.

The way we should view Satan is as the prototype antihero and Adam and Eve as the protagonist in the drama of life (a kind of morality piece). The antihero is one who, unlike Bloom or Earwicker, does not accept life as it is, things as they are, but who tries against incalculable odds to change the makeup of the world and his

puny position in it. An antihero is not simply a nonhero or one opposed to the hero; he is a specific personality, explainable in psychological terms. Dostoevsky's "underground man" notes that "the whole
work of man really seems to consist in nothing but proving to himself
every minute that he is a man and not a piano-key!" The constant
change sought he expresses thus: "perhaps the only goal on earth to
which mankind is striving lies in this incessant process of attaining, in
other words, in life itself, and not in the thing to be attained." Like
Satan, he reasons in extreme alternatives only: "Either to be a hero or
to grovel in the mud—there was nothing between. That was my ruin,
for when I was in the mud I comforted myself with the thought that
at other times I was a hero, and the hero was a cloak for the mud: for
an ordinary man it was shameful to defile himself, but a hero was too
lofty to be utterly defiled, and so he might defile himself." This
sounds like Milton's Satan in the first book in Hell, talking of his glorious past, so oblivious to the horrors of "immortal hate" and the self-
condemnation in arguing that "who overcomes / By force, hath
overcome but half his foe" (I, 648-649). His lack of acceptance of
things as they are can be seen when he criticizes God as thinking He
reigns securely on His throne because of "old repute, / Consent or
custom" (I, 639-640), which is his own goal, we know. The antihero
laments rank in the world and his insectlike condition; but, paradoxically, it is not a thoroughgoing democratic world he seeks. At the
base of Dostoevsky's protagonist's psychology is death wish ("Perhaps
suffering is just as great a benefit to him as well-being? Man is sometimes extraordinarily, passionately, in love with suffering, and that is
a fact"),[3] just as it is the driving force in Satan's personality. Satan's
bent toward uncreation can not possibly accord with the positivity
that heroic action demands. The antihero bemoans his existence because others have more power, more beauty, more talent, and so
forth; he hates himself ultimately and thus envies those around him.
Can his first view of Adam and Eve be any other way interpreted?

> O Hell! what doe mine eyes with grief behold,
> Into our room of bliss thus high advanc't
> Creatures of other mould, earth-born perhaps,
> Not Spirits, yet to heav'nly Spirits bright
> Little inferior. . . .
>
> (IV, 358-362)

But no one could possibly believe that Milton is condemning action to correct the evils and injustices of this world. The antihero is not the hero, yet that confusion is, I submit, the cause for the controversy over Satan and the detraction heaped on Milton as artist.

In *The Tenure of Kings and Magistrates,* Milton made quite clear the difference between the true David and the false David, for Charles I was heralded as a David by the Royalists, and his main line of argument is that when the power of kings and magistrates, which has been conferred upon them by the people in covenant for common peace and benefit, has been abused, it is the people's duty to reassume that power or to alter it in whatever way is most conducive to the public good. Satan and God pose a question almost impossible to answer until after the fact or by faith: who is the true God or leader? The portrait of Satan in Books I and II, as elsewhere, etches his falsity and duplicity, envy and egocentricity. He is neither God nor true leader, but rather the antitype of Corah, rebel against Moses, and thus antithesis of Moses. He would lead men into the bondage of Pharaoh (who is identified with Satan himself). Milton's Satan does not really allow us to misjudge whether he is true or leader. And much as some modern critics dislike Milton's God and the way that the theology he supports operates, the person of God, Father and Son and Spirit, that appears in *Paradise Lost* is the person of a true god and a true fountainhead of life. If one wants to argue with religion, that's one thing, but arguing with the literature which makes use of that philosophy is another.

The action to recover the people from the false kings and magistrates and to achieve the new commonweal is heroic and takes a hero to accomplish. It should be undertaken as the mid-century movement against the monarchy of the Stuarts attempted to reclaim the natural rights of man. Such a hero was not one who thought of himself as insect, who primarily wished position and acclaim for himself, who tried to change the world because of himself; he was one who thought of himself as an image of God, who aimed at the general good, and who deprecated the conditions of man's life (not man's fate), devolved to its present state through man's avarice and other sins. It is the confounding of the antiheroic Satan with the heroic-sounding lines he often speaks that has caused some to place Milton in Satan's camp. In a world of thwarted causes (the end of the eighteenth century or the 1960s and 1970s), it is easy to read hope into

"What though the field be lost? / All is not lost"; or even "courage never to submit or yield"; or even perhaps in the most depressed moments, "Better to reign in Hell, then serve in Heav'n" if Heaven is a middle-class 1930 Hollywood-like existence in a middle-class Norman Vincent Peale-like mind. Milton, I have no doubt whatsoever, would heartily approve and join those of the late eighteenth century or 1960s or 1970s who had the courage not to submit and not to give up hope and to live in the ghetto rather than on Elm Street near Winding Lane. Indeed, it is this quality of Milton's mind—and it comes through in so many works in addition to *Paradise Lost*—that has attracted the rebels of this world. But in the poem, it is Satan who says these things against God (a symbol at least of perfection) and against Heaven (also a symbol of perfection), and who follows them with repugnant concepts: "unconquerable Will" (even when proved wrong?), "study of revenge," "immortal hate," and the most horrendous of all, "A mind not to be chang'd by Place or Time."

Milton's aim in *Paradise Lost* is to achieve a spectrum of heroic action and its antithesis, as just outlined. In Satan we have the antithesis or heroic action, although he appropriates the language of that action. That some continue to be won over by Satan's arts of rhetoric either commends Milton's artistry or condemns those readers' ability to read and evaluate. In the Son are oppositions of purpose, achievement, and goals. The Son represents the doer of God's commands, not only in the defeat of Satan in the War in Heaven, or in the Creation, or in the judgment, but also in his role as man-God toward which Books XI and XII move and in his further role as Judge at the end of time. He becomes the exemplary hero, or prototype hero, for all men. Rather than death wish, his drive is love and creation. Since it is the Christ legend which subtends the folkloristic definition of hero described by Lord Raglan in *The Hero: A Study in Tradition, Myth, and Drama,* the Son and not Satan can be seen to function as this form of hero in the poem. Yet the Son is not the hero of *Paradise Lost* in the sense of being the central character of the work or the one to whom Milton has directed his energies, although he appears prominently in Books III, V, VI, VII–VIII (in the person of God), X, XI, and XII (as man-God).[4] As prototype hero he does, however, manifest elements which will appear in the "hero" of the poem.

Adam and Eve, as I have suggested before, together constitute the

protagonist of the poem in the same way that Everyman is protagonist in the morality play. They are buffeted by the antitheses of
Satan and God, that is, by the qualities exemplified by the Son. They
are the central characters—or rather, "hand in hand," character—
around whom the action revolves. They do not, I believe, function as
hero in the usual sense of "doer" or exemplar of achievement;[5] they
are one who plays out a part against great life forces and they are the
example of what life encompasses. Nor are they antihero, like Satan
fighting against those forces, although they are affected by and indicate that mankind embraces the qualities that give rise to heroism.
Their descendants in Books XI and XII illustrate the spectrum of
antihero through all grades of hero which exists potentially in man.
Rather than representing the folk hero, Adam and Eve represent the
archetypal elements of the outcast, banished from the world of Eden
for their crime against future man, becoming the wanderer until
such time as expiation be totally won.

> The World was all before them, where to choose
> Thir place of rest, and Providence thir guide:
> They hand in hand with wandring steps and slow,
> Through *Eden* took thir solitarie way.
>
> (XII, 646–649)

For Milton's "hero," we must turn to his remarks in the proem to
Book IX.

A comic mode for *Paradise Lost* demands an ending in hope and
joy; the only way in which the lost Eden will be regained is by complete realization

> that to obey is best,
> And love with fear the onely God, to walk
> As in his presence, ever to observe
> His providence, and on him sole depend,
> Mercifull over all his works, with good
> Still overcoming evil, and by small
> Accomplishing great things, by things deemd weak
> Subverting worldly strong, and worldly wise
> By simply meek; that suffering for Truths sake

Is fortitude to highest victorie,
And to the faithful Death the Gate of Life;
Taught this by his example whom I now
Acknowledge my Redeemer ever blest.

(XII, 561-573)

The path is laid out: obedience, love, acceptance of Providence, fortitude (which implies patience toward suffering when such suffering is for Truth, that is, God), and following the example of the Son by obedience, love, fortitude, small deeds, and meekness. By adding faith, virtue, patience, temperance, charity (XII, 581-585) will the happier internal paradise be found. Clearly Adam is counseled not to pursue the antiheroic life and is counseled toward the heroic life, which has been delineated by the actions of the Son. Satan and the Son offer archetypal views of these life styles, and man will vacillate between them till the end of the world. The comic mode is sustained by the hope that some will follow the path, for Adam has understood and so will many others.

The proem to Book IX reviews these ideas of heroism and allows us to conclude that what justly gives heroic name to person (or to poem) is the striving valiantly for good against opposing forces. When such forces of good and evil are archetypal or mythic, as within *Paradise Lost,* we have the root and prototype of all heroism. Milton says that his argument is not less but more heroic than the pursuit of Achilles' wrath or Turnus' rage. The heroism displayed in the *Iliad* or the *Aeneid* centers first on war ("hitherto the onely Argument / Heroic deem'd") rather than on love and charity, and second on trappings of feigned actions like jousts and splendid feasts. The heroism Milton chooses to depict is based on patience and martyrdom and is not fabled or feigned, since it represents the truth that he interprets from the Bible. Milton's subject, to achieve the name heroic for his poem, must be

foul distrust, and breach
Disloyal on the part of Man, revolt,
And disobedience: On the part of Heav'n
Now alienated, distance and distaste,
Anger and just rebuke and judgement giv'n,
That brought into this World a world of woe,

Sin and her shadow Death, and Miserie
Death's Harbinger. . . .

(IX, 6-13)

His higher argument, which is sufficient in itself to grant the name
heroic, remains untouched by other writers, and "this great Argument," as the proem to Book I relates, is that the lost seat of Eden
will be regained through the action of the Son and through the
brooding of dovelike creatures from the abyss within man. This argument had not yet been attempted in prose or rhyme. Heroic action is
thus patience (which is action to Milton and not inaction; it equates
"stand"), sacrifice of self for the love of mankind, and opposition to
the forces of evil that surround man and are within man. The name
"hero" is justly used for that person who exhibits the better fortitude.
The hero of *Paradise Lost* is thus not just an ordinary hero of literature, not a specific personage within the work, but rather every man
who follows the path, who learns like Adam the sum of wisdom. His
action is personal, significant for him alone, not exemplary, although he may, of course, become a type of Christ *figura* for the
mundane mind of man to follow. Although heroic action may also
lead others out of bondage through the reestablishment of a new
commonweal, it is the heroic action within the self that Milton is concerned with in *Paradise Lost*. Like Gerrard Winstanley and the Diggers, Milton aimed at the improvement of all mankind through the
improvement of each man individually, an unstated (perhaps unreal-
ized) goal of recent generations. The truly heroic, Milton urges, will
result from the rejection of the elements of antiheroism within man
and the pursuit of the "fairer Paradise" by "vanquishing / Temptation" (*Paradise Regain'd* IV, 610, 607-608). The hero of *Paradise
Lost* is the fit audience; the hero may be the reader.

· FIVE ·

Structural Patterns

PERHAPS ITS vastness, perhaps its overwhelming metaphor, perhaps the sheer weight of its ideas have prevailed in the past against anything more than occasional consideration of *Paradise Lost* as a well-structured, well-balanced, intricately organized whole. Only in recent years has an assault been made on the determination of its elemental composition through a study of imagery, myth, simile, language, and certain comparisons and contrasts. But the poem also evidences an involved skeletal patterning, the work of an astute master planner. The outlines of Milton's plan with its balanced quantities, narratives, images, and characterizations all lead to heightened awareness of the texture and concepts embodying this magnificent statement of God's purpose. I have already been referring to these structural patterns; here I shall discuss them in greater detail.

A recent study of the narrator of *Paradise Lost* by Anne Davidson Ferry summarizes many of the artistic elements of structure which have previously been noted.[1] The device of contrast, imitating the destruction of unity, is frequently encountered: Hell contrasts with Heaven and both with Eden; Satan with the Son; the relationships among Satan and Sin and Death with Adam and Eve and with the Father and the Son; Satan's offer to the infernal council to destroy man with the Son's offer in the heavenly assembly to save man; Hell's fires and ice with Heaven's radiance; eternal damnation with eternal bliss; the causeway to Hell with the stairs to Heaven; the glittering vaults of Hell with the golden pavements of Heaven; mankind and nature before the Fall with mankind and nature after the Fall; bliss with woe; light with dark; and ascent with descent.[2] Another device is repetition, which imitates the immortal world through unity and distinctiveness, as found in the following words all used for the same image: *sphere, globe, orb, arch, wheel*; and in movements associated with that image: *rise, climb, ascend, mount, descend, fall.* [3] The pattern with which this latter image is associated is the circle, the geometric form "especially suited to Milton's needs, as to Dante's, because it is a repeating pattern, turning endlessly upon itself, and because it is the traditional symbol of divine perfection, unity, eternity, infinity." [4] These devices and patterns are significant in any discussion of the poem's structure.

When it was first published in 1667, *Paradise Lost* contained 10,550 lines divided into ten books: present Books VII and VIII were one (VII), Book IX was then Book VIII, Book X was then Book IX, and Books XI and XII were one (X). With the second edition of 1674, a few lines were added, ostensibly to effect the division of the books. The division of the first edition will be the basis of the ensuing discussion, since it is in this that Milton's careful organization can first be seen; however, line reference will be to the books and lines in the second edition, since this is the text of all modern editions.

The exact middle of the first edition came with lines 761 and 762 of Book VI, 5,275 lines lying before and after. [5] At this point, the Son ascends as he goes out to defeat Satan and his cohorts on the third day in the battle in Heaven. The first half of the poem, devoted to the "cause" (I, 28) of the fall of Adam and Eve, is given over to the dominance of Satan; the last half, devoted to the "thing" ("effect") [6] which was the fortunate fall, is given over to the prescience of God. [7] Books I and II survey the devils' recovery from their fall, their decision to test the new creature man, and the nature of Sin and Death. There is an invocation in Book I. Book VII, providing the first full book of the second half and a separate invocation, surveys in balance with these the creation of all things out of chaos, specifically the universe in which man's world has been placed and the nature of love. Out of the flames of the burning lake has come the darkness which is Satan; out of the dark of Chaos has come the light which is God. Out of the decision to test man through perversion of faith and obedience will come the Fall of man and revenge on God; out of the decision to test man through the covenant of faith and obedience will come the awareness of how man will rise to God and thwart Satan. [8] The arms of Satan's warfare are Sin and Death, but these are balanced by the arms of God's warfare, love.[9] Book III, with a second invocation, moves us up to Heaven, where we hear the Father proclaim that his prescience foreknows man's transgression of His sole command, and then hear the Son offer Himself for the merciful redemption of man. In contrast, Satan is next seen winging through the air observing the Paradise of Fools and the Gate of Heaven (reached by Jacob's stairs) until he comes upon Uriel (the angel in the Sun) and finally Earth and Paradise. Balancing Book III is Book VIII, in which the fall of Adam and Eve takes place, God's prescience coming thus to pass. A fourth invocation alerts us to the inverse parallels in this book. First, we have a view of the beauty of Earth and Paradise through Satan's eyes (rather than Uriel's) and then through Adam and Eve's, who remind themselves of their means to ascend to Heaven, though of course they do not really comprehend this. Adam's statement of the doctrine of faith and free will iterates the theological matter of Book III and prepares for the Fall, which will soon ensue. Satan is seen in this book as incarnating himself as a serpent (through a kind of fraudulent kenosis) to win for his cohorts revenge on God. The Son, with whom he is thus paralleled, will incarnate himself as man (through a true kenosis) to win for man God's mercy, as He promised in Book III. The Son's pledge of incarnation and mercy *follows* the Father's announcement of Adam and Eve's disobedience; Satan's assumption of the serpent's body and deceit *precede* the acts of disobedience.

Book IV shows Satan confronting Paradise and observing the love of Adam and Eve, chaste and beautiful; Uriel descends to warn the watch to intercept an evil spirit escaped from Hell. Approaching Eve in a dream, Satan is driven off by Ithuriel and Zephon to Gabriel, and from thence by a Sign in Heaven. Book IX parallels in reverse and in opposing terms this previous book: now the angelic guard leaves Paradise and the judgment of God is given; Sin and Death descend to build a bridge from Hell to Earth, intercepting the stairs to Heaven. As they have succumbed to the temptation, Adam and Eve fall to quarreling, to remorse, to "weeping and gnashing of teeth." Books V and VI are primarily concerned with the relation by Raphael of the War in Heaven, in which Satan and his rebellious cohorts are defeated by the Son, bringing us in point of time to the beginning of the epic in Book I. First, however, Book V depicts the first parents' morning activities under the rising sun, and Eve describes her dream to Adam. Raphael's warning of obedience (after the middle point of the poem) ends Book VI. In contrast, Book X is devoted primarily to Michael's vision of the descendents of Adam, who will repeatedly succumb to evil because of Adam's transgression (and because they do not follow the Logos). It is a picture of the War on Earth. The warning of obedience is replaced at the beginning of Book X with God's decision for the removal of Adam and Eve from Eden and the placement of a celestial guard to protect the Tree of Life; warning and free will have not proved enough. The ending of Book X awakens Eve from her sleep of gentle dreams and submissiveness, and sends them forth to the East, with images of evening and heat.

Thus one line of organization of the poem is a balance of the books as here diagrammed:

    I, II — VII
    III — VIII
    IV — IX
    V, VI — X

Further symmetry, balancing, asymmetry, and reversals are discernible in an outline of sections of the poem as in Figure 1.

Another line of organization in *Paradise Lost* that emphasizes its bipartite form lies in location, direction, and time. Despite the three locations of Heaven, Hell, and Earth, we see the first two in contrast to each other or in relation to the third. The first half of the poem takes us from Hell in Books I, II to Heaven (and the heavens) in Book III, and to Earth in Book IV. Still on Earth in Books V, VI, the content primarily depicts Heaven. Balancing the first half, the last four books are devoted to the creation of Earth in VII (thus contrasting with the creation of Hell in Books I, II), to the loss of Paradise on Earth in Book VIII (thus contrasting with the idyllic Earth in Book IV), and to the future sinfulness of the Earth in Book X (thus contrasting with the earlier action in Heaven in Books V, VI). Diagrammatically we have:

    I, II — Hell   VII — Earth
    III — Heaven   VIII — Earth
    IV — Earth   IX — Heaven, Hell/Earth
    V, VI — Heaven   X — Earth

Figure 1
SYMMETRIES OF *PARADISE LOST*
(Based on the ten-book first edition; line references
to the second edition are given in italics)

Book VII

Books I, II

Invocation *I.1-26*
  Dove and the Abyss *I.19-22*
The Fallen Angels *I.27-330*
  Satan and Beelzebub *I.27-330*
Satan's Call *I.615-69*
Assemblage, Pandaemonium *I.670-798*
The Council *II.1-505*

Fallen Angels, Satan's Voyage to Hell
II.506-648
Creation of Hell, Sin and Death
II.648-884
Satan's Voyage through Chaos
II.884-1055

Book III

Invocation *III.1-55*
Theological Statement *III.56-415*
  Free Will *III.80-134*
  [Innocence of Uriel—see below]
  Disobedience *III.167-216*
  The Son's Mercy *III.227-343*
Satan's Voyage *III.416-742*
  [Free Will—see above]
  Paradise of Fools *III.418-98*
  Earth and Paradise *III.526-71, 722-42*
  Innocence of Uriel *III.613-721*

Book IV

Satan in Paradise *IV.1-775*
The Angelic Watch *IV.776-822*
Routing of Satan *IV.823-976*
Sign in Heaven *IV.977-1015*

Books V, VI

Morning, Eve's Dream *V.1-135*
Adam and Eve in Paradise *V.136-219*
Raphael's Visit *V.219-VI.912*
  Raphael *V.219-560*
  Typology *VI.561-76*
  War in Heaven *V.577-VI.892*
    Abdiel *V.803-907*
    Son's Victory *VI.669-892*
  Warning *VI.893-912*

Book VII

Invocation *VII.1-39*
  Spirit of God and the Abyss *VII.233-35*
Adam's Life and Story *VIII.249-559*
  Adam and Eve *VIII.357-559*
The Admonition *VIII.560-651*
Building of the Universe *VII.40-108*
Son's Commission from Father
VII.110-73
Son's Return, Greeting in Heaven
VII.548-640
Creation of Universe and Man
VII.243-547
Son's Voyage through Chaos
VII.174-242

Book VIII

Invocation *IX.1-47*
The Fall *IX.494-1189*
  [Free Will—see below]
  Guilt of Adam and Eve *IX.1034-1189*
  Disobedience *IX.745-1033*
  Satan's Seduction *IX.532-744*
Satan's Visit to Earth *IX.48-493*
  Free Will *IX.342-75*
  Vanity of Eve *IX.205-341*
  Earth and Paradise *IX.48-178, 417-54*
  [Guilt of Adam and Eve—see above]

Book IX

Adam and Eve *X.641-1104*
Sin and Death in Paradise *X.585-640*
Sin, Death, Hell *X.229-584*
The Judgment *X.1-228*

Book X

Eve's Dream, Evening *XII.607-49*
Adam and Eve in Paradise *XI.133-237*
Michael's Visit *XI.238-XII.605*
  Michael *XI.238-333*
  Means to Learn Patience *XI.334-67*
  Vision of Future *XI.370-XII.465*
    Noah *XI.719-901*
    Son's Victory on Earth *XII.285-465*
  Answer to Prayers *XI.1-133*

To sustain such relocations, Milton employed ascent and descent (with symbolic reference to man's redemption or resurrection and his fall); Satan moves from his low position in Books I, II upward and through the heavens in Book III; he proceeds downward to Earth and Paradise in Book IV; and he is shown at his former height in Heaven in Books V, VI. The second half sees him or his influence only on Earth except in Book IX, where from his success on Earth he descends to Hell (an archetypal pattern), Sin and Death having been thus enabled to ascend to Earth. But since there is a dislocation in time, we must rearrange this to see the parallel lying in the two halves. Satan has held a high position in Heaven, from which he falls to the depths of Hell; he can rise only toward Heaven, to descend then to Earth. Book IX concentrates an almost duplicate movement in shorter and familiar steps, for Satan descends from his middle height on Earth to Hell to return as Sin and Death do across the bridge, through the heavens, and down to Earth. First, however, in reverse balance with the evil movements, the guardian angels have ascended to Heaven and the Son has descended to Earth for the Judgment.

The narrator also provides directional movement as he begins on Earth "to soar / Above th' *Aonian* Mount" in Book I. Through Heaven's aid he is able to visit Hell and Chaos in Books I, II, proceed upward to Heaven for Book III, and then look down on Earth in Book IV, wishing for a voice like St. John's to warn Adam and Eve of Satan's presence. He holds this celestial vantage point through Books V, VI. Book VII invokes Urania to return him to his native element, where he remains in the ensuing books, except when the Spirit's continued guidance in Book IX allows him to observe the reactions to the Fall in Heaven and Hell. The narrator's bipartite scheme of *position : observation* may be shown thus:

I, II	Heaven : Hell	VII	Earth : Earth
III	Heaven : Heaven	VIII	Earth : Earth
IV	Heaven : Earth	IX	Earth : Heaven, Hell, Earth
V, VI	Heaven : Earth	X	Earth : Earth

The matter of time is equally significant. The narrator, of course, writes at a time postdating the end of the epic, that is, during the time to come which is implied in the vision of Book X. Though his material is of the past, his intent is of the future, and both are, we would say, contained in time present. The two times of past and future are constantly interwoven and constantly changing in the present, and thus so are the times of the epic. They appear as if disordered and ambient (that is, moving two different ways at the same time). But order lies in their fusion in the present; after all, time is comprehensible only to God. The epic starts *in medias res* (allegedly), for in relation to eternity, as Colie notes, man's life lies in the midst of time.

Time proceeds from the first book steadily through the tenth book; Satan and the fallen angels awaken, make plans, and prepare to assault Adam and Eve, who are forewarned, who are tempted and fall, and who are judged and repent. But time past, before the opening of the poem, is filled in by a narration within the basic plot by the angel Raphael in Books V, VI; in balance, time future, after the ending of the poem, is displayed by a vision within the basic plot by the angel Michael in parallel Book X. Thus, the first half stresses the past as the action leading up to the creation of sin, the means by which it will be spread (both in the fallen angels' resolve in Book II and in the observation of Eve and her dream in book IV), and the purposes of God in having given man free will. We should remember that in Hebrew, Raphael (as relater of the past and giver of warning) means "the medicine of God." The Son's offer of mercy in the future, while contrasting in time with the general pattern of the first six books, is foreshadowed in the past action of Abdiel reported in Books V, VI. Besides, there are numerous plot elements which prepare for what happens later in the poem. The second half stresses the future as the action leading up to the greater love (and thus faith in and obedience to God), the means by which it will be achieved (both through the creation of light out of darkness in Book VII and through the drawing of good out of evil in Book IX), and the rewards of God for those who abide by His Word. Here we should remember that in Hebrew, Michael (as foreteller of the future) means "Who is like God?" Elements of the past occur in Book VII as Raphael tells us of the creation of the universe and Adam relates what he remembers of his life until that time. They present us with God's truth and thus justify His judgment in Book IX; the actions of Adam and Eve in Book VIII will bring forth the future world of Book X. Indeed, we move backward and forward throughout the poem, despite its constant forward motion, with some elements of both times in each book, for time in eternity is all the same and we all undergo Adam's story each day of our lives.

In two additional ways the two halves of the poem complement each other: in the use of theme and the use of invocations. Books I, II look to the evil future which Satan, Sin, Death, and their cohorts will exact; bounding the first half is the evil but glorious past in Books V, VI, when the Son conquered Satan. Colie observes that Books I and VI begin and end with the same event differently understood. Between is the prediction of the Fall (evil) but also of mercy (good) in Book III and the avoidance (good) but imminence (evil) of Satan's assault in Book IV. In the obverse books, VII looks to the glorious past with the creation of the universe and of man; bounding the second half is the glorious but evil future in Book X, depending upon man's personal victory over the Devil. Here, Creation begins the second half and continuing re-creation ends the epic. Between is the Fall (evil) in Book VIII and the recovery (good) in Book IX.

The four invocations are all to the Spirit (or virtue and power) of God.[10] That in Book I invokes the Heavenly Muse and Spirit to aid the poet in the creation of his poem and in soaring to the heights that dominate the first half. Out of his darkness must come light, and what is low must be raised. The invocation in Book VII calls upon Urania to transport him from the heavens to his native element and to enable him to complete the half that yet remains unsung. Now, what has been raised must be lowered, without his own falling into error, and out of evil days (referring to the substance of the second half of the poem as well as to England after 1660) must come a song of good. The poet invokes Holy Light in Book III to dissolve his darkness so that he may "tell of things invisible to mortal sight." The entreaty appears here because he has sojourned in utter and middle darkness in the first two books, and Book III is to be placed in Heaven. The invocation operates only through this one book, for the next three, though he observes from the heavens, are placed on Earth. In the parallel Book VIII, the fourth invocation addresses his celestial patroness to change his notes to tragic in order that he may relate man's disloyalty, revolt, and disobedience. He needs special aid to accomplish his sad task, to achieve his higher argument.

Yet the foregoing bipartite construction shows us only one plan of organization for *Paradise Lost*. It is the warp of the cloth which Milton has spun as his tapestry. The woof lies in a pyramidic construction, a rising action within the poem to the central point in Book VI and a falling action thereafter to the point of departure from the secured existence of Paradise. The rising action is created by the development of the seeming success of Satan from the depths of Hell through his maneuvering of the fallen host to commission him to pervert mankind, through his relationship with Sin and Death, through his cosmic voyage, through his deceiving Uriel, through his arrival in Eden and approach of Eve, to his commanding leadership of the apostate angels and challenging of the Highest. As a result of the dislocation of time in Books V, VI, the movement is almost constantly upward to his height of former glory. Only the Father's statement in Book III is in real opposition to his success, for his routing in Book IV is temporary and superhuman, and Abdiel provides only a shadow of the resistance which the Son as Man will make.

From the middle point of the Son's victory where

> Hee in Celestial Panoplie all armd
> Of radiant *Urim,* work divinely wrought,
> Ascended, at his right hand Victorie
> Sate Eagle-wing'd, beside him hung his Bow
> And Quiver with three-bolted Thunder stor'd,
> And from about him fierce Effusion rowld
> Of smoak and bickering flame, and sparkles dire,
> (VI, 760-766)

there is a fairly constant falling off. For man falls in Book VIII from his idyllic state and perfect created universe of Book VII, which is followed by the dissension and remorse of Book IX. The world to come, as depicted in Book X, causes sorrow and despair until hope is evoked in Adam and he becomes aware "that suffering for Truths sake / Is fortitude to highest victorie" (XII, 569-570). The events that will occur after Adam and Eve have left Eden are purposefully placed before Adam's spiritual awakening and Eve's actual one so that the epic may end with an upsurge of hope. Only the promise of mercy in Book IX (restated toward the end of Book X) is in real opposition to this decline, Noah providing a shadow of the resistance which the Son as man will make. We have moved from Heaven to the created universe and astronomies, and finally to Earth, even for some four hundred lines in Book IX proceeding to the environs of Hell.

Under this construction we discern a general balance between Books I, II and X, III and IX, IV and VIII, and V, VI and VII.[11] Such balance does not oppose the bipartite arrangement but, rather, indicates the complex overply like the threads of a woven fabric. The roster of devils in the first two books is balanced by the biblical catalogue of man in the last book. The fallen angels are concerned with the New World (the Earth), which is about to be created, whereas Adam and his progeny are concerned with "New Heav'ns, new Earth, Ages of endless date / Founded in righteousness and peace and love" (XII, 549-550). The theologic statement of the Father (Book III) finds balance in his judgment and mercy (Book IX); the cosmic voyage of Satan is replaced by his return to Hell and the movement of Sin and Death to Earth; and the Son's love opposes the despair of Adam and Eve. Satan's thwarted attempt to seduce Eve at night after his first sight of Paradise and the happy couple in Book IV is transformed in Book VIII into Eve's fall at noon after he has viewed the couple's morning activities. He is routed in the earlier book by Gabriel and a sign from Heaven; his success in the later book brings lust and variance. Books V, VI, narrated by Raphael, examine the past in Heaven; in Book VII he tells of the more immediate past creation of the universe. Book VI ends with a warning ("fear to transgress") as does Book VII ("all temptation to transgress repel").

The effect of this pyramidic construction is dramatic and somewhat suspenseful. The antagonists, as in a kind of morality play, are God and Satan, that is, good and evil, light and dark, truth and falsehood. Satan and his arms of warfare are ranged through Books I, II, V, VI, with indication of his deception in Book III, when Uriel does not recognize his evil, and of his means of deception in Book IV, when he appears at the ear of Eve. God and his arms of warfare contravene Satan's activities in Books III, V, VI, with anticipation of the past defeat of Satan in the latter two books and of the potential future defeat of Satan in man's world when in Book IV Satan is driven from Paradise and his resistance is hindered by a sign from Heaven. The protagonist man—both as struggler and as one who acts out his part in the play of life—and the field of battle are introduced in Book IV, that book which most clearly presents the clashing forces of the antagonists to gain possession of man without man's active participation. It prepares for the knowledge of the warfare told in Books

V, VI. With the defeat of Satan in Book VI, one line of development is completed; a climax has been reached. Satan and his evil can be nothing glorious hereafter. But man's removal from active participation in this part of the drama — and the placement of it in the past — allows for the continuance of the warfare on the lower plane of man's present world. Surely, Milton implies that only active resistance to Satan and his temptations will insure virtue; a cloistered virtue, as he had written in *Areopagitica,* does not preclude one's falling into sin. Satan is seen in the first half, then, as growing in stature to his defeat in Book VI, a kind of drama unto itself, with a rapid falling off for him as the Son ascends in l. 762.

In the second half of the poem God's works are ranged through Books X and VII and presented by His emissaries Michael and Raphael, with indication of His justice and mercy in Book IX through the judgment and through the Son, "Destin'd restorer of Mankind," and of his truth (or prescience) in Book VIII, when Eve and Adam fall and introduce pride and lust and anger into their world. Satan's presence seems to contravene God's Word in Books X and VIII, with anticipation of his future successes in the former book and of his self-deception of the recent seeming success on Earth in Book IX. The protagonist is shown in his struggle and his acting out of life's play in Book VIII, which presents the drama of his succumbing to one of the antagonists. It prepares for the vision of Book X with its relation of the continued enactments of the Fall and the resistance which the Son or one of His types — like Noah — will exhibit. With Adam's awareness "that to obey is best" (XII, 561) comes another climax, which is again the defeat of Satan, Michael and Adam soon thereafter descending from the top of Speculation. Satan's climaxes have been placed roughly in the middle of both halves, in Books IV and VIII. But these are deceptive like Satan himself, those in VI and X representing the real and meaningful ones of life. There has been a downward movement from Book VI through the end of Book IX. Book X allows a rising action in the future (and so the prophetic vision), although the denouement appears to have cast down the protagonist, as Adam's progeny fall over and over as he leaves Eden. Man is seen in the second half, then, as declining in stature through Book X, a drama in itself, with a rapid rise of hope through his awareness of God's Word. Adam's descent oppositely balances the Son's ascension with His victory in Heaven, for man will rise only by means of the fortunate fall.

Only in recognizing the rising and falling action of the entire poem and the climax at its center are we able to see the drama of life as Milton wished us to view it. The epic is not drama, and it does not evidence Greek or Elizabethan five-act structure.[12] But it does retain dramatic effects and general development. To stress the climaxes of Satan's action, particularly that in Book VIII, and his "heroic" stature, is to be deceived by the adversary and to misread the sign in Heaven that closes Book IV. Here "Th' Eternal" has "Hung forth in Heav'n his golden Scales, yet seen / Betwixt *Astrea* and the *Scorpion* signe" (IV, 996-998); that is, the scales (Libra) lie between Innocence (Virgo) and Evil (Scorpio), and Mercy between Justice and Truth (that man is evil). Each of the latter is weighted with the outcome of succumbing to it or resisting it, and Satan can not unbalance this counterpoise: out of innocence may come evil, but out of evil will come good. On another level, of course, we have a statement of the beginning of man's Fall, for the Sun enters Libra at the autumnal equinox, proceeding through Scorpio (evil), Sagittarius (wounding), and Capricorn (lust) before "rebirth" with the rise of the ram in Aries at the vernal equinox. The ascendancy of the Son in Book VI and its attendant climax suggest a cyclic representation of the basic myth of life explored by Isabel G. MacCaffrey.[13] The interwoven solstices occur at the Fall ("Th' inclement seasons, Rain, Ice, Hail and Snow, / Which now the Skie with various Face begins / To shew us . . . ," X, 1063-1065) and at the departure from Eden ("with torrid heat, / And vapour as the *Libyan* Air adust, / Began to parch that temperate Clime," XII, 634-636). Direction is, of course, indicated with its good and evil connotations: vernal equinox, east; autumnal equinox, west; winter solstice, north; summer solstice, south.

The studies of Stanley E. Fish oppose the structural patterns of the poem only if one simplistically believes that one technique can not exist beside another and only if one denies that an author begins (or usually begins) with a pre-text or "foreconceit."[14] That is, the view that the reader, moving from the first line of the poem to the last, undergoes a constant education, one being readjusted and reevaluated, is not obviated by the larger overall structures and composition that Milton planned. For the reader does undergo changing perspectives (attitudes toward Satan offer the most obvious evidence) and he does move with Adam through the human pattern of observation-information, temptation, fall, and repentance. The repetitions — of language and the like — do cause the reader to remember prior occurrences, to reexamine and reevaluate them, and thus to pursue a newly learned and advanced path. But metaphor, imagery, and symbol do not simply provide a steady change as one reads through the poem, but also an overview, a perspective, as one moves away from the poem and sees it whole. The structures examined in the present chapter indicate a like view, and the compositional strata investigated by Allan H. Gilbert enhance the realization of what Milton was creating as a balanced and paralleled literary form. Besides, Fish's proposal implies that there is nothing to be gained from a second reading.

The basically simple view of the poem (and literature in general) which Fish's interpretation proposes in no way requires that no other schemes of composition are in operation. The "technique of discovery" (the term Mark Schorer used for the more complex writing device whereby the author manipulates the protagonist to undergo development and changed perspectives so that the reader's awareness and understanding are likewise altered) is important, but as one backs away from the piece of literature, after at least the first reading, that technique loses force, for the reader has been made aware previously of the manipulation of both the protagonist and himself. What appears instead (in well-wrought works) is a complex that is the literary artifact. Schorer's use of Joyce's *A Portrait of the Artist as a Young Man* is an excellent case in point, for as we move away from the work, we see the container which is the novel as a womb in which the protagonist is gestated from conception to delivery. The structures of the novel are considerably more than simply a pathfinding journey.[15]

The pyramidic construct which is *Paradise Lost* is a hieroglyph of the mountain of God; the Plains of Heaven imply that no further reaches extend above. The mountain, symbol of truth and virtue, depicts the difficulty of ascent, the ruggedness of the ascent, the danger of backsliding or sudden fall, the bareness and starkness of the upper regions — leaving behind the lushness of the valley and the ease of nonactiveness. The iconographic representations of the path to Heaven and of the path to Hell are obviously appropriate here. The aim of life for man is to return to the Plains of Heaven. In so doing, the creation of man *ex deo* will be reversed as Michael, a Hebraic equivalent of Hermes as conductor of the dead to the afterlife, "reduces" all the saints to become "Under thir Head imbodied all in one" (VI, 779). Thus is the prophecy fulfilled: "And when all things shall be subdued unto him, then shall the Son also himself be subject unto him that put all things under him, that God may be all in all" (1 Cor. 15:28).[16]

SIX

Numerological Relationships

ANOTHER facet of structuring within the poem lies in numerological relationships, which create geometries and arithmetic metaphors and which suggest mystic emanations arising from its creator. Milton's mathematical and Pythagorean interests are well known, and thus it is not strange to realize that the first edition of *Paradise Lost* totaled 10,550 lines, exemplifying the perfect number ten in various ways.[1] The original version of the epic (1667) was printed in ten books. To Pythagoras, ten indicated completeness, the total of all things; it and its multiplicity returned to unity. Ten was equivalent to the perfect circle and also to the tetraktys, the solid figure consisting of four triangles. The tetraktys represented the sum of 4, 3, 2 (the line), and 1 (the point of juncture of three sides), or 10. The ten books of the first edition emphasize the poem's completeness, its circularity, its perfection, and its unity. Medieval philosophy added the concept that ten represented (as perfection) the divine scheme. James Whaler has demonstrated[2] that the verse of *Paradise Lost* is built on units combined as 1, 2, 3, 4, or 4, 3, 2, 1. The ascent of the first combination "stresses or implies an affirmative idea of perfection, absolute completeness, order, truth, harmony, power, or some virtue" (p. 53), and the descent of the second combination "stresses or implies an idea of negation, imperfection, disorder, ruin, impotence, ignorance, hate, malice, abasement, or deadly sin" (p. 56).

Seen as ascent, the books of Milton's epic are arranged (with reference to the numbering of Edition 1) in the following pattern for the defeat of evil and the achievement of the divine scheme: Book I opens the epic with the recovery of evil through the awakening of the fallen angels; Books II and III contrast Hell and Satan, and Heaven

and the Son through parody, thus falsely emboldening evil; Books
IV, V, and VI present the heavenly defeat of evil as example through
the routing of Satan in Eden, the advice of Raphael and the resist-
ence of Abdiel, and the defeat by the Son; and Books VII, VIII, IX,
and X proceed to man's realization of what evil is through experience
and through contrast with the idyllic world before the Fall and then
to the means to find salvation. There is affirmation of the virtue of
fortitude as well as the other six. Seen as descent, for some do fall ir-
revocably, the books of Milton's epic are arranged in the following
pattern: Books I, II, III, and IV show the rise in power of Satan, a
parody of the Trinity, and his penetration into Eden and the mind of
man; Books V, VI, and VII, though Satan is defeated, present the
fallen angels in active contention with the Highest and a new universe in which all of God's expressed hopes will be dashed; Books
VIII and IX manifest the success of Satan; and Book X describes the
continued warfare on Earth and the repeated fall of man. But such
an arrangement means disorder in God's world and ruin and all the
other negative qualities associated with Satan. To see the epic thus is
to see it out of focus — to see it through a glass darkly. This is distor-
tion — and one wonders whether Milton was omnisciently aware of
the errant interpretations which were to be heaped upon it in later
years. Rather, Milton is writing to inculcate Christian virtue, and
such a negative reading as the latter is hardly consonant with his
thesis, but there are those who so read.

Individual books likewise exhibit a numerological orientation.
Whether one wants to think such numerological relationships as I
here suggest to be contrived and an abuse of intricate arithmetic
composition or not, the fact remains that these numerological relationships exist pragmatically. Numbers have had concepts attached
to them and still do,[3] and we can observe pragmatically that Milton
(as well as others prior to the eighteenth century and after the nine-
teenth — a hiatus to be explained in terms of a changing and changed
world of knowledge) knew of such inherent concepts and employed
them. As S.K. Heninger remarks, "In renaissance poetry, especially
that of the Elizabethans, the intellectual signification of symbolic
numbers heavily outweighs the visible image they present to the eye.
The palpability of symbolic numbers in a poem is but a means to a
far more serious end, and deciphering any code of number symbol —

ism is but the first step in the process of intellectualizing its significance."[4] Since, according to Philo and Pythagoras, six was the first
perfect number between one and ten (as it is the sum and product of
1, 2, 3), Milton placed the middle of his poem within that book. In
its perfection and incorruptibility, six was considered circular, and
the poem thus illustrates how past, present, and future—the Son at
the beginning of mortal time, during mortal time, and at the end of
mortal time—will see the defeat of evil. (The readings of Mother
Christopher and William Hunter cited above reinforce the point: see
n. 3 for Chap. 3) Then too, Philo wrote that mortal beings were mea-
sured by the number six. The first six books are heavenly and cover
those matters which will measure man. The number two was the
image of matter, thus eternal but not immutable—and therefore the
council in Hell, and Sin and Death. Two as the number of duplicity
becomes the number of the book in which duplicity is set forth in actual doubling as well as in deceit. According to Plutarch, it "is the
divell and evill" (*The Morals,* trans. Philemon Holland [London,
1603], p. 812). Four represents the Earth and man, just as the final
four books deal with earth and man. It is in Book IV that man and
Earth first enter the poem, although reference to them has been
made in the prior three books. The placement of man and Earth in
this book reinforces the conclusion that Milton was using number
concepts as one type of literary composition. Eight came to mean the
day of justice for Albertus Magnus, but as the cube of two, eight
seems to illustrate the triple action of the infernal trinity of Book II.
Four and eight, as feminine and thus weak numbers, subject to division and multiple concepts of duplicity, require that the assault and
fall of Eve take place in those books of the epic. Eight likewise represented providence and eternal regeneration. Three represents the
perfect unity of the Holy Trinity; seven is the universal, archetypal
number, the hebdomad of the created, and the sum of three (the
Godhead) and four (the symbol of man). Together, of course, three
and seven—the Godhead and the universe—represent totality and
perfection. It is thus obvious why the Council of Heaven appears in
Book III and why the creation takes place in Book VII.

Five was simply associated with six, the much more important of
the two combinations (addition and multiplication) of two and three.
Two indicates the female; three, the male. Milton unites the two
books, allowing part of Book V to illustrate the domestic love of

of Adam and Eve, Book VI to illustrate the pervasive love of the Son for the Father and God for mankind, and Books V and VI together to illustrate the action of duplicity upon the otherwise unified world which the mysterious Trinity of God through mutual love can beget. The Son so loved the Father that they begot the Holy Spirit, but another son of God, we understand, so envied his Father that he begot Sin at the moment of envious thought, and they together begot Death. Milton stresses the begetting of the Son and his love for his Father in Books V and VI, but we know from Sin's account in Book II that perverse generation was also taking place at exactly the same time. Since these books are numbers V and VI with their conceptual bases, Sin's account can not enter these books explicitly, but having learned of her generation before, we remember (or should remember) that account as we read. Satan's "Sleepst thou Companion dear" (V, 673), addressed to Beelzebub, an aspect of himself, and appropriate for a book numbered five, suggests perversion of love.[5] We should also note that a strong narcissistic love is the hinge of all good action and all evil action: it is through the prescient love of God for man, who was to be created *ex deo*, that providence (ultimately the providing of the Son) exists; it is through the love of Son and Father (two aspects of the same being) that the Holy Spirit is generated; and, one may add, it is through all God's sons' love of Him that the Holy Spirit will continue to be generated; but it is through the love of Satan for himself that Sin is generated, and then as Sin tells her Father (II, 763-767), it is through his narcissistic (and incestuous) love that Death is born; and finally it is through Adam's love of Eve ("Flesh of my Flesh, / Bone of my Bone thou art," IX, 914-915), basically a narcissistic love, that Satan, Sin, and Death are able to invade and control man's world. The reversals are, as everywhere in this poem, of great significance: Satan seduces Sin to beget Death, but Eve seduces Adam to allow death to come into existence. In the myth of Narcissus, death enters as Narcissus drowns for his self-love; but whereas water becomes the element of death (and so the desiccation of the end of Book X as Adam and Eve leave Paradise), water is also the element of resurrection and life when it represents repentance and the female quality of love. Self-love is evil only when it does not radiate outward to love of all creatures. Pride in the self becomes a love for the godliness within one. Books V and VI, operating together under concepts of love through combinations of femaleness and maleness, constitute Milton's version of the standard theme of love's war, the myth of Venus and Mars.

Nine, being just short of ten, shows defect amid perfection according to Christian symbolism, but as it is the square of three, it also exhibits God's will—and Book IX of *Paradise Lost* illustrates the ambivalence in the mysticism of this number. Undoubtedly, Milton placed certain themes and actions in certain books because of numerological concepts which were commonplace for the medieval and Renaissance mind. The skepticism that has been voiced over analyses of this kind of literary composition has arisen from two difficulties. Commentators have often presented their findings as if they were superimposing numerological schemes upon literature, and many modern readers simply are uninformed, first, about numerological beliefs common to the Renaissance, and second, about the way that literature is written. A literary work is rarely the result of putting pen to paper without outine, plan, devices—all those matters one can label a pre-text or a foreconceit—as Dorothy Canfield Fisher once alleged to be her method and as some so-called inspired inexperienced poets would suggest. I suspect that it is the belief that poetic writing needs merely inspiration that has often led to a damning of the Romantic poet—possibly Shelley more than any other—and it continues to plague critics as belief that all writing is but personal effusion—no compositional cerebration, no planning, no technique. The incompetent statements that have been made about such poets as Samuel Daniel, John Donne, and Henry Vaughan, for instance, manifest the truth of the thought. But the Renaissance poet knew differently and knew as a commonplace the symbolism of numbers and the geometric design that would effect a well-wrought urn.[6] The influence of numbers that I am suggesting is only a metaphor for meaning within a work of literature. The meaning is what is important, and the Renaissance poet used this device among so many others as one of the metaphors to underline that meaning. Milton's poem is a creation celebrating the greatest of creators and the greatest of His creations. Just as God's universe is intricately wrought and built on proportion and degree, so is *Paradise Lost.*

Such composition is not really arithmetic but, rather, symbolic. However, as Qvarnström has argued in *The Enchanted Palace,* other schemes of numerological patternings seem to exist in the poem. Whether one wishes to accept all of his (and others') suggestions—

and some become questionable through shifting of data and meanings attached to those data—nonetheless the kind of arithmetic composition that has been adduced in Vergil and Spenser, for two obvious examples whose works Milton knew well, seems to appertain in *Paradise Lost*. The kind of arithmetic composition which Qvarnström adduces, for example, notes that the important description in VI, 723-823, is preceded and followed by two 23-line speeches by the Son, and 23 signifies divine judgment upon sinners. Or, as another example, Butler remarks that "Uriel's speech in praise of the Creation (III, 694-735) takes 42 lines, that is, the number of days of creation, seven, times six, the number of perfection" (p. 151).

I would mention only two other ways in which Milton seems to have "counted lines." The introduction of Death into the narrative occurs at II, 666, a fact which can not simply be fortuitous. My remarks on the significance of two explains Death's entry in that book, but the specific line number loudly proclaims the Beast of Revelation: "Here is wisdom. Let him that hath understanding count the number of the beast: for it is the number of a man; and his number is Six hundred threescore and six" (Rev. 13:18). In terms of the balances and parallels which I have discussed in the preceding chapter, we know that Milton will compose his epic to balance the entry of Death at II, 666, appropriately as death enters man's world. And it is in Book VIII (IX of the second edition) that Adam falls and specifically at the reversed line 999:

> he scrupl'd not to eat
> Against his better knowledge, not deceav'd
> But fondly overcome with Femal charm.
>
> (IX, 997-999)

The very next lines indicate that the Fall has at that moment occurred.

> Earth trembl'd from her entrails, as again
> In pangs, and Nature gave a second groan,
> Skie lowr'd, and muttering Thunder, som sad drops
> Wept at compleating of the mortal Sin
> Original. . . .
>
> (IX, 1000-1004)

Note the birth imagery employed as well as the water (rain) imagery. The reversal of lines from 666 to 999 is not arithmetic of composition, of course, but hieroglyphic and symbolic.

Mathematical proportions may also exist in the poem through the employment of the golden mean (.618), a well-known concept in art but only rather recently recognized as significant in literature. The point of focal interest in a painting is not dead center, but a position offset in mathematical proportion, describable by the compass. The golden section, as it is traditionally called, is roughly .618 from two sides of the painting (thus roughly .382 from the other two sides). In literature, the golden mean is used as a balancing proportion between various sections of a work, yielding a ratio of relative importance between those sections and, what is most important, indicating that the two means exist in relationship. The golden mean for the first edition of *Paradise Lost* is VII, 1094 (that is, VIII, 477), and its surrounding lines. The twenty lines lying on either side of this present God's address to Adam concerning Adam's "fit help," his "other self," and the creation of Eve from Adam's rib as he sleeps. At line VIII, 478, he awakens. The placement of Eve's creation at the focal point of the total epic is clearly significant and, just as clearly, must have been planned. The first half of the poem had been devoted to an exposition of the cause; the first section of the epic poem in terms of the golden mean iterates cause in a secondary manner, for it is through weaker Eve that the seduction can take place and it is through Adam's view of her that he will succumb:

> so lovely fair,
> That what seemd fair in all the world, seemd now
> Mean, or in her summ'd up, in her containd
> And in her looks, which from that time infus'd
> Sweetness into my heart, unfelt before,
> And into all things from her Air inspir'd
> The spirit of love and amorous delight.
>
> (VIII, 471–477)

Indeed, just as Book III contrasts with Book VIII (of the first edition), as we have seen, so the mathematical proportion reinforces that contrast: Book VIII represents .616 of the total lines in the two books, and Book III, .384. Just as Book I contrasts with Book VII (of the first edition), so the mathematical proportion reinforces that contrast: Book VII represents .613 of the total lines of the two books, and Book I, .387.

Related to numerological considerations is the appearance of *Paradise Lost* as ten books in 1667 and as twelve books in 1674, and to this matter we should now attend. The reasons for change are speculative, and idolaters of Milton as one totally above crass judgments will be unhappy with one of my suggestions. But, on the one hand, no other explanation has been sufficiently cogent and, on the other, people seem to forget such facts as Milton's translation of *Declaration, or Letters Patents* in the same year as the second edition of *Paradise Lost,* a job done for the publisher Brabazon Aylmer for no seeming reason other than for money. And it is difficult to square Milton's allowing Dryden to tag his lines when "The Verse" states so categorically a position against tinkling rhyme and especially when "The Verse" may owe some of its existence to the controversy over rhyme and blank verse then being waged between Dryden and Sir Robert Howard, a friend of Milton.

The reorganization of *Paradise Lost* for its second edition of 1674 was effected by the division of Books VII and X into two and the addition of fifteen lines. Specifically, the changes were as follows: V, 636, 638–639 were added, and 637, 640 were altered; VII, 1–1290 became VII, 1–640 and VIII, 4–653, and VIII, 1–3 were added, l. 4 being altered; X, 1–1541 became XI, 1–901, with 485–487 being added and 551–552 being created from an alteration of one line in the first edition, and XII, 6–649 with 1–5 being added. Book VIII became Book IX; Book IX became Book X. (Alterations not affecting line count also occurred in I, 504–505, and XII, 238.) William B. Hunter, Jr., has argued that the additional lines were created, first, to effect the two book divisions, and, second, because these new eight lines changed the center of the poem, to maintain the center at VI, 761–762.[7] The center became shifted, however, in the second edition, Hunter shows, because of errors in printed line count in the first edition.

James Whaler suggested that Milton always had intended to present a twelve-book epic (thus emulating the *Aeneid*), but that numerological considerations influenced him to publish first as he did.[8] The thought is most insubstantial. Watson understandably assigned the renumbering of the books to the desire to make the symmetry of the poem more noticeable.[9] Arthur Barker proposed that redistribution was to accord with the *Aeneid* and with epic reconsiderations.[10] He views the ten-book form as a five-act drama with emphasis on the Fall as climax. The epic form which the poems had assumed called for twelve books (why is not clear, except as rival to the *Aeneid*) and for emphasis on the triad of disobedience, woe, and restoration. Barker's influential article tries to relate the ten-book form to Davenant's experiment in *Gondibert* and to view each two books as one act. It is impossible for me to see the unity of, say, old Book VII (new Books VII and VIII) with old Book VIII (new Book IX) in terms of dramatic structuring. The inclusion of the invocation in the latter book, alone, breaks up such a scheme. The only meaningfulness in reminding us of Davenant's abortive ten-book structure is recognition of the significance of ten as a unit, a point that Louis L. Martz has made in a recent examination of Sir Richard Fanshawe's translation of *The Lusiads* and its possible influence on Milton.[11] Further, Barker's belief that the twelve-book organization was felt by Milton to be necessary to emphasize the triad of disobedience, woe, and restoration in terms of three four-book units can be held, it seems to me, only by obfuscation of what the various books of *Paradise Lost* are concerned with. Book IV is hardly concerned with disobedience, and what the sections in Book X placed in Hell or descriptive of Sin and Death have to do with restoration escapes me. In any case, Milton had certainly decided well before 1665 (when the manuscript was apparently complete) to turn his dramatic attempts into an epic, and the suggested triad is not taken up in any organized order in the work. The redistribution may emphasize the Son's example for those who look only at things symmetrical as having balance, but this does not mean that such symmetry was necessary for Milton or even desirable in the poem. The drawing of good out of evil is seen also in terms of drawing order out of disorder (such as God's creation of light), of harmony out of disharmony, of proportion out of disproportion. Much more is thus achieved by a metaphor of structure where the seeming disorder, disharmony, and disproportion which the ten-book version allows disappear as the full structure is recognized. But man's finite perception has frequently failed to let him see that structure.

In view of the analysis of the balanced structure of the poem, it is difficult to believe that Milton was happy with the reorganization of the second edition, any more than he could have been happy with the addition of arguments which do not agree with the substance of the finished poem and which through three issues in 1668 and 1669 were gathered so ineffectually at the beginning of the volume. Just as he was then prevailed upon to bow down to the not very fit audience's deficiencies by supplying arguments, so was he reasoned into reorganization? The publication of seven college prolusions two months before in order to fill up a slim volume of familiar letters is not far removed from such hucksterism. As Pound would have said, "the Age demanded" an epic in supposed epic form, patterned in the way of the classics (the *Iliad* and the *Odyssey* in twenty-four books, the *Aeneid* in twelve), for the neoclassic world of literature had indeed arrived. It is not odd that within the ensuing age Dryden's translation of Vergil and Pope's of Homer would appear. The addition of Milton's remarks on the verse seem to add proof to the need to justify his work to a pedestrian reading public. For *Paradise Lost* did not sell well, as the six issues in three years attest, with their new title-pages to fool the public, and the problems for the age would lie in the vastness and complexity of the work (supposedly solved by the addition of the arguments) and in the unrhymed verse. Such reactions as Thomas Rymer's and John Dryden's,[12] and the implications in Andrew Marvell's commendatory verses written in heroic couplets, make clear the importance of the prosody for that conforming age.

Milton wrote, "This neglect then of Rime so little is to be taken for a defect, though it may seem so perhaps to vulgar Readers, that it rather is to be esteem'd an example set, the first in *English,* of ancient liberty recover'd to Heroic Poem from the troublesome and modern bondage of Riming." His annoyance with vulgar readers is clear, and though he did not himself "tag" his lines, he apparently allowed Dryden to do so in *The State of Innocence,* also sometime around 1674, but before Marvell wrote. I submit that such bowing down to the demands of the age as to justify himself in "The Verse," as well as to permit "lame Meeter" to be used on basically his "matter," is not far different from supplying the arguments as "ponies" and reorganizing the work to accord with supposed "Custom."

Yet another possibility does exist, although it may be rationalizing. Milton, deliberate artist that he was, may first have worked within the Christian epic framework: Dante's 100 became Ariosto's 50, which led to Tasso's 20, which in turn divided into Milton's 10. Possibly to create a clear rival to the classical epic and the *Aeneid* in particular, Milton revised to a twelve-book structure. His poem would thus move more patently to eclipse both Homer and Vergil. For *Paradise Lost,* beginning with the devil's arrival in Hell and the denunciation of the injustice of God, contrasts sharply with the *Odyssey,* whose last book (No. 24) shows the suitors' arrival in Hell and has them proclaim the justice of their fate and the righteousness of the divine order. Did, perhaps, Milton conceive of a two-stage epic, one to rival Dante and Tasso and one to rival Homer and Vergil, the ultimate epic, as it were?[13]

At least, the reason for the division of Books VII and X is implied in the previous discussions: Book VII paralleled and balanced either Books I, II or Books V, VI; and Book X paralleled and balanced either Books V, VI or I, II. Other single books paralleled or balanced only single books. Of course, VII and X were the longest books first published (although VII was only 101 lines longer than former Book VIII), but, needless to say, two of the most important for Milton's message. As a result of division, new Book VII became the shortest, new Book XII the next shortest (despite the five additional lines), and new Book VIII the third shortest (despite three additional lines). They are all roughly a hundred lines shorter than Book III. The parallels and balances of the earlier form are maintained, although the symmetry obfuscates a major symbolic motif. The numerology has been nullified in part and the center has been slightly offset, but, as Hunter demonstrated, through printing errors. Yet the aim of paralleling and balancing was maintained, as well.

A defensible text of *Paradise Lost* must grapple with the problems of the organization of the poem as well as the specific language and accidentals. As a study of the text has shown,[14] it should be based on a full collation of the manuscript of Book I, the first edition, and the second edition. This still requires decisions to be made, for none of the three versions is without error or probable error of all types. And then, too, one must decide whether to present a modernized text, a partially unmodernized text, a fully unmodernized text reproducing what answers one comes up with in his collation, or a fully unmodernized text offering what purports to be Milton's practice in such matters as spelling or punctuation, or intentions in such matters as capitalization and paragraphing. Yet, the only decision that is viable concerning the organization of the poem is to present it in twelve books with the added and altered lines of the second edition, for Milton did "allow" the poem to be published in this form. I caution, however, that we as readers should remember the earlier conception of the poem in its parallels, its balances, and its rejection of possible audience expectations in structure and form as well as in epic qualities and style. Not to remember is to overlook a major metaphor for meaning: structure and form.

SEVEN

Sources as Meaning
& Structure

IN MILTON scholarship, too frequently sources—by which I mean
allusive or paraphrased citation as well as analogues—have been
pointed out and discussed almost exclusively to demonstrate Milton's
breadth of reading, the wellspring of his language or ideas or characterizations, his indebtedness, or the nature of his humanistic
milieu. But the study of a more modern poet like T.S. Eliot, Milton's
sometime antagonist, should have suggested that a wealth of meaning may lie in an allusion or quotation, and that the author employed such sources to invoke a context pertinent to the thought or
emotion being communicated. However, few have delved into the
significance of source in Milton's poetry, yet the significance lies in
both meaning and structure.

Isn't mere footnotage what happens frequently for Milton?[1] For
instance, Todd cited Giles Fletcher's couplet from *Christ's Victory in
Heaven,* stanza 78 ("Heaven awaked all his eyes / To see another sun
at midnight rise") for V, 44 ("Heav'n wakes with all his eyes"). But no
contextual discussion appears from the relatively few editors who
have noted the correspondence of phraseology. Eve is recounting her
dream of the night before, presented in Book IV as Satan's infiltra-
tion of her subconscious in order to determine the means to seduce
the "new Race call'd *Man*" to Satan's party. She remembers a gentle
voice, supposedly Adam's, bidding her to come forth to be viewed by
the stars. The full orbed moon now reigns, and such light is given in
vain if none regard it. The voice plays upon seduction by vanity:
"Whom to behold but thee, Natures desire," "Attracted by thy
beauty." Milton is, of course, admonishing the reader not to succumb to a frequent and false premise underlying the voice's argu-

ment; that is, the premise that beauty, good, or like virtues have no substance, no meaning, if isolated from common view. This is not the same as the cloistered virtue of *Areopagitica*. Here in *Paradise Lost,* Milton is remarking that beauty is beauty regardless of circumstances; in *Areopagitica* he is remarking that after the Fall goodness can not be assumed to exist in one unless that goodness is put to the test, not that it does not exist in one. Satan repeats the false argument in IX, 542-546:

> but here
> In this enclosure wild, these Beasts among,
> Beholders rude, and shallow to discern
> Half what is thee is fair, one man except,
> Who sees thee?

In Milton's lines, when we remember Fletcher, the stars see Eve as "another sun at midnight," subtly insinuating part of the argument in Book IX that will seduce Eve: "Fairest resemblance of thy Maker fair, / Thee all things living gaze on . . . / and thy Celestial Beautie adore . . . / Empress of this fair World, resplendent *Eve,*" and "ye should be as Gods" (IX, 538-540, 568). The contrast between the dream at night—at midnight—and the Fall which will come during the day—at the hour of noon—is perhaps evoked here too in Book V by our remembrance of Fletcher's lines. But the lines come from Fletcher's account of Christ's nativity, the sun that rises at midnight being the Christ child born in the manger. Recalling this, we recognize that Eve in her dream was being tested for possibilities of envy. Satan, having assayed the organs of her fancy, can in Book IX move from praise of her beauty, as obvious here, to development of envy of the Gods. For Fletcher, the nativity "was never sight of pareil fame," and, as it were, for Milton the Fall was never sight of equal infamy. Fletcher says, "For God before, man like Himselfe, did frame, / But God Himselfe now like a mortall man became." The stars awake in *Christ's Victory* to behold the miracle of the Incarnation; in Eve's dream they awake to behold "Natures desire." The contrast is most extreme on all counts: humility / self-aggrandizement, beauty of soul / bodily beauty, selflessness / self. The verbs "awaked" and "wakes" particularly write an important thought in bold letters: the stars exist during the day but are simply not on view to man, and the fact that they "awake" at night from their sleep makes prominent the contrast with man who "wakes" at daybreak from his sleep. The lines allegorize the awakening stars as men who learn that God comes forth in darkness (with whatever metaphoric meaning is applicable) to lead the potentially misled traveler of life's path. The heavenly eyes in Milton's poem are as personified as possible for Eve's nonpopulated world. The allusion to *Christ's Victory* emphasizes the contrast between night / day, midnight / noon, sun / moon, and faith / demonstration.

In Satan's use of the stars as eyes, the metaphoric meaning of their existence is perverted. The "Eyes / That run through all the Heav'ns," identified with the seven around the throne of God (III, 648-651) and the eyes of the cherubim of Ezekiel's wheel (recurrent in the epic), are there for the purpose of guarding man. Through Satan, they become elements to vent man's vanity. The context of the lines in *Christ's Victory* make the stars part of the celebration of justice. The Son and his incarnation constitute the great Providence of God to achieve justice for man, who will err in the ways that are adumbrated in Eve's dream: through the hypocrisy of Satan, through wrong reason, through vanity, and through envy of God. Eve's dream supplies a double vision, once we remember this "source," the Fall and the nativity which will be necessary to counter its effect.

I would like to examine a passage from *Paradise Lost* that is afforded greater meaning once sources are fully brought to bear on it. It is the kind of examination needed throughout the poem. I choose a passage already discussed in part, IV, 970-1015 (Satan speaking first):

970	when I am thy captive talk of chains,
	Proud limitarie Cherub, but ere then
	Farr heavier load thy self expect to feel
	From my prevailing arm, though Heavens King
	Ride on thy wings, and thou with thy Compeers,
975	Us'd to the yoak, draw'st his triumphant wheels
	In progress through the rode of Heav'n Star-pav'd.
	While thus he spake, th' Angelic Squadron bright
	Turnd fierie red, sharpning in mooned horns
	Thir Phalanx, and began to hemm him round

980   With ported Spears, as thick as when a field
        Of *Ceres* ripe for harvest waving bends
        Her bearded Grove of ears, which way the wind
        Sways them; the careful Plowman doubting stands
        Least on the threshing floor his hopeful sheaves
985   Prove chaff. On th' other side *Satan* allarm'd
        Collecting all his might dilated stood,
        Like *Teneriff* or *Atlas* unremov'd:
        His stature reacht the Skie, and on his Crest
        Sat horror Plum'd; nor wanted in his grasp
990   What seemd both Spear and Shield: now dreadful deeds
        Might have ensu'd, nor onely Paradise
        In this commotion, but the Starrie Cope
        Of Heav'n perhaps, or all the Elements
        At least had gon to rack, disturb'd and torn
995   With violence of this conflict, had not soon
        Th' Eternal to prevent such horrid fray
        Hung forth in Heav'n his golden Scales, yet seen
        Betwixt *Astrea* and the *Scorpion* signe,
        Wherein all things created first he weigh'd,
1000   The pendulous round Earth with ballanc't Air
        In counterpoise, now ponders all events,
        Battels and Realms: in these he put two weights
        The sequel each of parting and of fight;
        The latter quick up flew, and kickt the beam;
1005   Which *Gabriel* spying, thus bespake the Fiend.
            Satan, I know thy strength, and thou knowst mine,
        Neither our own but giv'n; what follie then
        To boast what Arms can doe, since thine no more
        Then Heav'n permits, nor mine, though doubl'd now
1010   To trample thee as mire: for proof look up,
        And read thy Lot in yon celestial Sign
        Where thou art weigh'd, and shown how light, how weak,
        If thou resist. The Fiend lookt up and knew
        His mounted scale aloft: no more; but fled
1015   Murmuring, and with him fled the shades of night.

Sources have been offered from the Bible and classical literature, that is, Homer and Vergil, and these I shall reexamine. Line 974 has been referred to Ps. 18:10 by Henry John Todd: "And he rode upon a cherub, and did fly: yea, he did fly upon the wings of the wind." The irony that Milton intends can not be appreciated unless we remember that Psalm 18 is a song of David for God's deliverance of him "from the hand of all his enemies, and from the hand of Saul." Satan, the antitype of Saul, is boasting that until such time as he is captive of God, he will give battle to the good angels and will prevail, even though God accompanies them in their opposition. Milton has Satan specifically allude to a victory of God and man (David) over one who has become an instrument of Satan. He is reminding us in the biblical reference that God will prevail regardless of Satan's boast, regardless of his seeming victory. For Satan will seem to prevail over man until such time as he is captive, and he will be captive and in chains only when the millennium begins, at which time an angel will "come down from heaven, having the key to the bottomless pit and a great chain in his hand. And he laid hold on the dragon, that old serpent, which is the Devil, and Satan, and bound him a thousand years, and cast him into the bottomless pit, and shut him up, and set a seal upon him" (Rev. 20:1-3).[2] Milton has telescoped time here at the end of Book IV, soon after Satan has assayed the organs of Eve's fancy, by a veiled statement of Satan's success on earth and a clear reference to the conclusion of his reign when the reign of Christ begins—the subjects of the epic. The beginning of Book IX (Book VIII of the first version) balances the ending of Book IV by specific references to this passage, with language and figures repeated (see IX, 53-86). But further, the psalm makes clear that God delivers that man from his enemies who calls upon the Lord, as Adam and Eve must learn to do. The end of Book X (Book IX of the first version) here shows reverse parallels with the ending of Book IV, as Adam and Eve proceed to this realization:

> What better can we do, then to the place
> Repairing where he judg'd us, prostrate fall
> Before him reverent, and there confess
> Humbly our faults, and pardon beg, with tears
> Watering the ground, and with our sighs the Air
> Frequenting, sent from hearts contrite, in sign
> Of sorrow unfeign'd, and humiliation meek.
>
> (X, 1086-1092)

The water and air imagery may have some relationship to God's pavilion in the psalm (verse 11).

Line 974 has also been referred (by Bishop Thomas Newton) to Ezek. 1:24, all of chapter 10, and 11:22, which recite God's wheel in the heavens (see l. 975) and the cherubim whose wings lift them above the earth. The four cherubim, who are all eyes, had four faces each: one of a cherub, one of a man, one of a lion, and one of an eagle. While the emphasis on four suggests man, the progression of faces implied Christ to a later age, the latter two symbols being specifically identified with him, and with the four evangelists. These faces are, of course, the beasts, "full of eyes before and behind," around the throne of God: lion, calf, man, flying eagle (Rev. 4:6-7). Again Milton, for the informed reader, is alluding to the presence of God, His omniscience, and the triumph through Christ for men in their struggle with Satan. Not only does such hope emerge from the allusions, but Satan himself attests to its validity: "when I am thy captive," he says, and "ere then"—a clear acknowledgment that his arm will not always prevail.

There is also internal reference in the allusions of these seven lines (970-976). Satan has consciously reminded Gabriel that the chariot of God had been employed by the Son in the battle in Heaven. The Father addressed His Son after the stalemate between the opposing forces of angels:

> Go then thou Mightiest in thy Fathers might,
> Ascend my Chariot, guide the rapid Wheels
> That shake Heav'ns basis, bring forth all my Warr. . . .
> And the third sacred Morn began to shine
> Dawning through Heav'n: forth rush'd with whirlwind sound
> The Chariot of Paternal Deitie,
> Flashing thick flames, Wheel with Wheel undrawn,
> It self instinct with Spirit, but convoyd
> By four Cherubic shapes, four Faces each
> Had wondrous, as with Starrs thir bodies all
> And Wings were set with Eyes, with Eyes the Wheels
> Of Beril, and careering Fires between. . . .
> (VI, 710-712, 748-756)

With the ascendancy of the Son comes the fall of Satan; the Son advanced with twenty thousand "Chariots of God, half on each hand"

and "on the wings of Cherub rode sublime / On the Chrystallin Skie, in Saphir Thron'd" (VI, 769-771). In the War in Heaven God triumphed; now Satan, boastfully, though accurately where man is concerned, sneers at the symbol of the chariot, for he has discerned the means to triumph. While the cross-reference projects into the future of the poem and the past of the story,[3] it also points to the message for man inherent in Ezekiel's vision: only faith in God and joint action with God will allow "the spirit of the living creature" to be in man so that Satan's force of arms will be nullified. The image is used again specifically as the rebellious angels, now defeated, are expelled from Heaven (VI, 832-833, 844-852).

A reference for ll. 980-985 made by James Sims is 1 Cor. 9:10: "For our sakes, no doubt, this is written: that he that ploweth should plow in hope; and that he that thresheth in hope should be partaker of his hope." The angels with raised spears are first likened to a field of wheat ready for harvest; in the direction that the wind blows so bend the stalks. That is, as Satan moves, so do the spears to be immediately ready for action. This leads to the image of the Plowman overlooking his wheat field, anxious whether the ears will be nothing but chaff when finally threshed. So is the Angelic Squadron "careful" that their spears will prove worthy when finally put to the test. Just as the wheat may be damaged by such atmospheric conditions as wind, so may their spears be broken betimes by the windy boasts of Satan, provoking them to premature conflict. The squadron exhibit hope in their action of hemming in Satan, but they are also full of care (anxious) lest the balance not be on their side. (The whole of the verse paragraph, ll. 977-1005, is conditioned by its final image of the scales.) The biblical reference equates the angelic squadron with the apostles, who are given the right (or power) to do God's work and at the same time to be as ordinary men, eating, drinking, forbearing to work. Verses 11-12 ask, "If we have sown unto you spiritual things, is it a great thing if we shall reap your carnal things? If others be partakers of this power over you, are not we rather?" The reference to St. Paul's words makes clear that while the angels move to do what they have been bidden, they are still, without sin from doubt, liable to such humanly reactions as anxiety. Their partaking of hope is proper, but hope implies the possibility of failure (or "fear" as Satan had earlier remarked [IV, 108]). The biblical reference assures the reader that the angels' fear is not unworthy. And the immediately ensuing lines indicate that it is Satan who is alarmed, while the squadron feel but care. Satan, being alarmed, is experiencing fear, even though he had said farewell to it before.

In reaction, Satan makes himself seem huge, like the mountain Teneriff or Atlas, and his stature reaches the sky. Newton cited Wis. of Sol. 18:16: "And brought thine unfeigned commandment as a sharp sword, and stood up, and filled all things with death, and being come down to the earth, it reached unto the heavens." What is interesting about the citation, should it have been in Milton's mind as a figure on earth filling the skies, is the reversal again of an image of God, who here descends to deliver the faithful Israelites by smiting the Egyptians. (See Chapter Eleven for the significance of the myth of Exodus.) The Word of God which has leapt down from heaven, "as a fierce man of war in the midst of the land that was destroyed," is reflected in the epic as the golden scales set in the heavens, the celestial sign of Satan's lot. While the language of l. 988 may have specifically been suggested by this verse from Wisdom, the whole passage takes on meaning from the chapter. First, there is the equation of God's Word with the celestial sign. Second, as we see over and over in the poem, language relating to God is appropriated for Satan to emphasize his unlikeness to God, since he would have proceeded to actual combat ("now dreadful deeds / Might have ensu'd"). Third, the hidden allusion to the Exodus which the biblical reference implies suggests that the celestial sign for Satan is a metaphoric equivalent to the plagues visited on Pharaoh, who is identified mythically with Satan.

The scales themselves and the weighing of man derives, as Newton noted, from various biblical texts,[4] though classical literature supplied Milton with more direct matter. Line 1012, for which Newton recalled Dan. 5:27, can nonetheless be seen to imply for the reader that Satan, given the celestial sign, has like Belshazzar seen the handwriting on the wall. He realizes through the scales that "God hath numbered [his] kingdom, and finished it" and that "[He is] weighed in the balances, and [is] found wanting."[5] And this is the meaning of ll. 1013–1014: "The Fiend lookt up and knew / His mounted scale aloft." The numbering of Belshazzar's kingdom repeats the implication that Satan will be victorious for a while (as Belshazzar has been in lifting up himself against the Lord of Heaven), but that his "nation" will fall. The gloss of the Geneva Bible is particularly apt: "This worde [Mene] is twise writen for the certeintie of ye thing: shewing, that God hath moste surely counted: signifying also that God hathe appointed a terme for all kingdomes, & y^t a miserable end shal come on all that raise them selues against him." Not only is Satan given a sign, but all of hard heart are warned of the weightlessness of their opposing God. The biblical allusion makes most clear the application of the message beyond the literal narrative of the poem.

Opposing Satan's sign is the Son's at the height of the War in Heaven; "the great Ensign of *Messiah* blaz'd / Aloft by Angels born, his Sign in Heav'n" (VI, 775–776). Derived from Matt. 24:30 ("And then shall appear the sign of the Son of man in heaven: and then shall all the tribes of the earth mourn, and they shall see the Son of man coming in the clouds of heaven with power and great glory"), the sign avails to convince the proud (like Belshazzar) to relent. In the War of Heaven, Satan and his cohorts disdain flight or faint retreat ("parting" in Book IV); here Satan recognizes the sign and chooses to flee. The sign for Satan should bring to mind the signs and wonders presented to Pharaoh, referred to over and over again in the Bible. The end of Book IV therefore seems to be another facet of the basic motif of Exodus examined later. And the contrast with the sign of Book VI, which comes at what is the beginning of time for man and which is eschatological in its source (Matthew), should stress for the reader the need to observe and interpret signs. Although all uses of *sign* should be examined, we might here just note two uses in IV, 428–429, before Adam and Eve can understand the words' meanings as signs; two uses just after Eve's fall in IX, 783, and soon after Adam's fall in IX, 1077; three uses in XI, 182, 194 (where Adam recognizes them as signs though he does not understand fully), and 351; and finally the use in the midst of his discussion of the captivity of the Israelites by Pharaoh when Michael tells Adam,

> But first the lawless Tyrant, who denies
> To know thir God, or message to regard,
> Must be compell'd by Signes and Judgements dire.
>   (XII, 173–175)

For man, however, there will be signs to point the path to salvation, such as baptism (XII, 441–445), which washes from guilt of sin to life. One way of looking at *Paradise Lost* is that Milton has supplied his readers with signs both for those who would exercise lawless tyranny and for those who would love God. The scales will be tipped for each man by his attention to such signs.

Editors have also seen a number of classical sources in this final passage of Book IV. Line 980 was related by Newton to a passage in the *Iliad* II, 147 — in Pope's translation:

> And as on corn when western gusts descend,
> Before the blast the lofty harvests bend:
> Thus o'er the field the moving host appears,
> With nodding plumes and groves of waving spears.
>
> (II, 179–182)

This describes the Argive warriors, who have been stirred by Agamemnon's speech to set sail for home, abandoning assault on Troy as impossible of success. Their return, Homer says, would have been against the will of fate. This simile is used as an ironic description of the steadfastness toward duty which the guardian angels exhibit, for it is not the angels who flee or are even tempted to flee, but rather Satan. Their opposition to Satan, the further context of the Greek epic implies, is part of God's will. However, while the Greeks will be deterred by Athene (Wisdom) and will enter and conquer Troy, it is Satan who will return, reenter Eden, and conquer the first parents. The ruse of the Trojan horse and the serpent's body is worthy of note as well. The simile, predicating the wrong reason of the Greeks but the right reason of the angels, serves to underline the reversal in Satan's action: the admonition of Athene causes Odysseus to turn back the Greeks, and the sign in the heavens causes Satan to flee. But the allusion has further meaning for Milton's poem. Agamemnon's speech has arisen from a fraudulent dream implanted by Zeus; it is the first instance of the complex treachery that delineates the first half of Book II. Zeus has advised Agememnon to attack Troy at once, for he will supposedly win, but Agamemnon plans to rally the men by telling them to return home and by then expecting the commanders to resist and to incite the men to stay and fight. And this is what happens, for soon afterward Odysseus and Nestor interpret signs as indicative of success. Satan's insinuation into Eve's dream for fraudulent purposes and the sign in heaven which indicates Satan's lot reinforce Milton's remembrance of the simile from the *Iliad,* and the reader familiar with the passage will see the angels as agents of divine will and the episode as a necessary one to remind us of the reversals of truth which the wrong-reasoning Satan gathers about him.

Satan as a great mountain, l. 987, may reflect the *Aeneid* XII, 701 (Newton). Dryden's translation:

> Like Eryx, or like Athos, great he shows,
> Or Father Apennine, when, white with snows,
> His head divine obscure in clouds he hides,
> And shakes the sounding forest on his sides.
>
> (XII, 1020-1023)

The situation depicts Aeneas' final battle with Turnus in single fight while the nations stand awed. Aeneas is victorious but dies. He has appeared as a great mountain as he challenges Turnus, but in *Paradise Lost* it is Satan for whom the image is appropriated, and his challenge is nullified by God's hanging forth in heaven the golden scales. Is there an implication that Satan would have won against the guardian angels had not God intervened? At least he does win in the combat with Adam and Eve later in Book IX, returning to Hell in Book X to tell of his bad success. Or does the allusion only supply another heroic, though specious, image for Satan, the deceiver, the character of many appearances? Soon after Aeneas' fight begins (XII, 725),

> Jove sets the beam; in either scale he lays
> The champion's fate, and each exactly weighs,
> On this side life, and lucky chance ascends;
> Loaded with death, that other scale descends,
>
> (XII, 1054-1057)

which passage Masson noted for l. 997 and Newton for ll. 1003-1005. Satan's fate is likewise "death" (defeat) if he resist (see ll. 1012-1013). That Aeneas' and Turnus' fates are the same seems to be picked up in Gabriel's description of his and Satan's strength as dependent upon God. "Lucky chance" is light, and it is chance rather than providence by which Satan (and Chaos) work; God's providence is seen throughout *Paradise Lost* as the opposing force (as here in the sign) to all that Satan attempts. We can thus read the allusion as indicating that in the battle which will ensue between Satan and God's good creatures, Adam and Eve, neither will win and both will be defeated, but God's champions will, like Aeneas, found a new world.

The scales also derive from the *Iliad* (VIII, 69 and XXII, 209).

> The Sire of Gods his golden scales suspends,
> With equal hand: in these explor'd the fate
> Of Greece and Troy, and pois'd the mighty weight.
> Press'd with its load the Grecian balance lies
> Low sunk on earth, the Trojan strikes the skies.
>
> (VIII, 88–92)

> Jove lifts the golden balances, that show
> The fates of mortal men, and things below:
> Here each contending hero's lot he tries,
> And weighs with equal hand their destinies.
> Low sinks the scale surcharg'd with Hector's fate;
> Heavy with death it sinks, and Hell receives the weight.
>
> (XXII, 271–276)

Newton cited the first for ll. 997 and 1003; Addison cited the second for ll. 996–997 and Newton for l. 1003. In the first passage, Zeus weighs the scales in the advantage of the Trojans since the Greeks have been winning. The reference underlines the power of God and powerlessness of the combatants when he intervenes. The scales effect a postponement of the real battle that must be fought between Satan and Adam and Eve, just as in the *Iliad* Zeus's interference evens up the score until Book XXII, when Achilles will slay Hector (as in single combat Aeneas slew Turnus) and the Greeks will win. Again Milton's ironic usage of allusion is striking: while Satan's fate seems to be that of the Greeks here and in the next encounter (in Book IX), it is not Satan who ultimately succeeds. The passage in Book XXII of the *Iliad* places Achilles' and Hector's fate in the balance, and it is Hector's scale that descends, signifying death.[6]

Of course, the scales are also Libra, the sign of the zodiac for September 23–October 22, beginning therefore at the autumnal equinox. It suggests another level or kind of source, as mentioned before. The autumnal equinox is the diametrical opposite point from the vernal equinox, when the sun rises in Aries at the sign of the Ram. Just as that is the sign of the Son, so this is the sign of Satan, and thus at this point in the narrative we have the beginning of "ascendancy" of Satan. What lies before, symbolically implied in l. 998, is Innocence (Astrea, or Virgo), and what lies after is Evil (Scorpio). The balances, as in the Homeric parallels, are equalized at this time for Adam and Eve between Innocence and Evil. For the time beng God has tipped the scales, but Satan's next appearance in the "present" of the narrative (that is, in Book IX) will show the scales tipped in his favor. In terms of the zodiac, Milton has given the reader clues to what is to happen, a point also made earlier in a different context. After Satan's appearance as serpent (Scorpio) will come wounding and fall (Sagittarius), followed by lust (Capricorn)—all Book IX. Book X will bring repentance and renewed spirit (Aquarius) and the mercy of the Son (Pisces). In Book XII will be recounted for the couple the example of the Son incarnate (Aries) as they leave Eden to wend the beginning of man's recurrent journey through life.[7]

In contrast with the ending of Book IV is the ending of Book X, as already noted. Adam's speech (ll. 1013-1096) acknowledges God's judgment upon them and rejects death for the first parents as well as childlessness (both previously suggested), because either would allow the Foe to "scape his punishment ordain'd." Adam recognizes his lot ("the Curse aslope / Glanc'd on the ground") to labor for his bread and the eternal signs of their disobedience, "Th' inclement Seasons, Rain, Ice, Hail and Snow, etc.," things of the skies. Unlike Satan who rises to great, and false, height, Adam and Eve humble themselves, "with tears / Watering the ground." Their actions stated by Adam as about to occur are repeated by the narrative voice as actually occurring in the final lines of the book, and these actions become a "sign / Of sorrow unfeign'd, and humiliation meek." Therefore, we see that the passage in Book IV is related in sharp contrast to the final passage of Book X. But the contrast is also in the sources we have looked at.

The previous reference to Ps. 18:10 establishes that here Adam and Eve's prayer (delivered immediately afterward in Book XI) is like David's to God for deliverance from the hand of all God's enemies. God's wheel in Heaven and the eyes of the cherubim are not mentioned explicitly in Adam's speech, but he acknowledges God's presence and His "look serene" once they give sign of contriteness. The lines from 1 Cor. 9:10 echo, too, behind the ending of Book X, this time with direct meaning: "For our sakes, no doubt, this is written: that he that ploweth should plow in hope; and that he that thresheth in hope should be partaker of his hope." Like St. Paul in verse 11–12, Adam and Eve have already shown their "humanness"; and accordingly, the underlying fear that their hope will be dashed ("Undoubtedly he will relent and turn / From his displeasures") can not be condemned. The concept of a sign such as Milton describes in Book IV and which can be related variously to biblical texts plays an important role in Adam and Eve's understanding of the direness of their disobedience and at the same time is employed by them to demonstrate their repentance. Satan's sign, if you will, is his aggrandizement to mountain size and to armed warrior exhibiting horror. To see Satan in Book IV (and the various sources of his description) is to understand Adam and Eve in Book X as direct opposites. The passage in Book IV and its sources determine in reverse what Milton presents in the parallel (or contrastive) structure of Book X.

It is therefore most significant that this structurally parallel section, X, 1013–1104, has been almost totally unannotated. Illustrations of language have been offered (for *sere,* l. 1071; *Tine,* l. 1075); one of a cosmological ideal (for l. 1073, from Lucretius V, 1091–1094); and Hume's notation that the repetition of ll. 1098–1104 is common to Homer and Vergil. Sims has listed a number of biblical items (one of which had been previously noted by Keightley; John 16:21 for l. 1052), but these prove to supply biblical history (such as the prophecy that Jesus will bruise the serpent's head) or language (such as, "contrite heart" and "his ear will be open").[8] Two items, nonetheless, are worthy of special attention. Line 1053 talks of the "Fruit of thy Womb," the same phrase spoken by Elizabeth to Mary concerning Jesus (Luke 1:42). The phrase thus implicitly restates the prophecy, some lines after Adam and Eve have explicitly recited it. In ll. 1050–1053 Adam repeats that the judgment on Eve is the pain of childbearing and the joy that will ensue; similar is John 16:21: "Verily, verily, I say unto you, that ye shall weep and lament, but the world shall rejoice; and ye shall be sorrowful, but your sorrow shall be turned into joy." Milton thus emphasizes both the mystery and greatness of birth—his poem, after all, is as clearly about all kinds of creation as it is about Satan's destructiveness—and the underlying dialectic of the poem that out of evil will come good, out of darkness will come light, out of trial and sorrow will come joy and eternal bliss.

It is evident that these citations for the final passage of Book X are most unlike those for the parallel (contrastive) ending of Book IV. All this is consciously calculated, I am sure. The passage in IV is fabricated of signs, hidden and obverse meanings, accommodations to present the myth of Satan; this is the nonhuman world evoked to make sense of the human world. The passage in X is woven of truths, observable through all time; it need not be accommodated, need not be hidden, need not be metaphoric. This is the human world of us all. Read the passage anew and discover the ever-present: it is man's life "till we end / In dust, our final rest and native home." Until such time, the tears watering the ground will obviate mere dust. The ending of Book X should, of course, be compared with the end of the poem with its images of desiccation and the eschatological line, "Some natural tears they drop'd, but wip'd them soon," referring to Rev. 21:4: "And God shall wipe away all tears from their eyes; and there shall be no more death, neither sorrow, nor crying, neither shall there by any more pain; for the former things are passed away."

While the sources in this passage from Book IV influence the contrastive structure of the poem to eschew such sources in the passage from Book X, their echoes in the beginning of the complementary (balanced) Book IX condition the structure and explain why there has been a reversal in usage in Book IV. The classical parallels in Book IV, used with inverse meaning and generally applied to Satan, illustrate ironically Milton's rejection of the less heroic theme and champion, which he discusses in the proem to Book IX. Here he finds his subject more heroic than the wrath of Achilles and his fight with Hector, Aeneas' contention against Turnus, Neptune's revenge on Ulysses, and Juno's harassment of Aeneas. These kinds of subjects—wars, fabled knights, feigned battles—do not justly give a poem or person an heroic name. The assignment of these "heroic" acts to Satan in Book IV undermines the heroism of these works and their agents, and we have been prepared through such "sources" to understand Milton's rejection of the "hitherto . . . onely Argument / Heroic deem'd."

The view of sources for the poem suggested here makes reading complex and difficult. But this is not just any poem. The more we examine it, the more convinced we become that it, like God's creation, is mysteriously wrought, incapable of mere blue-printing, a constant and true fountain of light. It is a creation celebrating creation, and Milton has provided many avenues to its understanding. Source awareness, like its kin, metaphoric meaning, is but one.

EIGHT

The Genre

ALMOST consistently, Milton's poem has been termed tragic despite its hopeful thesis.[1] The concept of man's Fall with its introduction of sinning into man's world and its creation of mortality has been too overpowering for readers to remember that this was, for Milton and others, a most fortunate fall. The classification has led to discussion of the tragic hero—usually Satan, whose *hamartia* (or tragic flaw) was considered *hubris* (or overweening pride) as in so many Greek tragedies. Perhaps when *Paradise Lost* was first being planned in the 1640s, such interpretations of Aristotle applied, though not with Lucifer as hero. But as epic (from the late 1650s onward?), not only does the poem exhibit tragic formulas, but it offers various approaches to the comic mode, illustrating definitions proposed both before and after its composition.

The classification of *Paradise Lost* as tragedy is repeated in such a major study as O.B. Hardison Jr.'s *The Enduring Monument*,[2] which shortly thereafter discusses the comic mode in literature but not in Milton's poem.

First, comedy is a form that rebukes vice—as surely Satan and Sin are rebuked through the vision which Adam shares with Michael and through the example of the Son's warfare both in Heaven and later on Earth. (The temptation in the wilderness and the Son's rejection of Satan's wiles are never missing from the poem: I, 4–5, "till one greater Man / Restore us, and regain the blissful Seat," immediately sets forth the hope that "the Promis'd Seed shall all restore," XII, 623.) Vice in comic terms was a morality figure, who, like his descendent Sir John Falstaff, was repulsed in favor of Virtue (or specified virtues) after the protagonist had consorted with him. Adam's losing of Paradise had been first conceived in terms of a morality play, as the Trinity MS attests: the effect of Lucifer's seduction, which brought in mutes like "Labour, Sicknesse, Discontent, Ignorance, Feare, Death," and the like, is offset by the comfort and instruction of "Faith, Hope, Charity."[3] Following Michael's foretelling of the "return / Of him so lately promis'd to thy aid" (XII, 541-542), which will "bring forth fruits Joy and eternal Bliss" (XII, 551), Adam, in the completed epic, affirms his realization "that to obey is best, / And . . . ever to observe / His providence, . . . / that suffering for Truths sake / Is fortitude to highest victorie" (XII, 561-570).

Second, the object of comedy is "the reprehension of the sins and follies of the middle class."[4] That is, those sins which are common in ordinary man rather than those which derive from an exalted position (such as the sins of a noble leader, a Richard III) were to be purged by ridicule, parody, incongruities, and the like (as in *Volpone*). Aside from the general reprehension of Satan in the total fabric of *Paradise Lost,* the poem is built on such parody as that of the trinity of Satan-Sin-Death through contrast with the Holy Trinity and with Chaos-Night-Day and through comparison with Zeus-Athena and Adam-Eve. Etymological puns on "Sapience" (IX, 1018; both "knowledge" and "tasting"), "Pontifical" (X, 313; both "bridge building" and "papal"), "sinister" (X, 886; both "left side" and "evil"), and the like, are found alongside ironies like "accomplisht *Eve*" (IV, 660; the participle indicating her lack of need of further accoutrements such as those to which she later succumbs) and Satan's report to his cohorts that Adam's fall is "worth your laughter" (X, 488; alluding to II, 191, and other places, and Ps. 2:4). The sum total of Milton's humor is a ridiculing of sinners, sin itself, and sin-begetters. Milton's object lesson is the foolishness of men — the opposite of Comus's exclamation berating "lean and sallow abstinence."

Whereas tragedy is engendered by the wasting of good in the process of driving out evil, Milton shows that out of the abyss will come dovelike creatures and light (I, 19-22; VII, 233-245), and

> That all this good of evil shall produce,
> And evil turn to good; more wonderful
> Then that which by creation first brought forth
> Light out of darkness!
>
> (XII, 470-473)

In tragedy, evil must be driven out because it is imperfect, the order of the universe insisting on perfection; in *Paradise Lost,* evil has been the means of man's knowing truly what good is, so that from repentance "much more good thereof shall spring," and perfection will thus come full circle for the faithful through death, which is the Gate of Life (XII, 476, 571). Comedy, like Milton's epic poem, deals with temptation (Humanity), which is followed by sin (Evil), and most significantly ends in retribution or redemption (Divine Goodness). It is concerned with a happy ending on earth, and Milton shows the present material world its path to happiness:

> by small
> Accomplishing great things, by things deemd weak
> Subverting worldly strong, and worldly wise
> By simply meek.
>
> (XII, 566–569)

In his well-known book entitled *Laughter,* Henri Bergson adduces a number of structural principles of comic form that are pertinent to my discussion above of the structure of *Paradise Lost.*[5] Besides such concerns as we have already implied (human qualities, social significance, groups rather than individuals, a mechanization of life), the comic results in the imposition of geometrical form upon the living data of formless consciousness. It operates through reduplication, parallels, and antitheses — aspects of Milton's art which have already appeared in the larger, geometric structure of the poem and in its components of characterization, description, and language.[6] One process employed in comedy is the reciprocal interference of a series; that is, the simultaneous interpretation of two independent series of events in two different ways. This goes to the heart of the matter of *Paradise Lost.* While events move toward evil — the fall of the angels, the fall of man, the creation of sin and death, the act of disobedience — they lead to ultimate good. In man's fall is his means to rise; out of darkness (whether that of the abyss or that of the narrator) comes light; out of God's Truth and Justice come the Son's Mercy and the Peace, which will ultimately reign in Heaven (a shadow of which appeared with the birth of Jesus). This ambivalence is seen both in sweeping strokes (like direction: ascent and descent; east and south opposing west and north) and in seemingly simple word or phrase. For example, at midpoint Milton wrote, "half yet remains unsung but narrower bound / Within the visible Diurnal Sphear" (VII, 21-22). We are immediately reminded of the worlds of Heaven and Hell in the first half of the poem which are invisible, eternal, and formless. We hear opposites throughout the poem, of course, just as here we read "visible" and remember "invisible." Thus may we be sure that the invisible worlds of God and Satan have been concerned all along with the visible world of man, and that man in the second half of the poem will be concerned with the invisible world of God and subject to the invisible world of Satan. (Part of what is "seen" in the second half is, we should not forget, from the "top of Specula-tion.") The repetitions and inversions help create a geometric whole that is constantly in formation. This subtends the order achieved, ac-cording to Bergson, through the disorder of comic materials. The seeming disorder of such elements as time, location, movement, and plot, in *Paradise Lost* results in a complex order, like the universe it-self, when we understand it rightly.[7]

Yet the comic nature of *Paradise Lost* is most simply realized through comparison with a progenitor of some of its thought and of its title, Dante's *Commedia*. To Dante, "Comedy, indeed, beginneth with some adverse circumstances, but its theme hath a happy termi-nation."[8] Beginning in Hell, advancing through Purgatory, Dante arrives happily in Paradise; such resolution in joy, he wrote, reflects the fundamental pattern of human existence. In *Paradise Lost,* Mil-ton is showing the reason for Dante's dark journey and suggesting the hoped-for end of that journey. Literally, Dante's journey is the pro-gress of the soul after death, but allegorically, it represents man's life, subject to reward or punishment according to his worth through his exercise of free will.[9] Literally, *Paradise Lost* depicts the life of Adam and Eve progressing through adverse circumstances which, because of their exercise of free will to disobedience, alter their exis-tence to make them subject to reward or punishment. As they leave Eden, their earthly paradise, in reverse of Dante's epic, they set forth on the journey of life which Michael has brought to view in original Book X. But the purgation which living effects will end in joy for those who use Providence as their guide. Allegorically, of course, Milton presents the journey the soul must undertake to make death the Gate of Life. Like its medieval predecessor, *Paradise Lost* touches the potentially tragic,[10] for some will find death the Gate to

Hell, as had so many Florentines, but the Joy and eternal Bliss which come with the resolution "Founded in righteousness and peace and love" (XII, 550) place the Renaissance epic in the same genre as Dante's *Commedia*.

The realization of the comic mode of *Paradise Lost* leads us to a fuller awareness of Milton's thesis, of the meaning of the fortunate fall for him, and of the ineptness of the controversy over the epic's "hero." If the climax and theme are not the Fall, as I have argued, then the poem's classification under the tragic mode can not be accepted. If we can refrain from thinking of the poem as a drama with a hero, as if it were a *Hamlet,* and look upon it as a poem with dramatic elements, somewhat like a *Dr. Faustus,* but of course as a poem, we can see the movement going beyond Book IX with its tragic exercise of will, into the repentance and hope of Book X, and the faith in God's providence that Adam achieves in Books XI and XII. They who move through the poem and beyond have become figures in the divine comedy; they only are tragic who stop at Book IX.

A final point in the comic mode of the poem will obviate the tragic mode — the Fall as theme and climax — and combine the elements of the Son's triple defeat of Satan, the center of God as All in All, and the lack of dramatic suspense and heroism. Pervaded as *Paradise Lost* is with biblical concept and reference, it is significant to recognize the way that the first eight psalms, translated by Milton in August, 1653, work through the poem, the first contrasting the righteous and the wicked and the eighth meditating man's place in creation. But Psalm 2 is particularly worthy of note, not only because it is concerned with the reign of the Lord's anointed (a major consideration for the poem as we have seen), but because, in verse 4, it offers a text that weaves itself into the very being of the poem. "He that sitteth in the heavens shall laugh: the Lord shall have them in derision." It occurs directly, obliquely, and ironically. Belial first cites this verse when he says, "he from heav'ns highth / All these our motions vain, sees and derides" (II, 190-191), only a few lines to remark ironically that he, Belial, laughs

> when those who at the Spear are bold
> And vent'rous, if that fail them, shrink and fear
> What yet they know must follow, to endure

> Exile, or ignominy, or bonds, or pain,
> The sentence of thir Conquerour. . . .
>
> (II, 204-208)

Later in this same book, Sin tries to awaken her Father Satan to the uselessness of the deeds of his hand with the same scriptural text (II, 731), but he does not realize that he is not the one who can defeat Death. In Book V, as Raphael recounts the events leading up to the War in Heaven, we have first a glance at God's derision of the kings who set themselves against the Lord and his anointed, and then a direct reference. Noting first the multitudes banded to oppose God's high decree, Raphael relates what God the Father said, "smiling to his onely Son" (V, 718), who answers then "with calm aspect and cleer / Light'ning Divine,"

> Mightie Father, thou thy foes
> Justly hast in derision, and secure
> Laugh'st at thir vain designes and tumults vain. . . .
>
> (V, 735-737)

God's mockery in Book V is balanced by Satan's in Book VI; as the faithful angels are repulsed on the second day of battle, Raphael informs Adam that

> if on they rusht, repulse
> Repeated, and indecent overthrow
> Doubl'd, would render them yet more despis'd,
> And to their foes a laughter . . .
>
> .   .   .   .
>
> *Satan* beheld thir plight,
> And to his Mates thus in derision call'd.
> O Friends, why come not on these Victors proud?
>
> (VI, 600-609)

Yet after the Son's ascent in God's chariot, "Heav'n his wonted face renewd / And with fresh Flowrets Hill and Valley smil'd" (783-784).

Thereafter, in the half of the poem depicting the "effect" of the "cause" and moving toward the expulsion of Adam and Eve from the earthly paradise, references to Psalm 2 are generally appropriated by the satanic crew. But Michael makes clear that their laughter is specious and misdirected when he tells Adam that "The one just Man alive" "shall return / Of them derided" (XI, 816–818).

The derision that God directs against those who do not kiss the Son and who do not put their trust in him signalizes the omnipotence of God the Father. Satan's boasts, actions, and mockery are powerless against the Son and his triple victory. Such transcendence of the tragic by the Son throughout time yields a comic mode, and this is heavily underscored by such "derisive" lines and situations as the foregoing. The text from Psalm 2 implies God's presence above all things and his centrality; the holy hill of Zion upon which the Lord's king is set is the mountain of the poem itself, its summit (the Plains of Heaven) being reached by the Son's ascent from the right hand of Glory in Book VI. Both the lack of dramatic suspense and the spuriousness of the usual type of hero within the poem are explained by reference to God's omniscience and omnipresence.

The classification of *Paradise Lost* under the comic mode demands a new view of the poem as well as attention to comic effect and comic effects.[11] As Joseph Summers comments, after noting Stein's exposition of the comic metaphor in the War in Heaven, the war of good and evil is comic and absurd seen from God's point of view, heroic from the unfallen angels', and tragic from Satan's.[12] And for man, it will be heroic or tragic according to his exercise of free will. "To oppose the universe by our wills or our technology, as to oppose the good," Summers writes, "is not heroic but absurd. . . . It is impossible to imagine the truly heroic moments apart from love: Milton insists that it is impossible to imagine them apart from the love of God" (p. 137). Such classification corroborates through other means what I have advanced about climax, crisis, and theme; it further implies Milton's condition of mind, his hopes and philosophy, and for the literary critic another approach to the meaning of the poem.

What we have discussed is mode, an aspect of genre but not the same as genre. For *Paradise Lost* is not a comedy; it is an epic, but an epic with a difference. Though the poem abides by the rules, it modifies the epic tradition, a fact not always acknowledged.[13] Because the principles postulated by Aristotle and others are useful, though I believe a reexamination of their employment by Milton will counter usual interpretations, and because their technique of definition continues to be practiced in one form or another,[14] I choose to pursue my ideas of the genre of *Paradise Lost* within this framework.

Milton's modifying tradition while working within it can be observed in such poems as *Lycidas, Ode to John Rous,* and the translation of Psalms 1–8. Therefore, to assume that *Paradise Lost* necessarily was conditioned by what is "standard" for the epic tradition and what is "apt" for its alleged subject, as some do, is not justified. A more logical expectation would be that Milton created his own decorum, for he boasts that the poem "pursues things unattempted yet in Prose or Rime." First, however, the tradition must be investigated, and the full subject examined. Of significance in determining the tradition of the poem are its mode and its effect; this we have done earlier in this chapter. Of significance in determining the subject are its thesis, its theme, and its intention, which have already been examined. The intention is didactic, to inculcate virtue in man by showing God's truth, justice, and mercy, leading to peace, and Satan's deceit, injustice, and hate, leading to war. Fundamentally, the poem is concerned with the opposition of Eros and Thanatos, that is, the opposition of love and hate, life and death, creation and uncreation.[15] Thus, if the tradition within which Milton wrote is different from what it has been considered and if the full subject is also different, as my previous discussions urge, then the decorum of the poem must likewise differ.

Part of the tradition of the poem is genre. The classification of *Paradise Lost* as an epic has led to a number of predications: it is in the "high" style, it has a hero of noble status or virtue, it is concerned with heroic achievement. It is obvious to twentieth-century readers of Milton that the last two are the bases for the so-called Satanic interpretations of the poem and its alleged failure; fortunately, this implied censure of Milton's artistry has been laid to rest for most scholars (although not for the general reader). Satan, as we have seen in Chapter Four, is not a hero to the poem and, by the same reasoning, neither is the Son, who throughout is a contrast to Satan. The view that Adam (or Adam and Eve, that is, mankind) constitutes the hero, held by E.M.W. Tillyard and others, is not borne out by Adam's action or character. Adam is the kind of protagonist one finds in a morality play, a central character around whom the action revolves. The poem offers as antagonist the Son, with his attributes of love and faith, against Satan (whose name means "adversary"), with his attributes of hatred and unbelief. I do not wish to overstress the poem's relationship to the morality, although, appropriately, its major structural and imagistic pattern *is* balance through contrast; yet an awareness of this relationship moves us far from requiring a hero (in the usual sense) for the poem and thus from requiring the presence of certain traditional epic qualities.

Placing the poem in the epic tradition has also sent its readers in search of heroic achievement. But Adam neither achieves nor shows heroic action except at the end of Book X when he and Eve humble themselves to God. Satan corrupts, whether other angels or man, and intends uncreation; in no way can this be construed as fighting bravely for a cause against incalculable odds ("hitherto the onely Argument / Heroic deem'd," IX, 28-29). Positive Promethean action is the heroic action of the poem; such action sacrifices self for the love of others. It is the action of the Son or of man when he follows the Son's examples that predicates high achievement.[16] But the Son is greater than Prometheus, since he obeys the Father and shows faith. Full heroic action is magnanimous, in Aristotle's definition of the word.[17] Milton calls *Paradise Lost* a "Heroic Poem" in the forenote on the verse, and this he justifies in the proem to Book IX. He does not mention any hero. This passage alone, it seems to me, should direct readers to the differences from epic tradition that Milton was developing. His task is to tell of distrust, disloyalty, revolt, and disobedience—a sad task. In balance are the trust, loyalty, acceptance, and obedience of the Son throughout the poem and the admonitions (like Raphael's, "first of all / Him whom to love is to obey, and keep / His great command," just before in VIII, 633-635) which loom with ironic persistence. Here is an argument not less, but more heroic than those of the Greek and Roman epics. The word "argument" means "subject," as Milton indicates in line 24, but it also retains the meaning "proof" in a persuasive discourse. Quintilian (V. 8-11) called an argument the plot of a play or the theme of a speech but added that proof and credibility are not the result of reason only but of *signa* (i.e., "indications"). Book IX, with its recounting of the Fall and the immediate aftermath, gives best proof of how Satan works, how man is deceived, and what disobedience can bring.

Both as subject and as proof, this argument ranges throughout the poem. Book IX with the fall of Eve to Satan's blandishments and

Adam's fall through his love for Eve becomes the hinge of man's action in life. With this climax, Satan has seemingly triumphed and man must hew a path upward to God through repentance and faith, or through obedience and love. On the other hand, the climax of Book III indicates the Son's future victory on earth as man; in this way the argument of Book IX will be totally reversed. It is part of the great argument of the full poem, for the Son's action will furnish the means by which man will be saved. Those who will have preceded the Son as man will receive salvation through the harrowing of Hell; those who will come after will have learned the way to fly from woe. The climax of Book III is the hinge of man's salvation, but it is the climax of Book VI that is the keystone of the poem, as we have seen. With the rebellion and defeat of Satan and his cohorts, the need to create man has arisen. Without the falsely heroic action of the War in Heaven, there would have been no man, no Fall, no redemption, and no poem with its great argument.

Certainly man's action in life, whether Adam and Eve's in Book IX or most of their progeny's as related in Books XI and XII, is not heroic. The only heroic achievement is such as Noah's: faith in God, and love, implying obedience to Him. It is the example of the Son. But this does not constitute the narrative; it is, rather, the intended result of the narrative. Quintilian (V. 12) explicitly tells us that in each argument there is something requiring no proof, by means of which we can prove something else. What justly gives heroic name to person or to poem, Milton implies, is striving valiantly for good against opposing forces, and when those forces are basic, the term "heroic" is most suitable. What he will now present in Book IX gives higher argument (proof) to yield that name "heroic" for his poem. Though Adam and Eve fall, we see paradoxically the heroic action by which man may prove heroic. Milton is concerned only with the name of this poem, not for a person. The meaningfulness of the definition I am posing can be appreciated when we remember Dryden's remarks. He rejected *Paradise Lost* as a heroic poem in "Original and Progress of Satire" because "His design is the losing of our happiness; his event is not prosperous, like that of all other epic works. . . . "[18] It is thus understandable that Dryden was the first to cast Satan as hero, for he centers on the Fall rather than on the greater happiness that now may ensue, according to Michael in Book XII.

On the basis of the preceding, we can define the genre of the poem by looking at the properties of the epic-heroic poem found therein. First, there are the poem's sweep and length, its catalogues and war, and its organization of events. These are the elements that have so frequently categorized the poem for readers, but they are only narrative and structural motifs whose differences from epic form or use in *Paradise Lost* are more significant than their superficial likenesses. These elements we may label the "plot," which, according to Aristotle, is the arrangement of the incidents. In *Paradise Lost,* motifs are arranged in a contrasting form (for example, the creation of Pandaemonium in Book I and the creation of the Universe in Book VII) and in comparative (or repetitious) form (for example, the assault on Eve in Book IV and the actual Fall in Book IX). Contrast shows disorder (the world of Satan), as we have already said; comparison shows order (the world of God). Part of the meaningfulness of these devices of contrast which Milton employs is that all of life is made up of such opposites. The Spirit of God may be a dove and the meek may inherit the earth, but to defeat Satan one must be eagle-winged. A human being is the fusion of Man and Woman (the solitary being really embarking on his way through the wilderness of life as Adam and Eve leave Eden), and though he needs the power of the Father to achieve by great deeds, he also needs the compassion of the Mother to achieve by small. Through following the Son's example, one metaphorically takes on the Father's three-bolted thunder with which the Son defeated Satan in VI, 760–766, but one also takes on the Son's mercy and love.

The chronological disruption of narrative—the beginning *in medias res*—was a staple of epic, but Milton's use of it illustrates the thesis of the poem and becomes analogous to a major narrative element and motif. It is, in other words, a metaphor in the poem. We have a disordered poem out of which comes order, once we take perspective of the whole. A main problem for mankind is that it does not see clearly or fully or perspectively, only personally, delimitedly. For it is not just the poem that is disordered; it is man, too, who can be made an ordered person through Milton's leading him to acknowledge the poem's theme and its thesis. Those who will not be led are disordered eternally, in Milton's philosophy.[19]

Paradise Lost is itself a creation, a type of God's creation. All parts have importance in the full scheme; all parts look forward to the period after that creation has ceased to be: for God's creation, life after the final judgment; for Milton's creation, the life his readers are leading which will subtend their ultimate life after the final judgment. Of course, the poem can remain disordered for those who do not see its integrity, just as God's providence and ways, Milton would have surely felt, will not be acceptable to those who see from Satan's perspective only.

The structural motifs derive from epic example, but they are used more hieroglyphically, more metaphorically, more extensively and fully than in previous epics. *Paradise Lost* is epical but far from traditional.

Secondly, further properties of the epic-heroic poem can be discerned through consideration of other dicta for the epic. To Aristotle (*Poetics* XIII. 11-13) the poem should be embraced in one view; it should unify beginning, middle, and end. Only a perspective view, therefore, of the complete, received *Paradise Lost* will allow understanding of the poem as epic. The emphasis on one aspect of plot (the Fall) or the classification of certain sections as unnecessary (the vision of Books XI and XII) or the dismissal of other elements as poorly articulated (the War in Heaven) do not permit perspective.[20] When, however, we see it whole, the poem becomes unified and possible of embracement in one view. The theme that I have urged before is the view that thus arises, not the theme of the Fall, not the elements of the plot which are, rather, Quintilian's *signa*. Awareness of the preceding is necessary to progress to a discussion of two further epic qualities of this heroic poem.

First, epic affords great scope for the inexplicable, Aristotle observed (*Poetics* XXIV.15), because we do not actually see the persons of the story. The differences between *Samson Agonistes*, for example, where we are presented with definite persons speaking in character and performing specific actions (static as this dramatic poem is), and the *Aeneid*, where the epic voice comments and leads and unifies, illustrate what Aristotle was noting. In *Samson* we are limited by the dramatis personae, although the chorus at times — but certainly not always — seems to present part of Milton's message, and although close reading of the speeches of the main characters will lead us to understand the inexplicable that Milton was trying to enunciate. The epic allows the author to insert his view and to lead the reader to awareness of what is happening, what the characters are like, how what they say is to be interpreted, and how the work it-self should be read. The differences in point of view perhaps can be realized in this way: contrast what *Lycidas* says to us when we read the poem (the first ten verse paragraphs) as the author's direct and contemporary musing, and when we read it as the reflective musing of the uncouth swain of the last stanza observed by some superior voice (though swain and superior voice both be Milton).

In this regard, *Paradise Lost* falls between *Samson* and the *Aeneid*. The fact that it was first planned as a play surely was influ-ential in creating this dramatic-epic classification.[21] Allan H. Gilbert has shown evidence that earlier brief tragedies were incorporated into the final epic. If we minimize the narrator's position and stress the dramatic speeches of certain characters—of the fallen angels in Books I and II; of Satan, Eve, and Adam in Books IX and X—we read drama and tend to interpret the speeches as truth and the char-acters as real people. If we recognize the role of the narrator—and it is noteworthy that Anne Davidson Ferry's extensive discussion of *Mil-ton's Epic Voice* has caused many critics of the poem to reread it with surprising results—and realize that the characters are presented "in character," we read epic and, through perspective, see the range of truth from disobedience to obedience, and the characters as repre-sentative of ways of thinking and exercisers of will.

As drama, *Paradise Lost* allows us to go wrong in Milton's view (even if some may think we are broaching the intentional fallacy); as epic it allows us to choose right in Milton's view. The form of the heroic poem thus becomes the very embodiment of Milton's full mes-sage. This is another example of the break with tradition; it is neither drama nor epic in an unrelenting classic definition. As Roy Daniells has argued in *Milton, Mannerism and Baroque,* it is an example of the baroque by virtue, here, of its placement between the manneris-tic and the neoclassic (or late baroque), despite some tendency to-ward the latter. By casting his work in epic form, while deriving it from drama and retaining dramatic sections, Milton acquired great scope for the inexplicable and obtained answerable style.

Second, what is convincing though impossible, Aristotle wrote concerning epic (*Poetics* XXIV.19), should be preferred to what is possible and unconvincing. The application to a heroic poem like *Paradise Lost* as opposed to a drama like Jack Gelber's *The Connec-tion* (I do not say *all* dramas) is obvious. Of course, God can not be depicted and quoted, nor how angels eat or make love, but these achieve conviction for Milton's theme through anthropomorphism and accommodation or symbolic meaning. We are convinced that we ourselves are involved in the cosmic scene before us. Gelber's narcotic addicts are all too real—they even sit next to the audience during the play and approach them at intermission for money for a fix. Actuality is before and around the audience, but they are unconvinced that they may become addicts or that the "scene" is a basic philosophic problem. The drama has the defensible and most necessary effect of making us aware of a real problem, but it has reservations in scope and depth. Or we may look at *Samson* where the scope and depth of what Milton is saying arises from our interpretation of such phrases as "inward eyes." Proof that *Samson* remains unconvincing in the sense that Aristotle meant can be seen in the denial by a number of present-day critics that Samson is regenerated or that he is intended as a type of Christ. The difficulty for them lies in not being able to accept Samson as more than a folk hero of biblical writing, who is employed to delineate the conquering of self and despair in himself and only by vicarious projection in us. (Needless to say, I find this not a failure on Milton's part but a failure on the part of some readers as well as a characteristic inherent in the literary form.) *Paradise Lost* employs epic elements by moving into the impossible, which in the full view convinces that Eternal Providence exists and that God's ways are justified. It presents that which is possible only symbolically, but those who see Adam and Eve and Satan as true people doing real things have not been convinced of Milton's epical achievement.

A final point classifying the poem as epic is that it is a kind of praise, a praise of God rather than of hero and nation. We can call it epideictic because the example of the Son is seen and alluded to in Books III, VI, XII (or one like him—Abdiel, V, or Noah, XI) and because evil is shown so unfavorably in Books II, V, VI, IX, X, XI (the admonitory epic seen through blame). But besides this, the poem is an apostrophe to God's greatness and love for man, to the need and wisdom of obeying Him. Milton's admonishment is to join in the forces of life (Eros) and renounce the forces of death (Thanatos). Looked at thus, the epic is a full-scale argument leading to the Song of Moses and the Song of the Lamb, sung by those who have achieved victory over the beast and his image and his mark: "Great and marvelous are thy works, Lord God Almighty; just and true are thy ways, thou King of saints" (Rev. 15:3). Milton, in his divine inspiration, becomes the voice of the multitude, singing "Alleluia: for the Lord God omnipotent reigneth" (Rev. 19:6). The angelic praise of God figures prominently, of course, in the poem itself: III, 344-415; VI, 742-745, 882-888; VII, 180-192, 557-632; X, 641-648. The last is drawn from Rev. 15:3. This structure of praise in terms of the earlier ten-book version is balanced and paralleled.

Thus labeling *Paradise Lost* as epic, but an epic with a difference, we can examine (in the following chapter) what sense of decorum Milton would employ. The prior discussion suggests that Milton's decorum should be based on classical definitions of epic decorum but that it should also be altered within that framework in the direction of its more heroic argument.

Among the elements of the epic tradition (deriving largely from the *Iliad,* the *Odyssey,* and the *Aeneid*) which are found in *Paradise Lost* are the beginning *in medias res*; the disordering of time, place, and action in the narrow view; the narrating of the story through relation of past events as well as through prophecy of future events; the crossing of the appearances and actions of various characters; the quest and the voyage; the alternation of scenes; the alternation of dramatic dialogue and narrative; language, i.e., in the use of extended similes, parallels, and allusions; technical descriptions; heroic battle; councils; allegory; dreams; God-like visitants and divine guidance; epic games; and length and division into books, usually twenty-four or twelve. Milton employs all these elements but not in mere imitation. For example, at first reading *Paradise Lost* seems confused narratively because we have not seen why Satan and the fallen angels are on the burning lake, nor have we been presented with the creation of Adam and Eve and Earth when we meet them in Book IV, although they have been alluded to in the prior three books; or we forget that the War in Heaven is being told to Adam on Earth. But Milton so manipulates time and place that they only *seem* confused and begun *in medias res*. Actually the narrative moves steadily from the first appearance of Satan in I, 34, to Adam and Eve's expulsion in XII, 649. The quest and voyage seem to be appropriated for Satan in Book III, but the real quest and voyage occur after the poem ends. Milton gives us archetypes throughout *Paradise Lost* before they have become archetypal. The ironic use of such traditional epic elements, as one should expect from the proem to Book IX, is well illustrated by having the epic games played by the fallen angels in Hell while their leader wanders its expanse only to meet Sin and Death.

Further variations from the standard epic tradition include the lack of a clear hero who achieves heroic action; the uses to which epic elements are put, e.g., the enumeration of the fallen angels to allegorize the spread of idolatry, or the narration of Raphael to admonish by example and to explain the order and chain of being of the created universe; the greater presence of a narrator, who not only presents and comments upon the action, but who enters the poem personally as in the proems to Books III, VII and IX; invocations changing scene or focus; and the complexity of metaphoric elements which echo and reecho throughout the poem, not as "tags" but as keys to fuller meaning.

· NINE ·

Style

AS REMARKED before, one of the touchstones of epic genre is style, which classically requires decorum and certain lexical rules. But the difficulties inherent in discussing style grow out of individual preferences, knowledge, and point of view. No definition of style is quite acceptable, for the components of style, its techniques, and its effects do not seem determinable as a formula to satisfy all tastes. Yet the codifications which Aristotle and other rhetoricians devised have proved useful and have accordingly been "applied" to classify the style of such works as *Paradise Lost*. This technique of definition continues to underlie recent investigations of the style of the poem. Since literary style is discussed primarily through an author's language and uses of language, Milton's style has been termed "grand" and "sublime." Christopher Ricks, devoting an entire book to the subject, states the basic concept that places the poem in these categories: "Decorum (in the sense both of epic tradition and of aptness to Milton's subject) demanded that he should elevate his style by deviating greatly from common usage."[1] Elevation of style and wide deviation from common usage have confirmed the grandness and sublimity of Milton's verse for generations of readers, but I must demur not only because of the rather facile acceptance of this concept by so many students of *Paradise Lost* but because I am convinced that Milton's intentions and achievements are in opposition to the statement. Ricks implies a limitation upon Milton by "epic tradition" and by "aptness of subject." And, of course, he also begs the question of what that subject is. Rather, we can establish the style as complex in range and argue that the style is calculated to drive home Milton's "message." This last point fits the demands of decorum but in a different way from that advanced by critics in the past with a different view of the poem's subject, intention, and achievement. As in the discussion of genre, I shall turn my remarks on the principles postulated by Aristotle. The present chapter assumes many points made elsewhere in this study and illustrates what Milton's execution made of the various elements of his pre-text.

I have already suggested that Milton's decorum is based on classical definitions of epic decorum but that it is also altered within that framework in the direction of its more heroic argument. And we have seen that the subject and epic tradition employed by Milton are not what has commonly been assumed and what underlies, apparently, Ricks's comment. Literary decorum is defined as the fitting of the various parts of a poem together, the sound agreeing with the sense, the style with the thought. "Propriety of style will be obtained," wrote Aristotle (*Rhetoric* III.v.1-2), "by the expression of emotion and character, and by proportion to the subject matter. Style is proportionate to the subject matter when neither weighty matters are treated offhand nor trifling matters with dignity." Order, characterization, tone, vocabulary, style, and meter should all accord.

Classically, the epic (based on praise) should be in a high style and its subject matter should concern gods, heroes, members of the nobility, great men, great occasions, or noble abstractions. Comedy (based on blame) should be in a middle style and its subject matter should concern the middle class, the person of the poet, or middle-class occasions (such as birth, marriage, and death). High style in *Paradise Lost* adheres to the subject matter concerned with God and the Son; middle style adheres to the narratives concerned with Adam and Eve and their progeny, which includes Milton, the narrative voice. The scenes involving Satan pretend to the high style as Satan and his crew envision themselves noble and as they undertake their great action; but he is instead an *eiron*, a staple of a comic mode (satire), when viewed from man's reality, and an *alazon*, also a staple of comic mode (romance), when viewed with God's omniscience.[2]

The speech of God the Father (III, 274-343) is illustrative of the high style of the epic. The Father's joy at the Son's offer to become man to redeem mankind pervades the passage. By this act, heavenly love will overcome hellish hate; the Son will be more glorified thereby, and He will reign on God's throne as both God and man. The joy of judgment will peal forth when the sign of the Son appears in the sky; the world will dissolve in a great conflagration and from its ashes will spring a new Heaven and Earth for the Just, who will dwell with Joy and Love and Truth. Then the Son's scepter put by, all will have been reduced (led back) to God, who will once again be All in All.[3]

The language is most appropriate. Note the reduplication; for example, l. 292, "Thir own both *righteous* and un*righteous* deeds"; l. 301, "So easily *destroy'd*, and still *destroyes*"; l. 316, "*Both God and Man*, Son *both* of *God and Man*"; l. 337, "See *Golden d*ays, fruitful of *golden dee*ds"; ll. 339–340, "*Then* thou thy *regal Scepter shalt* lay by, / For *regal Scepter then* no more *shall* need"; l. 341, "*God* shall be *All* in *All*. But *all* ye *G*ods." Note the lack of resting places within the periods of this passage; there are grammatical pauses (such as ll. 280, 286, 289, 294, but there is no resting, as such a transition word as "So" in l. 294 or l. 298 makes clear. Note the specific words: "complacent," "transplanted," "ransomd," "fruition," "Humiliation," "incarnate," "dread," "tribulations," "compass"; the accents: l. 279, "Thée from my bósom and right hand tō sáve"; l. 320, "Thrónes, Princedoms, Powers, Dōminions Í rēduce"; l. 338, "Wīth Jóy and Love triúmphing, and fair Trúth"; and the sound: ll. 313–314, "Therefore thy Humiliation shall exalt / With thee thy Manhood also to this Throne"; l. 329, "Shall hast'n, such a peal shall rouse thir sleep." Indeed, a deliberate shifting of stress is developed with reference to the Father for contrast and for added meaning, particularly in duplications, as in

> For should Man finally be lost, should Man
> Thy creature late so lov'd, thy youngest Son
> Fall circumvented thus by fraud, though joynd
> With his own folly? that be from thee farr,
> That farr be from thee, Father, who art Judge
> Of all things made, and judgest onely right.
>
> (III, 150–155)

The diction is elevated as in "all Power / I give thee" (ll. 317–318); "All knees to thee shall bow" (l. 321); or "Then all thy Saints assembl'd" (l. 330). The symbol of the sign of the Son (to figure so importantly in Milton's account of the Son's previous defeat of Satan at the

beginnings of time [VI, 776] and drawn from Matt. 24:30) and of the
Phoenix along with allusions to Isa. 65:17-25, 2 Pet. 3:12-13, and 1
Cor. 15:28 manifest the high style of the passage.

Adam's denunciation of Eve in Book X, ll. 867-908, may not be
typical of the human sections, but it does indicate the mean style to
be found in the poem. The wallowing blame with which Adam as-
sails Eve pervades the passage; she is called a serpent and likened to
Satan; except for her, Adam now laments, he would have continued
happy. "O why did God create this noveltie on Earth?" God (who
now receives Adam's censure) should have filled the world with men
as angels or have found some other way to achieve generation.
(Adam has forgotten the omnipotence and omniscience of God.) To
Adam, woman (not man like himself) will be the cause of infinite ca-
lamity to human life.

The language again is appropriate. Note such puns as calling Eve
Serpent, her name supposedly being an unaspirated form of *Heva,*
"serpent"; or the line "to trust thee from my side" soon followed by
reference to his rib "More to the part sinister from me drawn," the
adjective meaning both from the "left" and "evil"; or the sexually
graphic "straight conjunction with this Sex"; or the word "fell" referring to Satan, who is both "dangerous" and "fallen." Note the way
duplication is made trivial and comic: "supernumerarie," "number,"
"innumerable"; "Serpent," "Serpentine"; "snare," l. 873, and
"Femal snares," l. 897. Hyperbole, employed by comic poets for
comic effect and yielding a "frigid" style, occurs throughout: "Out of
my sight, thou Serpent," "proof against all assaults," "Crooked by
nature, bent," "innumerable Disturbance," "infinite calamitie,"
"and houshold peace confound." There is a feeling of choppiness in
the passage, for phrases are interrupted and the flow of thought
tends toward an arid style: "nothing wants // but that thy
shape // Like his // and colour . . ."; "Fool'd and beguil'd // by
him thou // I by thee // To trust thee from my side // imagin'd
wise // Constant, / mature / proof against all assaults // And understood . . ."; "By a farr worse // or if she love // withheld By
Parents // or his. . . ." Symbols and allusions that are integral to
God's passage do not appear; the sounds are more plosive and sib-
ilant, and the words themselves are not generally unusual or unusual-
ly employed. The middle-class concern is especially emphasized by
the domestic strife lamented in the final lines of the passage.

Any one of his "glorious" speeches will suffice to show the false
high style of Satan, dissembler and buffoon. Look at I, 622-662.
Satan recounts his high exploit against God in the past and looks forward to further heroism in the future. Heroic war ("open or understood") has shown the rebellious angels to be "matchless" (except
against the Almighty) and "puissant"; they have "emptied Heav'n";
they have shown God that "who overcomes / By force, hath overcome but half his foe." They will now resolve by new war to "repossess thir native seat." We need not cite the high-sounding rhetoric
and language, or ringing accents, for those who have advanced Satan
as hero have done so frequently. Dissembling—and thus the irony
underlying all that Satan says—is always evident. The fallent angels
are not "matchless" against God or His presence in others. The power
of mind that could presage that they would be repulsed by God is in
everyone who admits God's omnipotence (which the fallen angels,
including Satan, on many occasions do). The War in Heaven has removed only a third of the angels (as Death and Raphael both report
in II, 692, and V, 710). None of the fallen angels should illogically
believe that they will reascend. In this speech, Satan implies that they
have lost hope (l. 637) and that they must come to a resolution because "Peace is despair'd" (note the etymological pun on "de-" and
"spero" [hope]), although in l. 190 he had been hopeful and denied
that resolution could come from despair. God's concealment of His
strength wrought their fall, according to Satan. They had hoped to
gain by force although now, defeated, Satan says, as if he always
knew, that force overcomes only half one's foe (note, too, his implied
denial of God's omniscience). And he will continue to push for force
(war open or understood) even so. A comic element is seen thus in his
self-deception; Milton is really so unsubtle that Satan becomes a caricature of the pompous braggart.

This effect is underlined by the contrasts that the poet builds.
When we hear Satan say that the Abyss can not long cover celestial
spirits under darkness, we remember shortly before the dovelike creature that sits on the vast abyss and makes it pregnant. The falseness
of Satan's images is impressed upon us by contrast; his calling the
fallen angels "Sons of Heav'n"—true though it may be—sharply reminds us of their unfilial love; the Son's filial love later will undercut
this epithet more patently.

But over all lies the hint of Satan's soliloquies that all this heroic, high-flown language is but trivia, for, Milton enunciates throughout the poem, God is omnipotent, omniscient, and omnipresent. The important text from Psalms 2, that the Lord will have the kings of the earth in derision, alluded to by Belial in II, 191, hangs over these sections and shows the self-aggrandized devils to be but the swarm of bees or pygmies they become about one hundred lines after this particular passage. The point is, they are giants only to themselves. Their pettiness is here seen in their "prying" (l. 655), their pride in their desired and heretical "self-raising" of themselves to Heaven; their envy appears everywhere. As vacuous orator, Satan becomes a buffoon; viewed with God's position, the fancifulness of Satan's speech is sheer romance and laughable besides. The rhetorical devices become obvious and contrived: the opening apostrophes, the rhetorical questions (ll. 626–630, 631–634, 661), the deliberate repetitions ("Warr then, Warr"). These caricature, when read fully. It is Milton's genius that has led so many astray, not Satan.

What then is the style? It is high, and it is middle, and it is falsely high but really low.[4] Its style depends on how we read the poem, but if we read it with Milton's thesis and theme firmly in mind, we see that the middle style predominates, the high offset by the low, though that is superficially high. (The style is a part of the total dialectic of the poem; it represents thesis, antithesis, and synthesis as much as the contrasts of good and evil, and the like. The point, of course, is that man partakes of both the thesis which is God and the antithesis which is Satan.) Yet we realize a striving upward and we have a feeling that as we accept the "message" we soar with Milton with no middle flight. As a heroic poem, *Paradise Lost* partakes of epical style, but it is not limited by what is epic style any more than its author is by other elements of epic tradition. Milton's style is appropriate to his subject, man's disobedience, but it also shifts aptly as the subject matter and characters shift. Milton has kept "propriety of style" if we recognize the shifts in expression of emotion and character and subject matter. Triviality does enter—when it should, and dignity is maintained—when it should be. The more heroic argument, encompassing *all* the basics of life, requires the full gamut of styles. It is not limited and it is a product of modified tradition.

Nonetheless, we can apply the terms "grand" and "sublime" to the whole rather than just to certain parts; but these terms will not mean quite what they summarized for the eighteenth century, under the influence of Longinus, Addison, and John Dennis. Rather than a mere equation of sublime with high or epic style, we have the sublimity of being upraised when the full effect and message of the poem is allowed to work upon us. It does not derive merely from language used and literary devices employed; it arises largely from the joy that pervades the whole poem when we recognize God's presence and the paradise within, happier far. It uplifts us when we see what is above the false grandeur of Satan and the mean existence of mankind. And we have this concept impressed upon us by the dignity (or grandness) of God's creation and ultimate plan. Justification of God's ways lies in recognition of true good, impossible before the Fall, and in recognition of the need for joint endeavor of man and God to reach high goals.

The poem is sublime in its elevation of the spirit and its tremendous joy; the elevation of the spirit is achieved through the style which moves from low to mean to high, and the joy is achieved by realizing that what has befallen man is not tragic but ultimately blissful, once the seat has been regained. Rhetorically the style is grand in part, but not all parts are stylistically grand. The total effect may reach grandness, but that is not the same thing as classifying Milton's style in one traditional category.

Milton's style is answerable to the Renaissance concept of epic, and it satisfies the expectations of decorum.[5] And though the impersonal and universal strain toward the individual and personal,[6] this is all carefully calculated to bring God's message down from high to the common man, thereby to raise man up. In fact, it is the individual and personal in the poem that are raised and supported. Man's habitat is the middle ground; the poet *intends* to soar with no middle flight above the Aonian mount. That he was successful is evident from the three centuries of readers who have soared with the poet. But the total view of the style of the poem and thus its answerability are not that simple.

The narrator inspired by God's spirit well exhibits the point being made in the poem: God works through man to reach Man; He purges and disperses the mists, and, as it were, with inward eyes illuminated, the poet can employ his intended wing, in no way depressed. Man's normal style is mean, his audience receives the mean best; but the spirit moves upward and the goal is upward, and fit audience will be led upward with the poet as he moves into the high and ultimately answerable style. The fusion of genres and the fusion of styles created a new genre and a new style, and thereby was wrought the only possible answer to argument above heroic. The epic as genre has always been mixed, and appropriately so would its style be mixed. Milton has gone beyond the more simple mixtures, however, and created a coherent whole that shapes up as something new. But I will not accept a modish label, like "anti-epic," for Milton's coherent whole, not only because the term has no real meaning and not only because it erroneously describes Milton's work, but largely because *Paradise Lost* is an epic and is in epical style.

Other matters, however, are also part of style — prosody, language in more general terms, form; and to these commonly discussed aspects of style I should like to turn briefly. Milton uses blank verse, or better, a ten-syllable line without rhyme, in *Paradise Lost,* except that a very few instances of scattered rhyme have been detected. They are so separated that rhyme seems hardly the right word. Milton's ten-syllable line generally has three to eight stresses and the incidence of run-on lines is high, with, accordingly, strong medial pauses, variously placed within the line. The effect is to create flowing passages and sustained thoughts, yielding heightened (or sublime) style.[7]

Good examples of the preceding statements can be found in IV, 720-735.

720   Thús at / thir shád/ie Lodge / arriv'd, // both stood, //
       Both túrnd, // and ún/der op/'n Skie / ador'd
       The God / that máde / both Skie, / Air, Earth, / and Héav'n,
       Which théy / behold, // the Moons / resplén/dent Globe
       And stár/rie Póle: // Thóu al/so mad'st / the Night,
725   Máker / Omní/potent, // and thóu / the Day,
       Which wé / in our / appoin/ted wórk / imployd
       Have fin/isht háp/pie in / our mú/tual hélp
       And mú/tual lóve, // the Crówn / of all / our bliss
       Ordaind / by thée, // and thís / deli/cious place
730   For ús / too lárge, // where thý / abún/dance wants
       Partá/kers, and / uncrópt / fálls to / the ground. //
       But thóu / hast pró/mis'd from / us twó / a Race

To fíll / thē Eárth, // whō shall / wǐth us´/ extóll
Thȳ goód/ness in´/finīte, // bōth whén / wē wáke, //
735   And whén / wē seék, // as now, // thy gíft / of sleép. //

(A ∧ indicates a brief pause; a // a strong pause, which occurs only at the end of a foot.) The lines are all built on iambs, five to a line, and are unrhymed, although trochees, pyrrhics, and spondees occur. Note "place" and "Race" separated by two lines; should we call this rhyme or not? Internal rhyming also occurs: "bliss," 728, and "this," 729; "-cious," 729, and "us," 730, for example. Although there seems to be five stresses in most lines, l. 722 has six and ll. 725, 727, 731, 734 seem to have only four. Run-on lines are frequent: ll. 721, 723, 726, 727, 728, 729, 730, 732, 733. Thus, rather than line-units we find phrase-units: "under op'n Skie ador'd The God that made both Skie, Air, Earth and Heav'n Which they behold"; "the Moons resplendent Globe and starrie Pole"; "the Crown of all our bliss Ordaind by thee"; and the like. In this way, the verse paragraph is developed as a unit and the style is heightened and sustained.

We might note a few pertinent points concerning general language. Emphasis is achieved in l. 722 partially by making each word a monosyllable; the creation being discussed is punctuated by the distinct quality of each word (Skie, Air, Earth, Heav'n) while the whole is part of a flowing idea begun in the preceding line and continued into the next. There is a kind of similitude of the creation itself coming in the midst of time. The longest word in this passage is, appropriately, "Omnipotent," four syllables. The two-syllable "mutual" of ll. 727 and 728, each modifying a one-syllable word ("help," "love"), suggests part of the thought which Milton is setting forth: together Adam and Eve can achieve unity which will make them true "helpmates" and create "love." At the same time, we have a compound here which suggests an equivalency; that is, help is love, either one begetting the other. In the last four lines of the passage, two sounds predominate: *s* and *l*, both soft, lulling, and continuant sounds. A form of onomatopoeia is evident.

The importance of choice of words may be represented by "delicious," "abundance," "partakers," and "uncropt." The meaning we first derive for "delicious" in this particular passage is "appealing to taste"; but the word also means, more generally, "alluring." The Edenic pair are praising God for the wonderful fruit that He allows to grow in their Garden, but this is the fruit that proves too alluring for them and which they partake of to bring death into the world, and all our woe. God's *abundance* is, first of all, the profusion of fruit he allows to grow, but when we recognize Milton's use of ambiguous language, it ironically suggests that God simply has given man too much—too much freedom of will, too much of material things, too much for His own good. (Of course, abundance is part of Satan's argument to which Eve will succumb in Book IX.) "Uncropt" takes on various meanings, besides suggesting the finality of death by its stopped final sound. That is, if the fruit is not brought to harvest, it will fall to the ground; if it is not pruned, it will overproduce and the tree will be weighted down. In terms of Adam and Eve, "uncropt" indicates the paradox of the fall: they will be "uncropt," in the sense of living forever, only if they do not fall. In addition, sexual significance adheres to the word and its use here when we think of the race they will beget after the Fall. Such use of ambiguous and paradoxic language adds texture to the poem and helps account for the label of "sublime."

Form, too, is part of style, when the literary work is looked at whole and in perspective. The structure of *Paradise Lost* and its inherence to the thesis suggests consideration of what is called Renaissance style, which includes Renaissance, Mannerist, Baroque, and Late Baroque. Renaissance composition is the formal domain of beauty regulated by algebraic equations and Platonic notions of harmony, according to Wylie Sypher.[8] Indeed, form means the imposition of a theory of proportion. The structure which we have observed places the poem close to Alexander Sackton's criterion for the neoclassical (or, more accurately, late baroque) style—symmetry produced not only as a function of construction, but by conscious design[9]—and under Sypher's tenet of the late baroque style—mutual actions of two bodies upon each other are presented as equal and directly opposite. The epic bridges the baroque, in its lavish treatment of space and determined areas (as Roy Daniells views it[10]), and the late baroque, in its organized, formal, geometric (if not symmetric until 1674) beauty.

· TEN ·

The Myth of Return

MYTHIC criticism has risen sharply in recent years. Myth in literature has emphasized the cycle of birth, growth, death, and rebirth, particularly as seen in the Christ figure. The form that such myth has taken is cyclic, a recurring cycle with its constant return, its circle imagery, and its attendant hope. Myth is seen in story elements, personages, imagery (and symbols), and patterns of narrative. Isabel G. MacCaffrey, in a book devoted to Milton's epical myth, writes, "As important to *Paradise Lost* as the fable itself are the myth's circular, returning shape, and its innocence of vision harking back to an experience older than any individual life. Milton made his poem from these elements, though he knew nothing of myth in the technical sense."[1] It goes without saying, then, that myth provides another avenue into the poem, one which exists as a pre-text and as both unconscious and conscious pattern, and which is realized largely by the execution of the poem. The myth of return provides the pattern on which much of the thesis and theme depend.

The definition of myth to which I would subscribe is: "It is the reiterated presentation of some event replete with power. . . . The mythic occurrence, then, is typical and eternal; it subsists apart from all that is temporal. If nevertheless we attempt to fix it in time, we must place it at either the beginning or the end of all happening, either in the primeval era or at the conclusion of time, that is before or after time. . . . Thus the event becomes 'eternal': it happens now and always and operates as a type."[2] Among the myths on which *Paradise Lost* rests are the Lost Eden, the Golden Age Restored, the Magic Mountain, and the Christ legend. These are narratives which recur in various forms in the literatures of the world, basically because of the hopes and fears of man, his observation of life and his attempt to explain life and its vicissitudes, and above all his desire to give life some meaning and reason. The answers that myths supply explain how and why life began and how and why life (as man knows it) will end. In between, that is, in life itself, will fall the action to reverse the beginning and to insure the desired ending. Man reasons that there must be some purpose in life, something besides void after death, and so conceives of an omnipotent God and an afterlife in His presence. *Paradise Lost,* rather than presenting these myths in disguised or in latter-day form, offers their archetypes as they supposedly occurred. Latter-day forms in the post-Edenic world appear in Adam's vision, e.g., Noah, Nimrod, Jesus (the clear example of myth undisguised within the human world). But Milton does not present these as myths in the sense of "false" or "made up"; rather they are the truth, though interpreted or elaborated or presented as the imagination can conceive they might (if not, must) have occurred. These myths derive from the Bible, a work of truth, written by the divine poet or poets (one like David), through the inspiration of God, who has accommodated Himself to man's incapacities by word, images, and parables, which are truth to the extent that human intellect is capable of grasping them. Since the Bible exists for all men in all times, it must be interpreted for the mundane mind of man in different ways, in different forms, and thus will God's revelation of the beginning and the end be understood. Milton in *Paradise Lost* is interpreting these myths for mankind. His interpretation is *utile*, since it is given to inculcate Christian virtue, and it is *dulce*, since it is given in narrative poetry, with dramatic potentialities. His creation becomes a type of the creation of God, and specifically of the Bible, created through the inspiration of God.

The poem does not present these myths in their usually accommodated form; the narrative seems to record the actual happenings in Heaven, in Hell, and on Earth, because of verisimilitude and also because the Bible records the basic narrative elements here extrapolated. Milton, surely, and his readers over the centuries have approached these myths as truth. Herein lies the difficulty that critics like John Peter and William Empson find with the poem and specifically with the Father and most specifically in Books III and V-VI. Some deny "Milton's" God; others accept Milton's "Satan." My quotation marks are meant to imply the problem: the figure of God is held accountable to Milton as artist and thinker, and since the religious precepts of this God are so unacceptable to some, Milton is criticized as artist and thinker; on the other hand, the figure of Satan epitomizes one's "unacceptance" of the tyrannic God and thus he is advanced as heroic figure, but Milton is condemned for not accepting Satan's position or accused of confusion in his attitude toward "Satan's party." The point is, the God and the Satan presented are mythic figures built on the elements of truth which are in the minds of men, and at the same time artistic creations which should be consistent unto themselves (and which are, when the entire poem is read with perception). What such critics as the foregoing will not accept are the concepts of Christianity that there is a God, that He can foresee though He does not foreordain, that revolt against Him for any reason and that disobedience to Him for any reason are wrong, that the sin of the race's progenitors is passed down through all time to the race, and that the means to remove that sin from one's human makeup is through trial of faith, obedience, and love. Somehow, such critics let their religious attitudes get in the way of their literary appreciation; Milton is deplored as writer because God is deplored as tyrant. To me, such critics are like young students who forget that this is an artifact of literature being read—not an expository theme on history or philosophy. Yet aside from this confusion of literature and life, there remains the fact, not too strong a word here, I believe, that the myths presented are accepted as truth by Milton and most of his readers, including his critics.

What is needed to read *Paradise Lost* without prejudice is, first, the recognition of what literature is and what it is not and, second, the acknowledgment that people do believe in the existence of God— a god who covenants and may be vindictive (the Old Testament god and in many ways Milton's Calvinistic Father) and a god of love and mercy (the New Testament god and Milton's Son).[3] Such recognition and acknowledgment will allow evaluation of the poem as poem and will set in motion those concerns of literature which allow the reader to examine, clarify, and evaluate his own beliefs, philosophy, appreciation of life and its people—those things which really make literature relevant or not. The myths on which the poem is fabricated have the dual function of presenting the truth (according to the rationalizations which have rested in human thought since the beginning of recorded histories) and of elaborating that truth to clarify it, fill in the gaps, and make it pertinent to the constantly changing temporal world of men.

A cliché of Miltonic criticism since Addison's and Voltaire's strictures has been Milton's misjudgment in inserting the allegory of Sin and Death into Book II.[4] Usually the further development of that allegory in Book X is slighted. (Perhaps we should not say "further development," of course; perhaps the germ of the idea was how to present Sin and Death's entry into man's world and the allegory of Book II became an extension and elaboration of that. Researches into the order of composition, at least, have concluded that X, 345-414 and 585-648, may be earlier than the corresponding section of Book II.) But the entire poem has the same allegoric proportions; what militates against a reader's acceptance of that statement is his belief that God exists, that He embodies the two aspects of Father and Son, that Satan exists, that angels exist, and that Adam and Eve existed. (The change in tense in that sentence should be noted.) To many, Sin and Death are on a totally different plane from other characters; they seem like characters in *Everyman* or *Pilgrim's Progress,* but Adam and Eve as well as Father, Son, and Satan do not seem like Everyman or Christian. What makes Sin and Death allegoric is that they are not and never were beings; what does not allow the others to be allegoric is that they are or were (supposedly) actual beings. Yet, for example, Sin's birth and pregnancy are not different in kind from the Son's creation or Eve's except that God, the omnipotent, is doing the creating; the bridge from Hell to Earth is a contrast with the equally allegoric stairs to Heaven, and the fissure in the wall of Heaven by which the rebellious angels are expelled contrasts with the Gate of Heaven, since only the faithful can leave and enter by that proper port; the kenneling of the hellhounds in Sin's womb is a parodic expression of the return of the faithful to the *substantia* of God at the end of time; and so forth. The criticisms of Milton's artistry against the "insertion" of the allegory of Sin and Death arise, then, from our attitude toward these obviously personified abstractions and toward the supposed realities of God, Satan, and Adam and Eve.

But are not God (Father and Son), Satan, and Adam and Eve also abstractions? Are they truly individualized, or are they not the essence of those concepts which they represent? Are Adam and Eve not detailed portraits of psychological man, portraits epitomizing (or allegorizing) man's hopes and fears, rationality and irrationality, sense of divinity and yet frailty when faced with the attractiveness of temptation? Exercise of the free will of mankind since Adam and Eve, Milton illustrates in Books XI and XII, requires great faith rather than reason to decide against the blandishments of bodily desires and temporality. (John Donne expressed the idea in a verse letter to the Countess of Bedford as "Reason is our Soules left hand, Faith her right.") The free will of Adam and Eve is meaningfully allegorized in Eve's fall as dependent upon man's rationality rather than his faith and in Adam's fall, upon man's personal, bodily, and temporal concerns.

Milton, I feel sure, accepted these narrative elements and psychological perceptions — these myths, if you will — as essential truth, but I hasten to add that he must have realized that his elaboration was but one accommodation of that truth in terms which he hoped would be (and indeed which have been) meaningful to mankind. Herein lies his concern with divine inspiration, which we have previously explored. Without such inspiration, his elaboration would be misleading, the meaningfulness of his poem but an empty dream. The dream-vision which the poem is, is not empty if it allows meaningful interpretation such as that afforded by a dream which man experiences, but it is empty if that interpretation is confused, evanescent, obscure. Unlike many of his readers, Milton saw his poem as truth accommodated to man and thus as essential truth rather than substantial truth.

Behind the specific myths employed in *Paradise Lost* is the basic myth of return. The cyclic structure of the myth combines observation of seasonal change with realization of birth, growth, and death. The analogy thus implies that rebirth will occur for man after death, as with vegetation, and the process begin again. This is interpreted as the change of generation and also rebirth at the end of time. Although the daily movement of the sun implies a similar progression (the imagery is used by Donne, for example, in "Song: Sweetest love, I do not goe"), to Adam and Eve the descent of night provided rest because of their "daily work of body or mind" (IV, 618). Almost punningly, Eve talks of forgetting "all time, / All seasons and thir change" (IV, 639-640), where she means only that she becomes almost oblivious to the movement from the first approach of daily light to its final departure. They do not yet know what death is (IV, 425), nor birth, nor growth (in the animal world), nor seasonal change. But with the Fall comes the "change / Of Seasons to each Clime" (X, 677-678) and death (X, 709); intermediately, Eve observes that "the Morn, / All unconcern'd with our unrest, begins / Her rosie progress smiling" (XI, 173-175), and Adam concludes that "we are dust, / And thither must return and be no more" (XI, 199-200). Only through the vision which Michael enables him to see can Adam talk hopefully of light (good) coming out of darkness (evil) (XII, 469-478), equate continuing generation with hope (XII, 375-385), and contemplate "the Race of time, / Till time stand fixt" (XII, 554-555).

The cyclic myth as man has delineated it is implicitly before us in the poem in its archetypal form. Although Milton does not have Adam draw the analogy between the seasons and man's life, the elements of the myth are present. The narrative structure which the myth predicates is the narrative structure of the poem: loss, quest, return. The good which man has known (seen in Books IV, V, VII, VIII, IX) is lost (seen in Books IX, X, XI, XII); he must quest after its rediscovery (seen in Books XI, XII, and specifically in the basic thought underlying the final lines on the expulsion); and rediscovery will bring return to the lost state of good in Heaven with God (iterated variously in Book XII). The cycle, it is assumed, rolls onward until the final Judgment. Man in his lifetime undergoes loss with the changes brought by adulthood; he quests in his lifetime for a return to a state of good and eventually to an Edenic life after death. The narrative triad is duplicated through the opposing dialectic offered by Satan. (The dialectic is the major literary device employed in the poem, as my remarks throughout this study have frequently shown.) Satan's loss of "that celestial light" (I, 245) has resulted from his pride and envy. Unlike Adam and Eve's loss, the result of deception, Satan's loss is self-tempted. His story occupies Books V and VI, though we learn much in Books I and II. His quest has been quite obvious to centuries of readers, it seems, in terms of his voyage through Hell, space, and the Created Universe (Books II, III) as well as his ride with darkness for seven continuous nights after his encounter with Gabriel. His quest is to determine (in Beelzebub's words) how

> To waste [God's] whole Creation, or possess
> All as our own, and drive as we were driv'n,

> The punie habitants, or if not drive,
> Seduce them to our Party.
>
> (II, 365–368)

Shortly before, Satan had expressed the hope that the fallen angels might "re-ascend / Self-rais'd, and repossess their native seat" (I, 633–634). But this is the hope of man's quest, not Satan's, for we quickly realize that Satan's oratory is meant to impress and soften up his audience for the plans to come. In other words, Satan's quest is a perversion of the questing theme of myth; it does not aim to return to God, it aims at thwarting return. Satan knows that return for him and his cohorts is impossible.

> all Good to me is lost;
> Evil be thou my Good; by thee at least
> Divided Empire with Heav'ns King I hold
> By thee, and more then half perhaps will reigne;
> As Man ere long, and this new World shall know.
>
> (IV, 109–113)

The return which Satan desires is uncreation, a return to the elements of chaos, as he tells Chaos and Old Night in Book II. This is uncreation only of the elements outside the heavenly square, not reformation of the *substantia* of God out of which all the sons of God (including Satan) have been created.

Despite its excellences, the study of Milton's myth by MacCaffrey misplaces emphasis on Satan's voyage and quest, as if this were the subject of Milton's poem and a true example of the myth of return. Indeed, this voyage, like Eve's recounting of her dream, equates a flying dream, and the implications are that this voyage along with its quest is one of anxiety, driven by compulsion and paranoid characteristics. We need not envision Milton as some kind of seventeenth-century Freud, surely; we need merely read Satan's motives as Milton expresses them, in Books I and II to recognize elements which have been present in man since the Fall and which modern analysis labels paranoid. In contrast is Eve's sleep in Book XII, in which there is no suggestion of flying or anxiety; there is only rest and quietude. MacCaffrey has allowed the "Satanic" critics and Satan's supposed heroism to fashion her approach to a major portion of her book, and though her discussion leads to significant insights, it does not recognize the inverse function of Satan and his quest. Satan's perversion of loss, quest, and return may represent the "antimyth" of the satanic people of this world, but it does not represent positively the myth of return which exists in *Paradise Lost.*

Another way of looking at the triad of the myth of return is separation, initiation, and return. Clearly, it is Adam and Eve's loss of innocence which brings separation (as in each man's life), for Satan loses no innocence though there is much that he should have learned from his act. Once separated from the secured world of the innocent Eden, Adam and Eve must be initiated into the world surrounding them outside Eden, as they are, before the fact, in Books XI and XII, through Adam's vision and Eve's dream. Only through man's initiation into the ways of the world will he be able to cope with the assaults of evil and effect return. (We are all probably well acquainted with the many initiation stories in modern literature; the various ways of the world to which Nick Adams is initiated in Ernest Hemingway's stories supply one good example of the variety of faces that "nongood" takes.) One significant way of looking at *Paradise Lost* is that it constitutes the myth of initiation (evil, death, sex, war, hate) for mankind, who, born separated, must find the means to return to the innocent Eden and the oneness of Adam and Eve.

Is it not therefore evident that the myth of return goes to the heart of Milton's message for man? Man has lost innocence through Adam and Eve (Milton said this explicitly in *Aereopagitica*); he must be initiated into the ways of evil (Milton's remarks on cloistered virtue come to mind), and thereby will he quest for the means to regain the lost paradise; he will, it is hoped, achieve return to the godhead at the end of time when God will again become All in All. The Lost Eden and the Golden Age Restored are the myths just described before; related are the Magic Mountain, which we have noted already as hieroglyphic structure (circle imagery also being noted), and the Christ legend. The Magic Mountain implies that the ascent to God is dangerous and steep, rocky and wearying; but that once there, one has reached a point (the Plains of Heaven) above which is nothing. (Only the Son as God the Father's agent at the center of the poem during the War in Heaven is able to "ascend.") The mountain is magical not only because it leads to Heaven, but because it may appear in many forms. In *Paradise Lost,* the poem itself becomes the magic mountain; it presents the action to be piled on action in life to reascend from the subjected plain (the world) to which Adam and Eve are expelled; and it suggests that movement upward for mankind may come as circular movement around the mountain (as in the myth of return) while progress in a rising direction, "light after light well spent" (as in the myth of exodus), will be made. The inverse is the vortex to Hell which Dante's Inferno allegorizes as circular movement involving stages of sinning while movement lies in a downward direction to the depth of Hell where Satan, encased in ice to his chest, stands amidst hellfire. Satan's awakening on the burning lake in Book I of Milton's epic, of course, recalls the end of the Inferno. Though Satan's quest and journey are purported to provide exodus from the fallen angels' infernal abode, the actions of Satan which Milton depicts in the total poem reveal the progression downward that any man will tread who pursues darkness after darkness ill spent.

The Christ legend, undisguised myth in the human world, insures man's recognition of the need for loss or separation (a version of the *felix culpa* which, however, avoids loss or fall while emphasizing the recognition of need), the nature of man's quest and the form that initiation takes (in the Temple, where the learned doctors may be confounded, as well as in the Wilderness), and the means to effect return. Paradise Found is available to all who comprehend Milton's mythmaking.

ELEVEN

The Myth of Exodus

WE HAVE just looked at the myth of return in *Paradise Lost* in the preceding chapter. But woven into the fabric of biblical thought is also the myth of exodus, made concrete as symbol by the delivery of the Israelites from Egypt under the leadership of Moses. It has been seldom discussed as a recurrent motif in the Bible and not at all specifically as a mythopoeic theme in literature. Exodus myth employs historical eras of life, but not as cycle; they are, rather, stages moving toward a blinding splendor (God). With each stage a dialectic has effected the (at least temporary) removal of all ills of the past and the passage into an advanced future. Herein lie the differences between these two myths: the myth of return repeats the ritual cyclically; the myth of exodus consists of repetitive stages of ritual moving linearly. Like other devices in this poem, the two myths, seemingly opposite, are combined to spin a cloth which will sustain all manner of imprint and dye, design or picture.

Over the years, ideas of myth have confounded these two basic myths by assigning an ending to the cycle at the end of time. The long seasons roll on, only to repeat themselves until the Second Coming occurs. But such a break in pattern, with the Second Coming, is inconsistent with the cyclic content of the myth of return; cycle, rather than being the basic myth of the Bible, is a metaphor drawn from natural observation. The problem of the confounding of the two myths can be seen in Revelation, when we learn that the serpent's bondage beneath the ground is not eternal (Chapter 20), for we had been led to see this as the end of mortal time and the beginning of eternity. The "author" of Revelation simply did not understand the myths he was reflecting. The myth of return incorporates no progression as it recurs eternally, and thus no point of completion of the endless rounds can be conceived. The Second Coming will not occur simply because time has elapsed. An equation has been made by founders of Christian thought between Christ's death and the death of vegetation or the daily descent of darkness and between Christ's resurrection and the rebirth of vegetation or the daily return of light. This has led to assignment of the time of resurrection on the basis of planetary motion (and conflation with the Passover) near the vernal equinox, with the symbolism of that equinox and the sign of the Ram (Aries) typifying a new beginning with its attendant hope. The end of the cycle, therefore, has become, in the interpretation of the New Testament, an eternal resurrection at the end of time; and Milton sees this as death's becoming the Gate of Life (XII, 571), or as an "endles morn of light" ("At a Solemn Music," l. 28). But these metaphors are not part of the myth of Exodus, although the concepts of eternity are, nor are they logical adjuncts to the myth of return.

Exodus as myth epitomizes (or typifies) the ritual that must constantly be undertaken to achieve the dream or reunion with the godhead. The significant differences in the myths lie in the achievements which exodus accomplishes. The ritual involved in exodus is a constant forward motion through successive stages of action and time, each a beginning again, an involvement in false security and error, and a removal from that involvement to a period of trial or purgation as things begin again. It is not cyclic. The mythic quest is thus mankind's constant striving forward to its dream through the ritual of exodus; the cyclic myth allows a questing theme only in the early hope that comes with rebirth. In *Paradise Lost,* the perverse quest of Satan, which takes on some of the attributes of the less heroic argument (see IX, 13ff.), is the obverse of man's quest, for his dream is uncreation—that is, a return of all created things to their chaotic state. The ritual by which he will hope to achieve his dream (for he does have hope, although he tries to deceive himself) is the constant corruption of mankind through the hardening of the heart.

A problem that one encounters in dealing with biblical myth is that one must interpret the Bible, seeing it not as revealed word but as archetypal literature. This is, of course, what exegetes have been doing for centuries while maintaining its truth, yet in the modern world of criticism there is still a tendency to read most biblical stories or events as unique. I would suggest instead that exodus, as well as Christ *figurae,* exists in the Old Testament because of its archetypal source in man's explanation of life in time, and as such, from a Christianized point of view, it is a type, whose antitype is the New Testament account of the Son's temptation in the wilderness.

The occurrence and recurrence of exodus before and after the symbolic event of Moses's leading the chosen people into a wilderness,[1] from thence to move ultimately to a land of milk and honey, are types of the leading of Jesus into the desert where he will be confronted by Satan. Heb. 3:7-19 justifies the typological argument I advance:

> Wherefore as the Holy Ghost saith, Today if ye will hear his voice, harden not your hearts, as in the provocation, in the day of temptation in the wilderness: when your fathers tempted me, proved me, and saw my works forty years. . . . For some, when they had heard, did provoke: howbeit not all that came out of Egypt by Moses. But with whom was he grieved forty years? was it not with them that had sinned, whose carcasses fell into the wilderness? And to whom sware he that they should not enter into his rest, but to them that believed not? So we see that they could not enter in because of unbelief.

The myths of birth-rebirth and of exodus exist together, the one serving as metaphor for repetition in time, the other as symbolic means to achieve return with the path by which return will be achieved clearly laid out. Whereas the cyclic myth takes on a chronological panorama of time (deriving largely from seasonal observation) and the monomyth crystallizes recurrence through resurrection, the exodus myth points to stages within time, renouncing the past and heralding the future. It is not cyclic but linear in time perspective, developed and advanced by stages which progress toward the millennium and its eschatological completion with the judgment of the Son. Here the messianic function of Christ crystallizes renewal through delivery from bondage, the final delivery antithetically binding "the dragon, that old serpent which is the Devil, and Satan" in "the bottomless pit" with "a great chain" (Rev. 20:1-2). The end of time will see the coincidence of resurrection and such renewal, and with this Milton believed would come the "reducing" (or "leading back" of the saints "Under thir Head imbodied all in one," VI, 779).[2]

The theme of exodus, thus seen, is patently significant to *Paradise*

Regain'd, where trial and resistance are emphasized if a type of Christ is involved; trial, fall, and repentance will be emphasized if a mere man is the subject, until time have a stop with the fall of the mystic Babylon.[3] In the fall and destruction of Babylon will be found "the blood of prophets, and of saints, and all that were slain upon the earth" (Rev. 18:24)—that is, those who have resisted the evil which Babylon represents. The belief in ultimate arrival at the land of milk and honey through such trial is symbolized by the angel's words to St. John, who has asked for the angel's open book of life: "Take it, and eat it up; and it shall make thy belly bitter, but it shall be in thy mouth as sweet as honey" (Rev. 10:9). The taste of honey prepares one, like Jonathan, to speak the Word of God, since thereby his eyes have been enlightened. It creates a paradise within and gives a preview of the ultimate paradise, for it moves through bitterness and through the renunciation of such false advisers as Saul, human but not spiritual father. With the end of time will come the end of exodus, for the trials and progressions forward will no more be needed and the unconscious remembrance of the race will have been blotted out. This view casts a further meaning on the prophecy that "God shall wipe away all tears from their eyes; and there shall be no more death, the former things are passed away" (Rev. 21:4). That the theme of exodus informs *Paradise Lost* will become clear as we explore the motif, particularly through the antitype of the temptation in the wilderness. Through this theme we will find greater meaning than heretofore for the "Paradise within . . . happier farr" (XII, 587).

Exodus is a leading out or a deliverance. As Eric Voegelin has noted,[4] the exodus is Israel's metaphor for its unique conception of faith. It represents a break not only with the Egyptian gods, but with the order they represent; it becomes a symbol of the replacement of false gods by true gods. Thus, it symbolically delivers one from the past which has become the secured existence of any established order, whether political or ideational. The past has created faith in an image (perhaps in an idol); the exodus dashes that image and replaces it with an image of faith. Exodus must occur frequently for the sons of Adam, for they repeatedly devise the various oracles and pagan gods enumerated in the *Nativity Ode,* be they Mammon or Dagon, material wealth or pleasure. The birth of the Son as man routed these false gods and prepared for the symbolic means of exodus for man from their control. Those who had preceded Christ in history had the memory of exodus as symbol. Those who have come after the age of Christ have not only that memory but the examples of the Son to create the fairer paradise within—that is, faith.

Yet exodus also underlies the Platonic myth of the cave, symbolizing man's self, his life, and his history.[5] The highest good, God, is not the goal attained by exodus; it is, rather, the means to renewal. And as one moves slowly upward from the cave through the dialectic, he is fortified to proceed to the next stage. One must grow accustomed to the new light before proceeding onward; it is only after many successive exoduses that man will reach the highest good. Analogue with the allegory of the cave is found in Exod. 33:20, when God says, "Thou canst not see my face: for there shall be no man see me, and live." God's blinding splendor would destroy in the same way that Zeus's appearance to Semele as himself (lightning) destroyed her. One must move by stages to be able to look on God, that is, the blinding splendor that answers the title question of a poem by Kenneth Patchen, "What Is The Beautiful?" The myth of exodus therefore acts as a symbol of the renewal of faith at certain stages of history through the renunciation of false beliefs, through the testing of man against the lures of Satan, and through leading him to a new promised land, each a successive type of God's Heaven. There successive stages advance from the specific (for Eden was the earthly heaven) to the more general, or from the local to the universal—the paradise within. According to Voegelin, "The promised land can be reached only by moving through history, but it cannot be conquered within history. The Kingdom of God lives in men who live in the world, but it is not of this world."[6] Studies of the Edenic quest—the attempts to fetch back the Age of Gold—are tangent to my argument, but they have not recognized the myth of exodus as here described.[7]

As the Israelites are delivered through the Red Sea, they enter a wilderness (or desert) which they must wander to reach the Promised Land. Of course, not all the Israelites accept Moses' leading forth (Exod. 14:11-12) any more than modern man accepts renunciation of the world outside the shadows of the cave. The period of wandering in the desert becomes a time of privation, to the extent of forty years (a generation): "And the children of Israel did eat manna forty years, until they came to a land inhabited; they did eat manna, until they came unto the borders of the land of Canaan" (Exod. 16:35). This symbol of privation repeats itself in the forty days and nights spent by Moses upon Mount Sinai (Exod. 24:18), those earlier of Noah's flood (Gen. 7:17), and those later fasted by Jesus in the wilderness (Matt. 4:2). The hoped-for rebirth of the nation of the chosen people of God through exodus becomes a symbol of the rebirth of the individual soul rededicating itself to God. The desert in which the people wander lies directly in the path of the Promised Land. The concept of "wander" itself implies errant steps, and indeed the Israelites "sin a great sin" (Exod. 32:30), as Adam had (XI, 427), and will repeatedly do so. Exodus—that is, deliverance from bondage—is therefore no guarantee for the future; it calls for continued exercise of the faith evoked by God's great hand in working deliverance. The meaningfulness of God's act of deliverance (whether through miracle or dialectic) is clearly seen when we remember the significance for Milton of Psalm 114, which commemorates the Passover: "Shake earth, and at the presence by agast / Of him that ever was, and ay shall last." "The memory of Israel preserved the otherwise unimportant story," Voegelin writes, "because the irruption of the spirit transfigured the pragmatic event into a drama of the soul and the acts of the drama into symbols of divine liberation. . . . Through the illumination by the spirit the house of institutional bondage became a house of spiritual death."[8]

Paradise Lost records the memory of exodus through specific references to it and to Moses,[9] through the theme which organizes and develops certain concepts of the poem, and through its "great Argument." Among the allusions to the book of Exodus are these:

> the Red-Sea Coast, whose waves orethrew
> *Busiris* and his *Memphian* Chivalry,
> While with perfidious hatred they pursu'd
> The Sojourners of Goshen, who beheld
> From the safe shore thir floating Carkases
> And broken Chariot Wheels.
>
> > (I, 306–311; Exod. 14:23–30)

> As when the potent Rod
> Of *Amrams* Son in *Egypts* evill day

Wav'd round the coast, up call'd a pitchy cloud
Of *Locusts,* warping on the Eastern Wind,
That ore the Realm of impious *Pharaoh* hung
Like Night, and darken'd all the Land of *Nile.*

(I, 338-343; Exod. 10:12-15)

Nor did Israel scape
Th' infection when thir borrow'd God compos'd
The Calf in *Oreb.*

(I, 482-484; Exod. 12:35, 32:4)

These references early in the poem equate Satan and the fallen angels with Pharaoh and the Egyptians, then with the locusts (recalling Apollyon and the locusts of the bottomless pit in Rev. 9:1-11), and with the false gods of Egypt and the idol fashioned by Aaron after the exodus.[10] The history of the exodus is retold in *Paradise Lost* in XII, 151-269. Although Satan and his cohorts are not mentioned in this passage, the attentive reader has been prepared from the beginning to recognize that this stage in history is analogic — indeed, almost allegoric. The chosen people, having fallen into bondage of a "sequent King" (XII, 165), a "lawless Tyrant, who denies / To know thir God, or message to regard" (XII, 173-174), can be seen not only as descendants of Adam and Eve but as representations of the first parents who had fallen into bondage of Satan through his envy. The bondage of the chosen people is a type of bondage of man by Satan; it repeats the pattern that the first fall set forth. And Milton alludes to this patterning which life undergoes by utilizing the equation of Satan and Pharaoh. God sends signs and judgments to Pharaoh (XII, 175ff.), just as Satan is shown a sign in the sky after he is found at the ear of Eve (IV, 995ff.) and at what becomes the beginning of mortal time when Satan is defeated in the War in Heaven (VI, 775-776, 789-790), and he has the judgment of serpentine nature placed on him (X, 164ff. and X, 504ff.) after the Fall. (Milton calls Pharaoh "The River-dragon" [XII, 191], and since the infernal locusts were identified with scorpions in Revelation, the transmutation of the fallen angels in Book X is into locust-like swarms including "Scorpion and Asp" [X, 522-524].) The history of the exodus recorded in Book XII is one statement of the constant fall that the descendants of Adam and Eve undergo. Each fall becomes a successive stage upward to the final judgment, for each fall discriminates for mankind another factor of the dialectic. At the end of time, man should be able to face God's bright splendor directly, not through shade or agencies, not through clouds (suggesting also repentance) or fire (suggesting also suffering). The pattern underlying the Fall integrates all history and argues for a linear progression of time, the past renounced and the future heralded.

Moses, a type of Christ in his role as prophet, appears frequently in *Paradise Lost*. Book XII, 235–244, explicitly indicates Moses' function as a *figura*.

> But the voice of God
> To mortal ear is dreadful; they beseech
> That *Moses* might report to them his will,
> And terror cease; he grants what they besaught
> Instructed that to God is no access
> Without Mediator, whose high Office now
> *Moses* in figure beares, to introduce
> One greater, of whose day he shall foretell,
> And all the Prophets in thir Age the times
> Of great *Messiah* shall sing.

A prophet is one who proclaims revelation. In Book I, Milton addresses the Heavenly Muse that inspired Moses to aid him in asserting Eternal Providence. The role of Moses itself is divided between Raphael and Michael, God's messengers to man, and is the artifact for one of the roles of the creator of the poem—the poet as narrator—a topic too complex for consideration here. Raphael in Hebrew means "medicine of God"; he is likened by Milton to Hermes, whose medical powers are symbolized in the caduceus he carries—two intertwined serpents around a winged staff, representing knowledge and wisdom. Milton emphasizes the fact that Hermes is a *figura* of Christ at this point in the narrative (V, 285–287) by calling him "*Maia's* son," that is, one born of mortal woman and the godhead. Moses' kinship with Hermes is seen in references to his rod in I, 338; XII, 198; and XII, 211–212. It had become a serpent when dashed to the ground (4:3) and with this rod Moses was empowered by the Lord to do signs (*signa*).[11] Such signs, of course, depict knowledge and the wisdom which should flow therefrom. When the signs were given "in the sight of the people . . . the people believed" (4:30–31). Raphael warns Adam to be obedient and have faith through example (*signum*), and to put the potential lure of Eve's beauty behind him. He offers knowledge and wisdom. The kinship of Raphael to Moses points to his prophetic role; God's ways are revealed and there is short-lived belief. But like the chosen people, Adam and Eve will fall into bondage.

In Adam and Eve's paradise, so markedly different from the wilderness faced by Moses and Jesus or even from Dante's "dark forest of life," which Milton expressed in *Comus* as a "wild surrounding wast" (l. 403), we are to see the original model of the antecedents to exodus. With exodus from Paradise will come desiccation, as the imagery of the final lines shows. Incapable of performing the prophetic role themselves, Adam and Eve fail in their test of faith by succumbing to *concupiscentia carnis,* that is, the bodily temptation of need usually seen through hunger. The doctrinal answer to this lure is that "man does not live by bread alone, but by every word that proceedeth out of the mouth of God" (Matt. 4:4). The role of the prophet is to present the Word of God to the people. The metaphor depends on the Word of God as food for the soul, just as actual food will strengthen the body and make it healthy. (The significance of the eating metaphor during Raphael's visit and revelation in Books V and VI is thus understood; the argument over the metaphor has been blind to symbolic language.[12]) The Fall occurs when Eve disregards God's Word by the partaking of actual food at noon, as if in need. (Eve's temptation, of course, also reflects, though imperfectly, the remaining two lures: *concupiscentia oculorum* and *superbia vitae,* the world and the devil.) Adam's temptation is likewise bodily and through supposed necessity. He succumbs to the lure of the flesh, "fondly overcome with Femal charm" (IX, 999). With their fall comes the loss of Paradise, that which had been, in Voegelin's words, "the secured existence of an established order."[13]

It is thus through Adam and Eve's inability to resist the formulation of false gods, through their negation of faith, and through their passive acceptance of a secured existence that the need for exodus was sown. Once fallen, they must be led forth to reformulate a concept of true godhead through repentance and then through further trial. Theirs will be uneasy thoughts and uneasy steps, though some will see only the mirage of security. Milton has worked into his narrative the cause of exodus and, as we will see, continuing exoduses and the great Christian antitype when Jesus is led into the wilderness.

Moses' role as Michael is equally instructive of the weaving of exodus into the fabric of the poem. Just as the trumpet had sounded when Moses gave the law of God to the people after the exodus, so a trumpet precedes God's commission to Michael to lead Adam and Eve out of Paradise (19:16-19, 20:18; XI, 72ff.) and to denounce their banishment and the future. Moses has been "sent from God to claim / His people from enthralment, and . . . return / With glory and spoil back to their promis'd Land" (XII, 170-172). So Michael, a Christianized form of Hermes as conductor of the dead to the Elysian fields, will start mankind out on its journey back to God with the expulsion. His ultimate Hermetic role is seen at the end of the War in Heaven, a role played by the Son—the antitype—at the end of time, when he leads the faithful angels back to God—reduces them—so that they become embodied within the Godhead whence all substances has derived in the creation *ex deo*. Michael like Moses is a revealer of God's law but neither is the exemplar that will lead the fallen into Canaan. For this we must wait for Christ. Milton wrote:

> So Law appears imperfet, and but giv'n
> With purpose to resign them in full time
> Up to a better Cov'nant, disciplin'd
> From shadowie Types to Truth, from Flesh to Spirit,
> From imposition of strict laws, to free
> Acceptance of large Grace, from servil fear
> To filial, works of Law to works of Faith.
> And therefore shall not *Moses,* though of God
> Highly belov'd, being but the Minister
> Of Law, his people into *Canaan* lead;
> But *Joshua* whom the Gentiles *Jesus* call,
> His Name and Office bearing, who shall quell
> The adversarie Serpent, and bring back
> Through the worlds wilderness long wandered man
> Safe to eternal Paradise of rest.
>
> (XII, 300-314)

The circumstances requiring the exodus of the Israelites out of Egypt is analogous to the expulsion of Adam and Eve out of Paradise; each had fallen into bondage to a false god through lack of faith and wisdom. The house of institutional bondage, whether Egypt or Eden, had become a house of spiritual death, in Eden literally through the sin which "Brought Death into the World, and all our woe." The excesses following the Fall in Book IX symbolize that spiritual death. Fisch notes that "the Jewish commentators had glossed the word *play (saheq)* as a reference to sexual orgies following the violation of the divine command. This again serves to relate the corruption of Adam and Eve to the archetypal frame of the Exodus."[14] His references are to IX, 1027–1028 ("But come, so well refresh't, now let us play, / As meet is, after such delicious Fare") and to Exod. 22:6, after the exodus ("And they rose up early on the morrow, and offered burnt offerings, and brought peace offerings; and the people sat down to eat and to drink, and rose up to play"). Echoes of the Red Sea with its stretches of wilderness (Exod. 13:18), the dried land of passage through which they move eastward to their final home with a cloud by day and a pillar of fire by night to lead them, can be seen in Milton's description of the expulsion.

> The Cherubim descended; on the ground
> Gliding meteorous, and Ev'ning Mist
> Ris'n from a River o're the marish glides,
> And gathers ground fast at the Laborers heel
> Homeward returning. High in Front advanc't,
> The brandisht Sword of God before them blaz'd
> Fierce as a Comet; which with torrid heat,
> And vapour as the *Libyan* Air adust,
> Began to parch that temperate Clime; whereat
> In either hand the hastning Angel caught
> Our lingring Parents, and to th' Eastern Gate
> Led them direct, and down the Cliff as fast
> To the subjected Plain.
>
> (XII, 628–640)

With this we should compare Milton's description of Moses's leading the chosen people forth under the guidance of God.

> Such wondrous power God to his Saint will lend,
> Though present in his Angel, who shall goe

Before them in a Cloud, and Pillar of Fire,
By day a Cloud, by night a Pillar of Fire,
To guide them in thir journey, and remove
Behind them, while th' obdurat King pursues:
All night he will pursue, but his approach
Darkness defends between till morning Watch;
Then through the Firey Pillar and the Cloud
God looking forth will trouble all his Host
And craze thir Chariot wheels: when by command
Moses once more his potent Rod extends
Over the Sea; the Sea his Rod obeys;
On thir imbattell'd ranks the Waves return,
And overwhelm thir Warr: the Race elect
Safe towards *Canaan* from the shoar advance
Through the wild Desert, not the readiest way,
Least entring on the *Canaanite* allarmd
Warr terrifie them inexpert, and fear
Return them back to *Egypt,* choosing rather
Inglorious life with servitude.
(XII, 200–220; Exod. 14:19–29)

We have moved from references to Exodus and Moses in *Paradise Lost* to the theme itself. It is by the temptation in the wilderness which Jesus will undergo that the Son will overcome Satan by simply obeying God. Man's obedience and the Son's example appear in I, 1–15; III, 94–95, 107, 203–205; V, 501, 512–514, 522, 536–537, 541, 611–612; VI, 687, 902, 912; VII, 159; VIII, 325; and XII, 386–435.[15] The last citation is especially pertinent here.

nor so is overcome
Satan, whose fall from Heav'n, a deadlier bruise,
Disabl'd not to give thee thy deaths wound:
Which hee, who comes thy Savior, shall recure,
Not by destroying *Satan,* but his works
In thee and in thy Seed: nor can this be,
But by fulfilling that which thou didst want,
Obedience to the Law of God, impos'd
On penaltie of death. . . .

The Law of God exact he shall fulfill
Both by obedience and by love, though love
Alone fulfill the Law.

On the one hand, the garden itself has been the place of temptation, though not a wilderness because the Fall has not yet occurred, and man has fallen to that temptation. On the other hand, the wilderness that Adam and Eve face as they leave Paradise becomes the theater for continued temptation—with resistance by some and fall by others. The rejection of the security which their world afforded before has given rise to uncertainty and possible fears in the future. Only reliance upon God's Word—that is, upon God's providence—will allay such perturbations of the mind and soul. The exodus or expulsion in the poem has been preceded by avowals of faith by both Adam and Eve. They greet the new world before them with hope and faith. The final lines are replete metaphorically.

Som natural tears they drop'd, but wip'd them soon;
The World was all before them, where to choose
Thir place of rest, and Providence thir guide:
They hand in hand with wandring steps and slow,
Through *Eden* took their solitarie way.

(XII, 645-649)

The last line, deriving as it does from Ps. 17:4, reinforces the deliverance by God and alludes to the exodus again, for this is one of the psalms dealing with the freedom from Egyptian bondage. "O give thanks unto the Lord, for he is good: for his mercy endureth for ever. Let the redeemed of the Lord say so, whom he hath redeemed from the hand of the enemy. . . . They wandered in the wilderness in a solitary way." Adam and Eve's wandering in the wilderness is equated with the chosen people's wandering in their wilderness, quite unmistakably. The place of rest that Adam and Eve and their progeny shall take is metaphoric, not simply a reference to daily rest. Whether they rest in Heaven or in Hell is for them to choose by obedience and faith, or not. Their steps will be wandering (errant, unsteady) and they will be slow, but eventually, many exoduses onward, man will be able to arrive at the land of milk and honey and enter in to bliss. This exodus, solitary as it is, becomes a rededication of the

individual to God through renewal and rebirth. The sum of wisdom,
Michael has told Adam, is to know that

> to obey is best,
> And love with fear the onely God, to walk
> As in his presence, ever to observe
> His providence, and on him sole depend
>
> .   .   .   .
>
> . . . suffering for Truths sake
> Is fortitude to highest victorie.
>
>   (XII, 561–570)

Perhaps we are reminded that "Blessed is the man that walketh not
in the counsel of the ungodly, nor standeth in the way of sinners, . . . But his delight is in the law of the Lord" (Ps. 1:1–2). The
dropping of the natural tears and the wiping of them soon away recalls the prophecy of Revelation already quoted. Recognition of the
allusion restresses that the former things are passed away, and that a
new life lies before mankind. The significance of exodus as a beginning again in a stage in time is unavoidable.[16]

   The vision that Adam has of the world to come in Books XI and
XII consists of a number of stages in time separated by various exoduses, with a major break in continuity as we reach the story of Noah
and the flood. Michael's words to Adam shortly thereafter define
exodus as suggested here:

> Thus thou hast seen one World begin and end;
> And Man as from a second stock proceed.
> Much thou hast yet to see, . . .
>
> .   .   .   .
>
> This second sours of Men, while yet but few;
> And while the dread of judgement past remains
> Fresh in thir minds, fearing the Deitie,
> With some regard to what is just and right
> Shall lead thir lives, . . .
>
> .   .   .   .
>
> . . . till one shall rise [Nimrod]
> Of proud ambitious heart, who not content
> With fair equalitie, fraternal state,

Will arrogate Dominion undeserv'd
Over his brethren, and quite dispossess
Concord and law of Nature from the Earth,
Hunting (and Men not Beasts shall be his game)
With Warr and hostile snare such as refuse
Subjection to his Empire tyrannous.

(XII, 6-32)

Milton's language indicates that Nimrod is a type of Satan, who again enthralls the chosen people. We may be sure that others in the future will rise Satan-like to pervert, although Michael, after reciting the Mosaic exodus, comes swiftly to David the King and then to Jesus. Adam's reaction to all he sees through these two books articulates with the polarities of good and evil as the stages of history are played out. There are steps forward — sometimes even large ones for Adam and thus for the attentive reader — but the journey will not end until the Son

shall come
When this worlds dissolution shall be ripe.
With glory and power to judge both quick and dead.
To judge th' unfaithful dead, but to reward
His faithful, and receave them into bliss,
Whether in Heav'n or Earth, for then the Earth
Shall all be Paradise, far happier place
Then this of *Eden,* and far happier daies.

(XII, 458-465)

This paradise, the paradise within which those who emulate the Son will achieve, can emerge only through successive trials and transformation of the hard heart into "th' upright heart and pure" (I, 18).[17]

After the Judgment on Adam and Eve in Book X and their repentance, they stand "in lowliest plight . . . Praying, for from the Mercie-seat above / Prevenient Grace descending had remov'd / The stonie from thir hearts" (XI, 1-4). God's miraculous powers were frequently seen in a kind of alchemical transformation of making "glassy flouds [flow] from rugged rocks . . . and . . . soft rills from fiery flint stones gush," as Milton paraphrased Psalm 114.[18] The well-known emblem printed on the title page of Henry Vaughan's *Silex Scintillans* depicts the same miracle of removing the stony from a heart. The hardened heart and the means to transform it are mentioned often by Milton. Just after the defeat of Satan in the War in Heaven, for example, we read:

> In heav'nly Spirits could such perverseness dwell?
> But to convince the proud what Signs avail,
> Or Wonders move th' obdurate to relent?
> They hard'n'd more by what might most reclame,
> Grieving to see his Glorie.
>
> (VI, 788-792)

The hardening of Pharaoh's heart (read Satan's) is repeated often in the verse of Exodus 14, and these supply Milton's lines when describing the Exodus: "and of [God] / Humbles his stubborn heart, but still as Ice / More hard'n'd after thaw" (XII, 192-194). It is the pure in heart that are blessed, Jesus says in the Sermon on the Mount, for they shall see God; that is, they will be able to face His bright splendor once all hardness of heart has been transformed.

To effect this, God will send a Comforter (the Holy Spirit of John 15:26)

> who shall dwell
> His Spirit within them, and the Law of Faith
> Working through love, upon thir hearts shall write,
> To guide them in all truth, and also arm
> With spiritual Armour, able to resist
> *Satans* assaults, and quench his fierie darts.
>
> (XII, 488-492)

This passage occurs almost at the end of the poem, but the thought had initiated the poem as well—another factor bringing the poem into a circle and a continuum. The poet has asked instruction from the Spirit, "that does prefer / Before all Temples th' upright heart and pure" (I, 17-18). By the end of the poem, we see the beginning of the search for the means to that purification which the latter-day poet professes. The means to such purification of heart, which the poet admonishes his readers to seek, lies in 1 John 3:2-3: "we know that, when he [the Messiah] shall appear, we shall be like him; for we shall see him as he is pure." The role of the Son throughout *Paradise Lost* is the center of God's Eternal Providence, which Milton wishes to assert and which will thereby justify God's way toward men to men. The Son encompasses the Eternal Providence of God, as we have seen in Chapter Five, and the theme of the poem, as we have noted, is love. The temptation in the wilderness will exemplify the means for a man to make exodus effectual, and the resurrection will assure all men of faith. Thus, have we moved to the "great Argument" of the poem in its relationship to the theme of exodus.

The message of exodus is that the stony must be purged from fallen man's heart and he must believe that his redeemer liveth. My reading of the poem thus gives special urgency to the Father's words in VII, 154–161:

> in a moment [I] will create
> Another World, out of one man a Race
> Of men innumerable, there to dwell,
> Not here, till by degrees of merit rais'd
> They open to themselves at length the way
> Up hither, under long obedience tri'd,
> And Earth be chang'd to Heav'n, and Heav'n to Earth,
> One Kingdom, Joy and Union without end.

The "degrees" are the stages which successive exoduses will reach continuously through time, until the Second Coming. The process of purification of heart which is symbolized in the myth of exodus is expressed by the Father in III, 188–202 (my italics):

> for I will *clear thir senses* dark,
> What may suffice, and *soft'n stonie hearts*
> To pray, repent, and bring obedience due
>
> . . . .
>
> And I will place *within* them as a *guide*
> My Umpire Conscience, whom if they will hear,
> *Light after light* well us'd they shall attain,
> And *to the end persisting, safe arrive.*
> This my *long sufferance* and my day of grace
> They who neglect and scorn, shall never taste;
> But *hard* be *hard'n'd, blind* be *blinded* more,
> That they may *stumble on,* and deeper fall;
> And none but such from mercy I exclude.

The purgative way, through successive trials and exoduses of the race of men, will lead to illumination by truth and, finally at the end of time, to reunion with God. The trials mankind will undergo (see specifically those in Books XI and XII) will be trials by potential drowning (Noah's flood) and trials by potential burning (the conflagration of 2 Pet. 3:10). These successive stages partake of alchemy, an object of which was to produce pure and indestructible gold from baser metal.[19] Alchemical transformation resulted from "killing" the base metal and then from experimentation involving water and fire and the philosopher's stone. "Killing" alchemically represented sexual union, the partners of which were Sol and Luna, symbols of fire and water. Too much dominance of either of the two Great Sexes would destroy the experiment. The desirable union of Adam and Eve would agree with these principles, and so we must see them go forth solitary, hand in hand; they are as one and must continue as one, lest either destroy the other. The way in which Milton transposes the imagery of water and fire is astounding,[20] but just the final lines of the poem will underscore its importance to the theme of exodus: the mist, the river, the marish, the tears; the blazing sword, the torrid heat, the Libyan air adust, the parching of the temperate clime. The pure heart, like indestructible gold, will result from its "killing"—from humility—and its reformation through the amalgam of suffering and repentence. Through such trial will come the paradise within as and when the pure heart is forged. The philosopher's stone—the catalyst, as it were—in these trials is faith, seen as obedience and love, both in God and in one's marriage partner.

The sexual connotation of the alchemical lore is related to exodus through birth symbolism. The repeated vision of the New Heavens and Earth that will emerge out of the phoenix-like final conflagration, or the myth of creation (often alchemically expressed in the poem) is sufficiently well known not to be cited. But we can note, first, the presage of the birth of the Promised Seed (that which brings forth repentance and hope in the poem), and it is the Promised Seed that will lead man out from bondage to Satan; and, second, the graphic delivery of Adam and Eve from the *hortus conclusus*, or enclosed garden, which is Paradise. Here the "great Argument" and the theme of exodus coincide. The *hortus conclusus* of Song of Songs 4:12 has usually been interpreted as a womb symbol and as the garden of Paradise. Like the child who has come to depend upon a secured existence within its mother's womb with its amniotic waters of life, Adam and Eve issue forth to a desiccated world adust (with its obvious pun on mortality, dust). They proceed "to th' Eastern Gate" (again, a womb symbol), moving fast down the cliff to the subjected plain. Like the child who must grow into manhood, Adam and Eve and their progeny must face the wilderness of life with each successive generation.

The exodus of Moses is expressed in similar birth metaphor, once we recognize it — the sea, of course, being a female archetype.

> [God] them lets pass
> As on drie land between two christal walls,
> Aw'd by the rod of *Moses* so to stand
> Divided.
>
> (XII, 196-199)

This graphic symbolism is startling, but the pervasiveness of the myth of creation in the poem should obviate disbelief. The myth of exodus, we see, has derived from man's attempt to explain his life in time; it owes much in the recesses of human thought to the observation of human gestation. The myth of exodus is plainly an archetype of birth; its stages through history are the movement of generations through history, each, it is hoped, an advance over the preceding generation. And the forty days or years of biblical privation and trial are the days of generation. A modern example of this use of exodus can be seen in Joyce's *A Portrait of the Artist as a Young Man*, a novel which is a womb in which the gestation of its hero is expressed in imagery following the course of pregnancy. The novel ends with the exodus of Stephen Dedalus from his maternal life — from mother and country — to a world to be forged into the artifacts of immortality.

Milton as creator of the poem and as prophet reveals God's Word in order to lead man to purification of heart. The book of life is bitter, and the poem has its tragic effect. But it can also be as sweet as honey. Milton is able to act as creator through the inspiration of the Celestial Patroness, who brings God's Word nightly to his ear. The poem we are reading is the fruit of the union of poet and Spirit as we have seen in Chapter Seven; it is delivered forth to the wilderness of man's world as Adam and Eve descend to the subjected plain from the cliff above. Its envoi might be: Go forth; "be fruitful, multiplie, and fill the Earth, Subdue it" (VII, 531–532).

A myth of linear time and the continuum of life, the theme of exodus is remarkable in *Paradise Lost,* for it opposes the cyclic myth of birth-rebirth while it lies hidden, obscure, through strategic manipulations of time. The displacement of time in the poem at first yields a confused time-perspective for the reader; once recognizing the uses of time in the poem, the reader feels enjoined to conclude a pattern of cyclic time, since it seems to repeat itself in various ways. Yet Milton, I suggest, does this consciously to mislead those who wish to believe that "the future would be like the past" and that "no single event could have universal significance."[21] The fact is, the poem moves steadily forward from the first line to the last with only a few countable days elapsing. All events are momentous, and all are unique. Time, Milton is urging, moves forward constantly to the final day of judgment so prominently discussed in Books III, VI, X, and XII.[22] The citation in Book X comes after we have seen the effects of judgment, when the heavenly audience sings Halleluia: "Just are thy ways, / Righteous are thy Decrees on all thy Works" (X, 643–644). Milton is quoting Rev. 15:3: "And they sing the song of Moses the servant of God, and the song of the Lamb, saying, Great and marvellous are thy works, Lord, God Almighty; just and true are thy ways, thou King of Saints." The making of saints, which is the intention of exodus, will result from God's just ways. The myth of exodus—certainly not that of return—asserts eternal providence and justifies God's ways toward men.

TWELVE

The Poem as
Novelistic Technique

THE STRUCTURE of *Paradise Lost,* its story and treatment, the
techniques of relation and the narrative voice, the repetitions of language and its verbal arts, the portraits drawn (dramatic and psychological), the humor which is often missed, and its extensive myth —
all contribute in such a way to the totality of this literary masterpiece
which breaks so strongly with conventions while employing those conventions that some critics have not been aware of them. F.R. Leavis,
for example, has said, amazingly enough, that "Milton's inadequacy
to myth, in fact, is so inescapable, and so much is conceded in sanc-
tioned comment, that the routine eulogy of his 'architectonic" power
is plainly a matter of mere inert convention."[1] Much of the assault on
Milton has derived from the transference to him of the inadequacy of
those influenced by him, for example, in such dreary poetry as William Mason's or Robert Lloyd's, or from the anti-Romantic bias of
influential critics like T.S. Eliot who had followed Irving Babbitt's
biased strictures. Indeed, Milton's influence on Eliot — including language — is so pervasive that one must pause on this count alone to
question Eliot's abilities as a critic. And one wonders whether Ezra
Pound, whose remarks on Milton are few, scattered, and unoriginal,
ever really read Yeats appreciatively.[2] A recent collection of comments and more developed statements concerning Milton made by
the Romantics, and the judicious analysis introducing them by
Joseph A. Wittreich, Jr.,[3] should correct the misreading of such
authors as Blake, Coleridge, and Shelley on Milton, and the more
valid understanding of these authors which has been emerging in the
last decade or so may eventually turn the popular mind away from
using them as the whipping boys of all that is bad in poetic expression. Some of the considerations we have looked at in this study of

Paradise Lost will suggest that, while there may be in the poem problems of an artistic or ideational nature for some readers and while the literary experience of the poem may not be agreeable to all readers, nonetheless the poem is not the work that some have viewed and accordingly criticized. I believe it is not inaccurate to say that some of the artistic approaches and fusion of art and thought which this study explores have not been commonplace in Miltonic criticism. A rereading of the criticism of Eliot, Pound, Leavis, Waldock, Broadbent, Peter, and Empson will validate this statement.

The literary challenge which A.J.A. Waldock leveled against the poem and which basically remains unanswered will serve to suggest the way in which *Paradise Lost* has achieved literary wholeness and especial significance in its "newness" of result. He wrote:

> It is possible, I think, to overrate very much Milton's *awareness* of the peculiar difficulties of his theme. . . . It is not absurd to mention the novel in connection with *Paradise Lost,* for the problems of such a poem and the characteristic problems of the novel have much in common. . . . We have only to look at the material that he was bent on disposing in his epic to see that some of the problems he faced were virtually insoluble. . . . Could any writer with an instinct for narrative, we ask ourselves, have failed to see what problems those first three chapters of Genesis held, and to shrink back deterred?[4]

On one level, Waldock sees difficulties in the presentation of a story based on miracle and fabulous action, a story whose main characters are nonhuman or suprahuman, a story which requires philosophic proof and acceptance. On another level, he contrasts the novel form emerging during the seventeenth century with the compositional cruxes which Milton had to solve: the method of presenting narrative and character, the language to sustain such presentation, and the means of keeping strands of action, place, and time straight, yet intertwined. The novel form of the seventeenth century was not much of an advance over the episodic tales or romances of an era before (for example, Alexander Hart's *The Tragi-Comicall History of Alexto and Angelica*) or the true picaresque (for example, Richard Head's *The English Rogue*), and it is not until the mid-eighteenth century that the kind of complexity that *Paradise Lost* engages enters the novel. Bernard Bergonzi, who counters Waldock's criticism by disallowing comparison of two such disparate literary forms, remarks: "A successful answer to Waldock would have to show that the narrative stsructure of *Paradise Lost does* possess the kind of coherence and psychological plausibility that we have come to expect from the novel. Again, there can be no doubt that it does not."[5] Yet the poem can, I believe, be viewed in terms of novel technique, and to Milton's advantage.

The novel form as we generally think of it is a consistent narrative moving in time, involving sustained characterizations with psychological validity and, as the novel developed, with complexities of action, time, place, and purpose. The narrative of *Paradise Lost* exists in the time-present of the poem, beginning with the awakening of the fallen angels in Hell, their council to debate the means of revenge or escape, their appointment of Satan as envoy to determine and effect that means, and his voyage through Hell, through Chaos, and to the created universe. The omniscient God co-temporaneously observes and discusses the situation with Heaven's inhabitants, and His Son offers himself as ransom for an event to occur in the future as a result of Satan's discovery and effecting of the means of revenge and escape. Time is not human time, and so, though these narrative elements may have taken a long period of chronological time in human reckoning, the reader has no awareness of the length. But neither does he have a sense of brevity, for the language is so manipulated that time does not become a consideration as one reads, and even when one returns and ponders the time element, he has no sense of immediacy of one action after another. Sometime after Satan has begun his journey and just before the council in Heaven, the universe has been created as well as Adam and Eve. All time is but a thought in God's mind and the narrative supports this orthodox concept. Time has moved, but we do not know how far. The narrative then proceeds to view Paradise and its inhabitants through the eyes of the narrator and through a third-person technique as if the scenes were directly before the eyes of the reader, including Satan soliloquizing. The use of a narrator for description or comment has been common enough in the novel since its inception. In only a few places does the first person become unavoidable as one reads the epic. Usually, the third-person point of view takes on the rather dramatic feeling that a specific character's position is the main point of view of the work.

Here, we have Satan, in the beginning of Book V we have Adam. The contrast between Raphael's dramatic story-telling of the War in Heaven and Michael's recitation of highlights of the War on Earth emphasizes the difference; we often forget that the War of Heaven is not occurring in the time-present; we are well aware that Adam is being told about the future world. This occurs partially because Michael's vision is punctuated by comment by Adam. Yet the point of view throughout is consistently that of the narrator, who directly enters at times, as in many eighteenth- and nineteenth-century novels.

The fallen angels' envoy, Satan, achieves his mission by determining that revenge against God lies in winning man from God, and by discovering the means to that end through the fancy of Eve, but Eve by herself. Because Satan has penetrated Paradise, though he is routed, God sends His envoy Raphael to warn the inhabitants by relating to them the evil which may attempt to attack them, the way in which that evil has come about and why, and God's counteraction (the universe). Since the whole of the counteraction is unavailable through Raphael, Adam supplements the account with a human and limited view of his own first existence and the creation of his mate. (The variety that a switch in story-teller provides, of course, is also of artistic significance.) Although the reason for the creation (the rebellion of the false angels) and the purpose of the creation (to replenish Heaven with truly worthy beings) have been in God's prescience for all time, the reader is not made to feel that these have been planned actions from before the fact, primarily because they are not so presented (for God foresees but does not foreordain) and because of the technique of flashback — story-telling of what occurred at some time past as if it were happening at that time. This technique has been with narrative art in some form for as long as we have evidence.

Next, the narrative moves in time to an occasion when the warning previously given can be put to the test. The time-lapse is "The space of seven Continu'd Nights," perhaps, that is, seven units of whatever human thought equates with "night" since the creation of Sun and Moon have taken place. Finding the woman alone, playing upon the "Organs of her Fancy," Satan is able to tempt her and effect a stage of the Fall, which must, however, wait for Adam, the Root of Man, to turn against Raphael's warning and succumb to the charms of Eve, his narcissism having already been displayed in his account of her creation. The Organs of Eve's Fancy have shown a latent pride (and pride *is* good) by which Satan deceives. Eve, quite innocent, is not prepared for the deceit of Satan. The way in which Uriel, Regent in the Sun, is taken in by Satan's hypocrisy shortly before underscores Eve's lack of culpability in being deceived; she is culpable in her lack of obedience regardless of the reasons offered for disobedience, and that disobedience—and thus her sinning—occurs only at the moment that she tastes the fruit. Adam, on the other hand, sins more disastrously for him and us, for he is presented clearly with a choice of obedience or disobedience, without the deceit of Satan being practiced upon him directly. Adam's love for "Bone of his Bone, Flesh of his Flesh" is also good, until such time that it becomes intemperate, as here, and forces a disobedient decision. He falls at the point of making that decision and of thus tasting the fruit. He falls through deceit, although once removed. Milton could not be expected to speculate on what would have happened if Adam had not fallen although Eve had; but psychologically the portraits drawn of both make their individual choices consistent for them while at the same time Milton's handling of both temptations would have allowed different decisions to be made had the people involved been different. But man is man: deceivable, born innocent, sensate, needful of love, and subject to wrong reason. The portraits we are given before the point of temptation—Eve's in her recounting of her awakening from creation in Book IV, as well as her dream recalled in Book V and Adam's remembrance of her in Book VIII; Adam's in his remarks in Book IV and his recollection of Eve's creation in Book VIII as well as his accession to her blandishments in the beginning of Book IX—lead inevitably to the choices each makes. We do not experience suspense for the outcome in the sense of not knowing what happens (just as we do not when we reread anything or read that which is historically based); the sense of suspense comes with the motives developed prior to the act—suspense as to when and how and under what circumstances the act will take place. The characterizations of Adam and Eve and the acts that they commit leading to their Fall are sustained and psychologically valid.

The narrative immediately continues in time to present the fallen pair's ensuing actions, then their reactions to their lust, and, indeed, the complexes of guilt and self-hate and recrimination that mankind has inherited, and their attempts to rationalize their situation (since they now have not only reason but knowledge). The reactions in Heaven, the judgment on Earth, and the reactions in Hell (both in the Hell of Satan's offspring and in the Hell of his governance) follow in logical order. Man's repentance — in the normal theological and psychological sequence of act, guilt, repentance — balances in Book X the negative (ultimately positive) reaction in Heaven, the compensational results on Earth, and the positive (ultimately negative) reaction in Hell. To follow must be two things: a firming-up of the realization on the part of man of what the crime against God has been and what it has brought into being, and an unequivocal statement of the means to regain what has been lost. The narrative thus portrays the world that will ensue upon Adam and Eve's leaving Eden, as they do shortly after their repentance. The device of envisioning the future has become common enough in dream visions and novels bordering on science fiction. The narrative techniques are thus basically three: a report on happenings as if they were before the readers' eyes — the time development from the first line of the poem to the last; a view of what has occurred to make the present what it is — the narratives of past action encased within the poem, primarily by Raphael in Books V and VI, by Raphael in Book VII, and by Adam in Book VIII (although throughout the past is filled in, as it often is in novels, by remarks of various characters, e.g., Sin's account of her own and Death's births); and a view of what will come as a result of what we have read about — the narratives of future action encased in the poem, related by the Father in Book III, by Eve in her recounting of her dream in Book V, and largely by Michael through the vision of future history in Books XI and XII (although again foreviews are given throughout in little ways, often ironically).

The narrative line is represented diagrammatically in Figure 2. There is obvious consistency in the narrative line, although it digresses as so many novels do by recounting events of the past and by presenting the future as very few do, except for certain effects. The complexity of time created by these two devices is a great advance over such novels as Samuel Richardson's but comes nowhere near the kind of thing one finds in Thomas Pynchon's *V.* or even William Faulkner's more easily rearranged *The Sound and the Fury*. The devices are not difficult to follow, but Milton's employment of them does not rigidly follow the patterns laid down in the *Odyssey*. They are so integrated into the poem that we the readers, not Milton the

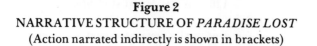

Figure 2
NARRATIVE STRUCTURE OF *PARADISE LOST*
(Action narrated indirectly is shown in brackets)

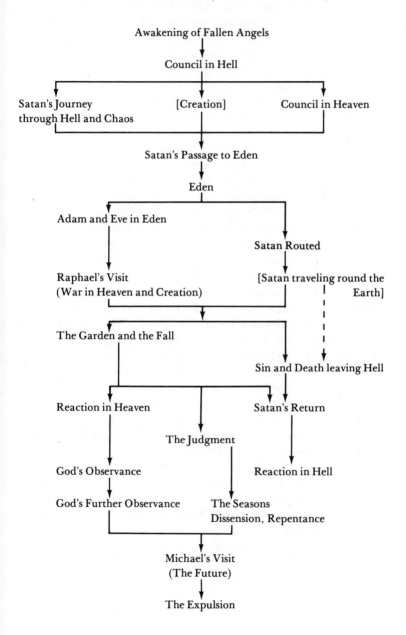

author, have not continually separated and ordered these intertwined strands of time and narrative. The diagram also makes clear
that the narrative line divides into simultaneous actions (it is somewhat more complex than a diagram can show). Again, the use suggested in something like the *Iliad* is much simpler to follow because it
is presented with accompanying language that breaks more firmly
with the preceding section than does, say, the lines concerning Sin
and Death readying themselves to leave Hell, "ere thus was sin'd and
judg'd on Earth" (X, 229). The point is, Milton is dealing with time
that has no duration in human count, and thus at the point when the
Fall is being set up in Book IX, Sin and Death who will thus be enabled to leave Hell to roam on Earth at large must, to maintain the
allegory, be preparing to leave. As the Fall occurs in Book IX they
must leave, intercept Satan, and reach Earth to coincide with the
aftermath of the Fall (IX, 1034-1189). The Divine sees all this in an
instant and the reaction in Heaven and the judgment are thus
logically given as soon as possible, pushing the section on Sin and
Death later; conveniently, this action then easily leads to the reaction
in Hell. This kind of simultaneous action has often appeared in the
novel in only broad strokes with authorial indications of "Mean-
while" (which Milton also uses) and the like. The modern novel, however, like Joyce's *Ulysses* or Kenneth Patchen's *The Journal of Albion
Moonlight*, is more frequently built on such complex polymorphic
and polyphonic techniques, yielding much greater complexity than
Paradise Lost. These manipulations of time extend the narrative line
and develop it, making it something unassociated with the novel of
the seventeenth century or even the early eighteenth.

The narrative of *Paradise Lost* is coherent, although I do not
doubt that many readers have not found it so. The fault lies in the
reader; I daresay such a reader expected a clear-cut story (with the
connotations of "story" that narrative does not require) of Adam and
Eve's Fall, and of course he did not find it. Part of the problem is, as
I have tried to show, the misfocus on Book IX rather than on the
whole poem and specifically on Book VI as climax of the poem. The
full narrative line should include the theme toward which it drives,
and that requires close attention to the whole poem and specifically
to Book VI. The question of psychological plausibility seems well
enough documented if we think only of Adam and Eve. But since the
Adam and Eve story is not the full narrative and does not constitute,

in my view, the full thesis and theme of the poem, we must look at God the Father, God the Son, and Satan in terms of characterization and psychology. It is humorously amazing to me that those who have objected to the poem largely because of the portraits of God and Satan have nonetheless continued to view it as the story of Adam and Eve in Genesis only.

I must disagree with Waldock that Milton was not aware of the peculiar difficulties of his subject matter (a better term for what he meant than theme). Even so, the difficulties which Genesis offered and which would make Waldock shrink back did not make Milton do so, and one wonders whether even partial success under such conditions is not more to be admired than undertaking the kind of self-portrayal that someone like Thomas Wolfe found to be his only subject? The difficulties in presentation of a story based on miracle and fabulous action and whose main characters are nonhuman or suprahuman need ask only one thing of the reader: belief in the fable and its actors *for the duration of reading that piece of literature.* This may be suspension of disbelief, but only of a very basic kind. When I read *The Tempest* I suspend my disbelief that Prospero has magical power and that a creature like Ariel can exist. But once this basic suspension is made, we can proceed to read, understand, and evaluate the play as literature, as message-bearer, as mythic artifact, as what-you-will. Milton's problem was not in using the story of Genesis, but in his readers who believe that there is a God, that there is a Devil, and that Adam and Eve actually existed. As remarked before, there is not one character in the poem (with the exception of the narrator) who is real. All take on allegoric proportions in being and action, and the way in which people like Addison and Voltaire missed this clearly indicates my point: only Sin and Death are allegoric because Addison and Voltaire, *et al.,* did not conceive of them as having bodily form; but in contrast God is God, and the Devil is the Devil, and Adam and Eve existed because the Bible tells us so. *Paradise Lost* requires nothing more than any piece of creative literature — something made up by the author which is not true regardless of its supposed closeness to fact, like Truman Capote's *In Cold Blood,* or closeness to natural or realistic elements, like Emile Zola's *Germinal,* and that is, that we accept as true that which the piece of literature presents *for the duration of reading that piece of literature.* Christina Stead's *The Man Who Loved Children* is one of the great allegoric masterpieces of the novel, but the reader believes implicitly that the Pollitts exist just as presented because he sees himself and those he is associated with in their portrayal. Most readers do not recognize the full allegory of *Paradise Lost* and see in the characters and actions things which they do not believe (or rather do not want to believe).

For J.B. Broadbent, "the most serious" fault that Milton shows in *Paradise Lost* "is failure to motivate Satan evilly. Satan's immediate motive for sin, the 'begetting' of the Son, is ambiguous, vague . . . and confused by the ceremony after the war in time but before it in the poem when the Son assumes the office of Redeemer. . . . [H]e does not give us any vision of the germinal defection of Satan himself, such as the birth of Sin provides in Book II and such as we have for Eve."[6] It would seem Broadbent desires a straight story with a steady plodding forward of time and, besides, he has not understood what Raphael reports along with Sin's account in Book II. To John Peter, much of the problem for poet and reader alike is a matter of indecision as to the plane on which the poem's characters exist.[7] Behind these criticisms are the lack of identification of the reader with the Father or the Son; the identification of the reader with his view of Satan as antagonist to injustice; and the alleged vindictive action of God in "begetting" the Son and Satan's unpsychologically realized reaction. The allegoric (or mythic) nature of the poem is overlooked because God is God, not an allegoric figure, and the Devil is the Devil, not an allegoric force. All actions of these characters (taken as real beings) must be identifiable with actions which the reader might undertake. (Somehow readers have been able to identify with Adam and Eve just as they can with Stead's characters, without recognizing their mythic proportions.) The polarities of God and Satan are reversed mirror surfaces: where God foresees, Satan merely hopes the outcome will be as arranged for; where God provides, Satan leaves things to chance; where God acts through reason, Satan acts through emotion. Human readers can certainly not identify with a being who foresees (yet we accept, say, a Tiresias or Cassandra as literary conventions to create dramatic irony); but Satan's delusions, self-contradictions, and purposes would not equate man's hopes if readers recognized them for what they are. The providence of God depends on foresight, and since this is outside man's experience (except for those believing in some form of clairvoyance), the acceptance of providence must rest on one's faith in God and His om-

nipotence. Man reduces chance by preparations for an end he believes is good and desirable; readers of *Paradise Lost* seem to see
Satan's moves toward his goal as representative of such preparations
and thus accept his actions unanalytically. Yet Satan's goal of uncreation, of revenge and harm, are not good and desirable and if the
end is wrong, the means must be too; here lie his preparations for the
corruption of mankind. His moves toward his goal are representative
of some men's actions, but these are the preparations of the con man,
the thief, the vice-lord. Satan reduces chance by underhanded
means, as in the implanting in Beelzebub's mind his advancement as
envoy to seek revenge on God. His goal is really self-aggrandizement;
still, if one assumes, out of some sense of justice against a vindictive
God, that his goal is the righting of a grievous wrong, the means by
which he seeks to achieve it are nefarious and should give one pause
in accepting the assumption. Milton's answer to the question of
whether the end justifies the means will be read in Adam's observation "That all this good of evil shall produce / And evil turn to good"
(XII, 470–471) and in his belief in the justification of God's way toward men, although means to a worthy end would not be nefarious,
though possibly militant and harsh. *But it is not means that are in
question, it is the end.* Satan's means to reach his goal—subtle implications, deceit (as of Uriel), hypocrisy, all of which are his means of
subversion not only in the Adam and Eve narrative but in the winning over of some of the angels in the War in Heaven—are the archetypes, again, of the con man, the demagogue, the morally bankrupt.
Satan becomes an archetype of the antihero and particularly of the
recurrent guilt-ridden self-hater. If the reader believes that the equation between Satan's rebellion against God, and mimetically, man's
against the political or social or economic tyranny of an establishment is valid, I can only say that he has read a poem of his own making, not Milton's. Milton does not believe that the equation is valid
and largely because God is not equivalent to the Establishment. Indeed, the kind of man-subjugating Establishment that one finds in a
police state or a stratified society is a result of the corruption of those
who, like Satan, aggrandize themselves at the expense of their
brothers. Milton would consider rebellion against "God"—whatever
the word denotes—and the peace and love and happy immortality
that the term connotes is an example of death wish, self-hate,
Thanatos (in Freud's sense). For Milton "God" is God, but the poem

does not demand that we read this equation. God in *Paradise Lost* is readable as metaphor for love and peace and all that is good. But as I have pointed out, Milton's critics will not admit to themselves that "God" is not God or at least that "god" may be metaphoric, as well as Sin and Death. The question is not the means, but the end.

The two difficulties in connection with God and the foregoing comments are that critics have seen God's statement of justice as a form of the police state and His "begetting" of the Son as a form of stratification in society. They overlook Raphael's equation of "to obey" and "to love" and the freedom of love that the angels have. Had they not such freedom, Satan could not have rebelled; like Satan and his cohorts, the critics have forgotten God's omniscience, omnipresence, and omnipotence. The stratification they infer overlooks the fact that the Son is God and the realization that Satan himself has functioned in the position of leader among the angels *but without any sense of stratification among them.* Indeed, in the War in Heaven itself, an equal number of good angels can fight only to a stalemate with the rebellious angels because of their equivalence. Only God is the superior, and the subordinate position of the Son, who lacks omniscience, omnipresence, and omnipotence, underscores this fact of the poem. Taking Satan's side, critics have been able to hoodwink themselves into believing that God's begetting of His Son has changed the ground rules and is an example of nepotism. The Son's begetting is the result of God's prescience and thus His Providence.

Of importance to this discussion is Milton's meaning when he says "the Paradise within." The concepts of the Diggers, particularly as envisioned by Gerrard Winstanley, or of people like Robert Owen or of the commune-oriented youth of recent years are not different. Milton, *Paradise Lost* well illustrates, believed that man must develop within a love of all mankind, that such love is the equivalent of the metaphor "God," and that this "means" ultimately is the "end." The story of Christ is an exemplar of what man must do. Adam realized it (see XII, 469ff.), but Milton knew that most men — being unfit audience — did not, and so (thankfully), we have *Paradise Regain'd* as unequivocal parable.

The criticisms which Broadbent and Peter level at the poem are answered, it seems to me, in my previous remarks. Peter places the poem and its characters on various planes but accuses Milton of doing so. He has identified with Adam and Eve perhaps, undoubtedly with Satan, and has equated God and his actions with all that he finds unacceptable in the Establishment of our contemporary world. He (along with so many others) has not recognized Milton's assertion of God's Providence in the begetting of the Son, who is God also, before need arises. Perhaps evaluation of the poem must be lowered because of Milton's lack of success in this and related matters for so many readers. But any teacher or parent knows that the lack of communication may be the consequence of the recipient's mind-set and psychological *Affekt*. The metaphysical problem of good and evil is at the base of Milton's epic and the criticism; good is observable and evil is observable, and pragmatically one must accept their existence. What is good and what is evil? Milton is asking and answering. That he cannot ultimately do away with mirror-existence for the two concepts should not, I believe, be charged against him, for who can explain them further? Since all observable things yield a perspective of mirror-existence — the positive implying the negative — Milton has used the rhetorical device of antithesis (or dialectic) throughout. The "cause" of evil is that it is the opposite of good.

In Satan's rebellious thought lies the observation of what we today call the id and in God's "presence" in man (who is the "ego") lies what we call the superego.[8] Like a Zoroastrian canvas, *Paradise Lost* presents the psychological life of man through the suprahuman, allegoric actions of myth. Man born into the world (like Adam and Eve leaving their *hortus conclusus*) has both id and superego as he starts his journey through life; what occurs in the battle of forces within us is man's history. We cannot deny the existence of these forces within us, nor the myth that Milton employs as objective correlative.

The sources of Satan's rebellion are the sources of such opaque criticism as Broadbent's. What such critics want is a definite cause (beyond which they will not think) for every action; their mind-set demands the expectable and applicable to themselves. Satan reacts against God's "begetting" of His Son; thus this thought and its ensuing action must have as cause this "begetting." We must remind ourselves that Eve's dream in Book IV is not sin, that sinning on her part does not occur until she partakes of the fruit. The cause is the intemperance of the id in the person of Satan as serpent, playing on the "Organs of her Fancy" — through temptations of pride in self, coveting of material position and its accoutrements, and supposed neces-

sity (for the Fall occurs at noon). The cause is Satan on the level of
prelapsarian logic in man's world; he is the dramatic and personified
cause, without whose existence the creations of innocence would not
have changed. But the cause that is allegorized is the imbalance that
may come to exist within man, should the superego become weak,
should the excesses of the libido overtake their checks. The poem and
its characters exist on one level, but the importance for man in this
life is another level; it is not different from the meaning in most literature, for example, Eliot's Prufrock. I cannot see an indecision over
plane because a fourfold interpretation may be elicited.

Likewise, in Sin's account of her birth, we see that she (allegoric
Sin or Evil) did not exist until

> All on a sudden miserable pain
> Surpris'd thee, dim thine eyes, and dizzie Swumm
> In darkness, while thy head flames thick and fast
> Threw forth, till on the left side op'ning wide,
> Likest to thee in shape and count'nance bright,
> Then shining heav'nly fair, a Goddess arm'd
> Out of thy head I sprung. . . .
>
> (II, 752–758)

The implication is that the seeds for such birth had existed before.
The seeds, like Eve's pride, will be good when moderated, for Satan
has assumed, apparently through ability, a superior position of
leadership to other angels. Pride in such position and ability is good,
but once that pride steps over into dominance over those one leads,
evil has come into being. Here is an archetypal situation that has
always plagued the communal concept, the "we-are-all-brothers"
belief; those who by dint of ability have moved into a position of
leadership have time and time again appropriated unto themselves
superiority, command, domination, authority. This is the problem
that the younger generation of the last ten years has been grappling
with; they have not really reached the answer, they know, whether in
mountain-top commune or in constantly changing constituency in an
urban pad. The hope of achievement is still there; the need is still
there. Milton's poem is subtended by this hope and is clear in the
ways in which it is defeated and the ways by which it will be gained.
Sin tells us what happened with Satan: he no longer could see

clearly and his blood pressure rose through anger. He loses perspective of the situation, that is, because he did not anticipate God's announcement and he assumed that it was equivalent to what it would have meant had he, as leader of many of the angels, made the announcement. (The relationship with Beelzebub is instructive here.) It thus was an announcement understood as placing him in a new and different position, but of course this is not true since the Son is God, and Satan has the same relationship with God as before. The psychological step behind this loss of perspective and dimming of sight and rising anger is that Satan had been moving toward appropriation of superiority, command, domination, and authority over the other angels, although all that was supposed to exist was leadership, since all were sons of God — as he at other times insists, all brothers. The announcement is an inflection point. Like Eve, Satan has not fallen yet despite his moving toward such position, any more than Macbeth is fallen when he cogitates the witches' prophecies in Act I. Satan may not be motivated by someone or something other than the announcement, but to be so would have required the existence prior to that inflection point of someone or something that was already fallen. It is difficult to understand how Satan could be motivated evilly in terms that would satisfy Broadbent. The point that Milton makes, I think, is that Satan has assumed omniscience as a son of God (even the Son, as subordinate, does not have omniscience) but is suddenly surprised to learn something from God's announcement that he had not foreknown, and he reads that "begetting" from his, not God's, point of view. The situation is the psychological epitome of the cause for self-hate, played over and over in time when we become angry at others for what we ourselves have committed or omitted. The germinal defection of Satan exists in Raphael's account, Sin's remarks, and the implications of the words used. Any further narrative would be redundant.

To me, the question of Satan's motivation is a nonquestion: (1) the material is allegoric; (2) the "begetting" is the inflection point of Satan's assertion of id and bad pride rather than motivating cause; and (3) the situation is intended to point out other significant matters, as suggested before. If Milton has not supplied us with a human equivalent to motivating cause, neither has anyone else. The Father labels the motivating cause as well as one can, I suppose: the angels fell self-deceived. They, or more properly Satan, have been deceived by themselves as to their status, although it is no different from any other angel's, and they have deceived themselves over the meaning of the Son's begetting. The implications in the term "self-deceiv'd" are that the seeds for self-deceit, for that which is destructive, are always present through the inherent quality of substance, which in order to be positive must contain the elements of negativity. Yes, this suggests that the substance which is God contains such qualities, but the stasis (or equilibrium) which is achievable is maintained by Right Reason and moderation.

If we can acknowledge the allegoric as well as the dramatically literal levels of the work (not, of course, to deny the tropological or anagogic), and if we can bring interpretation to bear upon the poem as we do with other pieces of literature so that we can see what is going on in Satan's mind when he "rebels" (the word is the wrong word, of course; it should be something like "misunderstands" or "succumbs to wrongful pride"), and if we encompass the entire poem and not just the Adam and Eve sections, and if we do not demand of a work of literature a prescribed form and development, then and, I suppose, only then can we proceed to understand certain novelistic ideas which *Paradise Lost* does engage. For the reader who still believes after the last page of a novel is read that the couple live happily ever after, or that David Copperfield (any *bildungsroman* will do) moves into a life of love and peace, or that the hero's death solves all problems which henceforth will not rear up for those who remain, *Paradise Lost* must be a horrifying experience. For nothing is solved, nothing is ended, everything is potential and beginning and sadly hanging out there in the metaphysical future. Though I still hold that Milton is hopeful in his work and that its effect is ultimately uplifting, no one, surely, can finish those last lines without experiencing the tears that Adam and Eve brush away. But they are brushed away, for the vista of the new life is before Adam and Eve and, Milton would hope, before us, the readers. The significance of the poem is not the poem itself but its effect, the results it will work, the guide and corrector and inspiration it will become for some, at least. In this, perhaps *Paradise Lost* is most novel, most modern. In this, *Paradise Lost* classifies itself as a work exemplifying the basic analysis that Georg Lukács and Lucien Goldmann made of the novel: an ironic narrative of a demoniac quest for authentic values pursued by a problematic hero in a decadent society.[9] The quest of *Paradise Lost* has always been thought of as that of Satan, and it exists in its mirror world as such; but the quest of importance is man's as he is born into the world outside Eden. Man's quest is as Lukács describes it, and the tension that the novel depicts is shown within the vision of Michael. The tension lies in the total break that is always imminent between those authentic values and the everyday world that surrounds man. The demands of living, the demands of the superego as well as the id, constantly tend to degrade man and his quest. Milton must have dreamed of the "Light after light well us'd" for Everyman and hoped that his noble task would lead some through the world's vain mask, though he knew some (most?) would become fodder for death and others would convert to inaction, would as we say today "cop out." For me, the vision of Milton in *Paradise Lost* is still so frighteningly present and futural! His concern in the epic has certainly encompassed the concerns of the novelists of our time; of itself this may be answer enough to Waldock's charge.

THIRTEEN

The Poem as Entity

WHAT is the poem that many people read as *Paradise Lost*? Unfortunately, the length of the epic has often caused it to be excerpted to a few books, some other sections, and summaries. This study has been written for the reader who has pursued the full poem, or will; it is not an introduction to the poem but an introduction to ways to approach the poem — not all the ways, but the literary ways. The reader should have his text at hand and should be briefed sufficiently in the narrative to follow discussions without having to reread. A condition an author should not exact? Perhaps so, but when one deals with one of the most complex works of literature that has been fashioned, some assumptions must be made to progress anywhere. And *Paradise Lost* is such a masterpiece, as the intricacies described manifest. Such manifestation for me is most significant when I can see the author in control of his work, employing techniques and devices that achieve his intentions, the effects desired, the meaning implied, and when this is discerned in the full work, not just some of its parts.

One key to the unity of a poem is the use of metaphoric meaning, that is, the meaning imbued in a word or phrase and determined by its usage and particularly its continued usage throughout the work. The meaning of the parts of the work is conditioned by the metaphoric meaning of its words when the author is in control of his tools. Part of the metaphoric meaning may describe the author's subconscious meanings for a word or phrase, but in any case its artistic usage is consciously controlled. We may look at a word like "Omnipotent" (or "Omnipotence"), applied only to God in the epic, and define it as "unlimitedly (and singularly) powerful"; the action of God in the poem expresses his omnipotence and makes the definition meaningful. The seventeen uses of the word partake only of this denotation of the word, and this is appropriate for the concept of a god who is unambiguous and truth unvarnished. Milton's control of such language throughout his massive poem is a sure sign of the creative artist constantly at work. In contrast is a word like "meek," with its primary meaning for Milton of "submission," as in the beatitude that the meek shall inherit the earth. In all eleven uses, the word has this positive meaning. The first occurrence should have made that positive meaning clear; it is used of the Son's "aspect" (face, demeanor) when he completes his offer to redeem future fallen man (III, 266). While some play of the meaning "mild" lies about the word here (appropriate to the Son, who represents in his own language his potential to become man, since his language shows some overlay of connotation), it is the Son's unwitting submission to the Father's will that is paramount. The word is used here first in the epic because it is the first occurrence of submission to God's will in the epic. The Son's submission to the Father is the archetype of all submission. The Son's meek aspect speaks though he is silent, for silence is the highest eloquence. His meek aspect breathes immortal love to mortal men. And above his love shines only "Filial obedience: as a sacrifice / Glad to be offer'd, he attends the will / Of his great Father" (III, 269-271). Note that in this passage Milton progresses from mouth to nose to eyes (even graphically citing *above*). The word "meek" is used of others, though, unlike "Omnipotent," because others too can be submissive to the word of God. It is used of Eve, Adam, Raphael, and Eve's "meek surrender" to Adam, and in XII, 597, which notes her spirits that have all been composed to "meek submission." The message that each use of the word is to proclaim to the aware reader throughout the poem is stated most succinctly by Adam in XII, 569, when he concludes that the way to overcome the worldly wise is "By simply meek."

Parts of the poem and its characters are unified by the use of the word and its metaphoric meaning. Opposed to "meek," but serving also as a unitive factor, is "bold"; twenty-seven times it has a pejorative meaning, being used of Satan or the satanic. It is not submitting, it is opposing God's will, it is assertion of the self. It exposes an action of the id. The first occurrence (I, 82) defines Satan's words to Beelzebub when they awaken on the burning lake; the last (XI, 642), the actions of the Giants of the Earth (identified with the fallen angels). The transference of the term to man occurs as descriptive of Eve's disobedience; "Bold deed thou hast presum'd, adventrous *Eve*," laments Adam (IX, 921). The sin is presumption. And we thus should know that "bold," each time we meet it in the epic, stands in opposition to "meek" and smacks therefore of evil influence through assertion of the id, whether the subject is the Champions who defied the Paynim (I, 763), or Eve who, though now not bold or loquacious, is only "abasht," not yet submissive (X, 161). (Incidentally, the word "abasht" is used only four other times, once each of the fallen angels, of Satan, of Adam ["half abash't" at Raphael's admonition concerning his apparently excessive love of Eve, VIII, 595], and of Adam and Eve after their lustfulness in Book IX. The connotation of the word is never positive; it suggests shame for having been found in some action deemed unworthy at the time by the persons who are thus abashed.)

But there are three further uses of the word "bold" which seem not to fit the foregoing remarks: III, 13; IV, 854; V, 876. Taking these in reverse, the word describes Abdiel's answer to Satan, who has just warned him to "fly, ere evil intercept thy flight." Abdiel instead speaks angrily and threateningly, alleging that God's Golden Scepter has now become an Iron Rod "to bruise and break / Thy disobedience." Evil, or its shadow, has intercepted Abdiel, though his faithfulness to God be praised. He has presumed to make God a god of war. He has indeed been infected by the foes who encompass him round, and it is appropriate enough a word for one who has, even unknowingly, approached disobedience to God himself. Abdiel may show some affinities with the Son, as many commentators have urged, but we should not dismiss his near-defection. A similar case is found in IV, 854, where Zephon speaks boldly to Satan, who has penetrated Paradise. He challenges (or "singles") Satan, while noting that Satan's fear will cause such a challenge not to be tried. The evilness of Satan has infected Zephon as well, we see Milton subtly suggesting, once we recognize the metaphoric meaning of the word "bold." But the most significantly changed meaning which this realization creates is in III, 13: "Thee I revisit now with bolder wing." "Thee" is the Holy Light (the Son or the Spirit of God), and the poet now has ascended to light from out the Stygian Pool. The poet

has been tinged with some of the evil of the realms and their inhabitants that he has visited in Books I and II. He is making clear by using the word "bolder" that his own knowledge of the good which he
will now discourse comes from his knowledge of evil. Compare XI,
84–93:

> O Sons, like one of us Man is become
> To know both Good and Evil, since his taste
> Of that defended Fruit; but let him boast
> His knowledge of Good lost, and Evil got,
> Happier, had it suffic'd him to have known
> Good by it self, and Evil not at all.
> He sorrows now, repents, and prayes contrite,
> My motions in him, longer then they move,
> His heart I know, how variable and vain
> Self-left.

The proem understandably continues with Milton's personal sorrows,
repentance, and prayers. But "bolder" also announces the exercise of
the id within the poet. His tinge of sinfulness is presumption—a presumption to ascend to the pure Empyrean, to depict God the Father,
to offer in the ensuing lines of Book III the truth of God's Word. The
word used here is "bolder," implying that he has been "bold" ("pre-
sumptive") as well in descending to Hell, though taught by the Muse.

These three uses of "bold" indicate that, while it may be necessary
to insinuate oneself into certain situations, such presumption is
nevertheless not the good that God prefers. The initial move to
achieve good by what might appear boldness must derive from God,
not from others themselves, and thus only would there be submission
to God's will. It is understandable why Milton viewed (or tried to
view) his actions as being within his great taskmaster's eye.

The poem is clearly made an entity by such metaphoric meaning.
The use of certain words is not haphazard or solitary; it is controlled
and it informs the whole poem, not just a passage here or there. It
can collapse the poem into its metaphoric entity or it can detail the
numerous facets of a single idea for which the whole poem has become vehicle. I have previously called attention to the significance of
the word "stand," its opposite "sit," and their related cluster of image
words like "upright," "easy" and "uneasy," and "seat."[1] For Milton,

the concept of "stand" is active, restive, suggestive of man on guard against temptation, vigilantly alert; faithful man is one who is "upright" and "steadfast"; and his steps are "uneasy" steps because he is not certain that potential danger does not surround them or lie before them. But when "sit" is positive, it is inactive, restful, suggestive that danger does not surround one; it implies in the noun "seat" the Edenic world sought by man and in "easy" steps those taken without peril from the evils of this world. These concepts, however, may take on opposite values. Man must stand, be upright in mind and body, move by uneasy steps, until such time as he can sit unafraid. Such verbal concepts can be derived from an examination of Milton's use of language throughout a work or throughout the full range of his works. It indicates that connotations adhere to words for Milton (as for all of us) and such connotations yield a greater texture of meaning as well as point up a technique of composition to weld a work together. For with each repeated use, the reader brings to bear his accumulated connotations of a word, in comparison or, when varied, in contrast, and with each repeated use in which the same character is involved a progression toward fuller understanding is accomplished.[2] Important, too, is omission of a conceptual word where we might think it could normally occur.

We need look only at I, 4–5, to see that the connotations described above exist in the use of language in *Paradise Lost*: "With loss of *Eden*, till one greater Man / Restore us, and regain the blissful Seat. . . ." "Seat" is equivalent to Eden or Heaven and partakes of the glorious concept of peace associated with them. The modifier implies the nonblissful seat which ordinary man may experience and which all would experience did not Christ restore us and regain a viable heaven for us. As is common in this poem built on antitheses, the noun is appropriated for Hell and thus partakes of the infamous evil associated with Satan. Thirty-two uses refer directly to Eden or Heaven or imply such relationship.[3] It is particularly important, however, to note the connotation of the word in a seemingly ordinary use,[4] as in the following, which helps create a total vision of the paradisiac.

> Rais'd of grassie terf
> Thir Table was, and mossie seats had round,
> And on her ample Square from side to side

All *Autumn* piled, though *Spring* and *Autumn* here
Danc'd hand in hand.

(V, 391–395)

We have long been aware of the motif of Adam and Eve hand in
hand, as one before the Fall but separated in Book IX except when
Adam seizes Eve's hand at IX, 1037, in sexual lust, to be joined as
one again only by Michael at XII, 648. Here in Book V, the vision of
Spring and Autumn dancing hand in hand makes explicit the oneness of the year and the lack of seasonal change; this world is idyllic,
partaking of the peace and temperance which the image connotes.
The mossy seats on which the Edenic inhabitants and their angelic
guest sit remind us of that blissful seat which Eden is and which is
soon to be lost. Prepared by these images, we suddenly become aware
of the image of the square of their table. Although the circle was well
known as a symbol of perfection, it is squareness that connotes Heaven.[5] Accordingly, the word "round" is reconsidered, for it implies
both the placement of their sitting spots around the sides of the
square table and at the same time a circumscription of that square,
and thus the image of the squaring of the circle (impossible by ordinary means) iterates the perfection of the Earthly Paradise.[6] In Heaven there is the square unaccommodated; on Earth, Heaven can be
approached only by the circle that may hold within it the shadow of
that which is heavenly. Another noteworthy appearance here is that
of VIII, 590:

love refines
The thoughts, and heart enlarges, hath his seat
In Reason, and is judicious, is the scale
By which to heav'nly Love thou maist ascend. . . .

(VIII, 589–592)

True love lies in reason, not in passion, not sunk in carnal pleasure;
love goes hand in hand (see VIII, 510–511) rather than in lustful sei-
zure. Love is accordingly Edenic or Hellish, of God or of Satan.

We find the word appropriated directly for Hell,[7] as in this
example, which effects the transference of image.

Is this the Region, this the Soil, the Clime,
Said then the lost Arch-Angel, this the seat

That we must change for Heav'n, this mournful gloom
For that celestial light?

(I, 242-245)

Interestingly, the examples of the word in Book XI, once we are
alerted to the pejorative metaphoric content, remark the satanic influence behind the glorious kingdoms of the Earth: for we are to remember that, according to Psalm 2, the Lord will have the earthly
kings in derision through the begetting of his Son on the Holy Hill of
Sion. Observe how this applies in XI, 385-420, where, before realization of the pejorative meaning and reference to Psalm 2 that Milton
attaches to the word, "seat" had only the denotation of location
(italics removed and others added).

His Eye might there command wherever *stood*
City of old or modern Fame, the *Seat*
Of mightiest Empire, from the destind Walls
Of Cambalu, *seat* of Cathaian Can
And Samarchand by Oxus, Temirs Throne,
To Paquin of Sinaean Kings, and thence
To Agra and Lahor of Great Mogul
Down to the Golden Chersonese, or where
The Persian in Ecbatan *sate,* or since
In Hispahan, or where the Russian Ksar
In Mosco, or the Sultan in Bizance,
Turchestan-born; . . .

.   .   .   .   .   .

. . . in Spirit perhaps he also saw
Rich Mexico the *seat* of Motezume,
And Cusco in Peru, the richer *seat*
Of Atabalipa, and yet Unspoil'd
Guiana, whose great Citie Ceryons Sons
Call El Dorado: but to nobler sights
Michael from Adams eyes the Film remov'd
Which that false Fruit that promis'd clearer sight
Had bred . . .

.   .   .   .

. . . So deep the power of these Ingredients pierc'd,
Eevn to the inmost *seat* of mental sight,

That Adam now enforc't to close his eyes,
Sunk down and all his Spirits became intranst.

The appearance of the word in l. 418 contrasts the positive connotation, as a shadow of Heaven within man, with the four pejorative uses within the catalogue of the earthly kings. The heavenly seat is reason; the false seat is the symbol of man's subjugation of men.

The word "sit" is often imbued with the metaphoric meaning suggested, although it also appears as a rather colorless term (as in the line "the Bee / Sits on the Bloom extracting liquid sweet," V, 24–25). Often it refers to being in Heaven, but it may also be appropriated by or for infernal beings.[8] In II, 859, it relates to Chaos. Satan, though he uses the word with its heavenly meaning, is made to reflect his lack of full understanding of that meaning in IX, 163–165: "O foul descent! that I who erst contended / With Gods to sit the highest, am now constrained / Into a Beast." Two seemingly general occurrences imply much more by this connotation than we at first thought. In IV, 578, Gabriel calms Uriel's self-reproach at allowing one of the banished crew to pass on by remarking,

> *Uriel,* no wonder if thy perfet sight,
> Amidst the Suns bright circle where thou sitst,
> See farr and wide: in at this Gate none pass
> The vigilance here plac't, but such as come
> Well known from Heav'n. . . .
>
> (IV, 577–581)

Uriel is supposed to be vigilant, aware that danger is at hand, but he has lapsed. His error has come through the hypocrisy of Satan, yes, but Gabriel's word "sitst" reminds us subtly that this is a lapse and ironically comments on the lapse of vigilance at the gate to Paradise. These guardians of Earth and Eden should have been standing. Eve's use of the word in VIII, 210 ("For while I sit with thee, I seem in Heav'n") encompasses its basic meaning and indicates the reduced need for vigilance before the Fall when she and Adam are together. It is only when she separates herself from Adam in Book IX that the temptation can proceed. It should be noted that the word is used only three times after the Fall, once in reference to Shame for genital bareness, twice in reference to Sin and Death guarding the Gate of

Hell. The womb is considered a symbol of a gate (and vice versa), and the collocation of the word in these three places implies that sexual intercourse (since not now conditioned by reason but a result of carnal pleasure) must be guarded against lest it lead to Hell. Adam is later to learn that man must make death (a popular synonym for sexual intercourse) the Gate to Life. Significantly, the word "sit" does not appear in Books XI and XII, which envision the world after mankind has left Eden to wander the wilderness beyond.

The word "stand" is contrasted by its more frequent general usage and by only one real appropriation by the infernal world: "against all force / Death ready stands to interpose his dart" (II, 853–854), an appropriation from which we infer the alertness and constant activity of Death to capture man as a cohabitant of Hell. The metaphoric meaning for man is basic in ten uses of the word.[9] It may be used for the faithful angels, as in VI, 801 ("Stand still in bright array ye Saints, here stand / Ye Angels arm'd, this day from Battel rest") or for man, as in VIII, 640 ("stand fast; to stand or fall / Free in thine own Arbitrement it lies"), but its message is clear. That message unites the poem and yields texture. For example, Adam, unaware, tells us that "to sit" is no longer possible on Earth, which is part of the philosophy of the poem: "in mee all / Posteritie stands curst" (X, 817–818). The language demands close reading and rereading, indeed, a "standing" of the mind to the meanings it imparts.

It is through standing that uprightness is achieved, not only in graphic terms but symbolically. The "upright heart and pure" (I, 18, from Ps. 15:1–2 and 1 Cor. 3:16) which the Spirit of God prefers before material symbols dedicated to a love for God, such as temples (implying that man is the Temple of the Holy Spirit as in 1 Cor. 6:19), is equivalent to the paradise within (XII, 587). This uprightness of the faithful is invoked seven times.[10] Gabriel's reference to Satan's uprightness before the fall of the angels in IV, 837, shows that uprightness may become the groveling of the serpent once the pure heart has hardened. The term is used three times to suggest steadfastness to evil, a perverse uprightness (I, 221; II, 72; VI, 82), although in the first two instances we are not really aware of Milton's meaningful usage. By the third, however, we should be able to infer the mirrored terms of the poem, for the word is used of "beams" (generally a reference to the Sun's / Son's rays of light and mercy) created by innumerable spears, helmets, and shields employed to assault the faithful and protect "the banded Powers of *Satan*." Raphael's admonition to Adam after his account of the creation lays forth unambiguously the connotation of the word.

> Thrice happie men,
> And sons of men, whom God hath thus advanc't,
> Created in his Image, there to dwell
> And worship him, and in reward to rule
> Over his Works, on Earth, in Sea, or Air,
> And multiply a Race of Worshippers
> Holy and just: thrice happie if they know
> Thir happiness, and persevere upright.
>
> (VII, 625-632)

It is used only once more in the poem, when Adam describes himself at his own creation.

But it is not just specific words that are fraught with special metaphoric meanings; imagery, too, accounts for much of the depth of the poem. The three uses of "red" (aside from the Red Sea in I, 306, and Love's proper hue in VIII, 619) point to war and thus allude to one of the horses of the Apocalypse: "and power was given to him that sat thereon to take peace from the earth, and that they should kill one another: and there was given unto him a great sword" (Rev. 6:4). The images are all assigned to God's war against the evil spirits, directly or through his angelic agents, for Milton develops in the poem the archetypes of such modern-day concepts as war. Michael's sword (VI, 250, 278, 320ff.) as well as that worn by the Son (VI, 714) recall the same sense of God's wrath and vengeance and evince that war may be good or bad, depending upon its sources and its motives. Satan recalls to Beelzebub God's "Thunder, / Wing'd with red Lightning and impetuous rage" (I, 175), now "perhaps" spent; Belial reminds the council that God's "intermitted vengeance" might "arm again / His red right hand to plague us" (II, 173-174); and "th' Angelic Squadron bright / Turnd fierie red" (IV, 977-978) surround Satan in the Garden "With ported Spears."[11] The significance of calling it the Red Sea can be understood in these same terms through the discussion of the myth of exodus.

The word, as used for Raphael when he answers Adam's question concerning how angels express their love, defines "blush": "To whom the Angel with a smile that glow'd / Celestial rosie red, Loves proper hue, / Answer'd" (VIII, 618-620). Spirits' love-making is total mixture of their being, unlike man's partial fusion with woman. Qualified as "rosie red" here, "blush" means, of course, reddening of the face and significantly from shame or modesty. Shortly before this, Adam had described Eve as blushing like the morn when he first led her to their nuptial bower (VIII, 510-511). In Book XI, after Adam and Eve have spent a restless night because of their guilt, "the Morn, / All unconcern'd with our unrest, begins / Her rosie progress smiling," and Eve wishes to remain as they are, "though in fallen state, content." But that this would not come to pass is first given sign by nature "After short blush of Morn" (XI, 173-175, 180, 184). All these uses of the word "blush" or its concomitant images fuse into a metaphoric meaning, quite far beyond the one-dimensional kind of idea conveyed by a word like "Omnipotent," and that metaphoric meaning unites the poem, making of it something more than mere words and images important only for their own specific passages. These three references to blushing lead to a number of realizations of meaning and of psychological significance for Milton: (1) Love-making should be accompanied by blushing, apparently out of modesty? out of shame? The sexual orientation which allows such a statement implies guilt and anxiety over sexual activity, as well as inhibition. It is psychologically significant for the author and accordingly renders a psychological level to all discussions of love in the poem, an area worthy of detailed investigation. (2) To talk of blushing as "Loves *proper* hue" suggests appropriateness (implying shame), propriety (socially acceptable and thus universal), liturgical correctness (as appointed for a religious rite), and heraldic insignia. Thus love (or sexual activity) for Milton becomes a pattern to be followed ritualistically as necessity, not as enjoyment, and not openly but somewhat covered by the disguise of color. Love not accompanied by blushing seems, therefore, not to be "morally" oriented (as Milton would seem to believe it should be). (3) The Morn (Aurora) reflects the fire of the Sun (a male symbol), preliminary to the union of Sun and Earth during the light of the day. The "Air suddenly eclips'd" indicates that Adam and Eve will not live content, and that their sexual activity (unlike that of Morn) will not be "innocent" or "proper" but covert and shameful. The conjunction of the three passages leads to a view of sexual activity that probably underlay Milton's own attitudes toward sex, but such a topic cannot be examined here. Where "red" connotes war, "rosie red" (blushing) concerns sexual activity, and we remember the traditional union of War and Love to which this metaphoric yoking adds meaning. Love pits male against female, male as aggressor, female as submitter; but love's war is not the strong color of war: it is mollified to only a rosy hue.

Imagery of the moon is another clear-cut example of Milton's artistry of language, although Banks describes the occurrences of moon imagery as merely referring to a natural means of dispelling night or clouds (pp. 112-113). The moon provides light, pale though it be, to aid life's voyager when the darkness which is Satan's world walks the Earth. It becomes an emblem of God's omnipresence and mercy toward man.[12] Milton has Uriel describe this office of the moon, though an awareness of metaphor on the part of the reader must exist if communication is to occur.

> Look downward on that Globe whose hither side
> With light from hence, though but reflected, shines;
> That place is Earth the seat of Man, that light
> His day, which else as th' other Hemisphere
> Night would invade, but there the neighbouring Moon
> (So call that opposite fair Starr) her aid
> Timely interposes, and her monthly round
> Still ending, still renewing through mid Heav'n,
> With borrowd light her countenance triform
> Hence fills and empties to enlighten th' Earth,
> And in her pale dominion checks the night.
>
> (III, 722-732)

The moon's triform countenance depends on its phases: increasing, full, and waning. While increasing, it (Diana) was thought of as representing female virginity; while at the full, she was the patroness of chastity, pertinent here as aider in dispelling the evil of the night; and when waning she became, after the Fall, patroness of childbirth, the chase, and nocturnal incantations. This latter phase, with its declining light, allowed usurpation of the moon as symbol (but symbol only) by the infernal host or their followers on Earth; compare I, 440, 596, 784; II, 665, and XI, 486. The eclipsing of the sun by the moon at the crucifixion of Christ epitomizes that usurpation.

Like the preceding in demonstrating the meanings and changed meanings of word clusters in *Paradise Lost* are "hair" and "vine" (or "wine"). These charged symbols underscore the loss brought by the Fall, and Milton was aware, as he hoped his readers would be, of their symbolic use in aftertimes. "Hair" suggests youth (and thus eternality), sex (and thus generation), and power. One of the vows made by those of biblical times who consecrated themselves to God (like Samson) was to avoid cutting their hair. A Nazirite (from the Hebrew *nazir,* "consecrated") symbolized one dedicated to God, to following God's bidding and to leading forth or inspiriting others to a firm faith in God's word; such power—whether physical or internal—derived from God's beneficence. I am not implying, of course, that Adam and Eve are like latter-day Nazirites; I am indicating that the vows of the Nazirites derive from age-old patterns and attitudes which Milton explores as imagery indicating Adam and Eve's obedience or disobedience to God. Our first glimpse of Adam and Eve in Eden, therefore, describes them thus:

> His fair large Front and Eye sublime declar'd
> Absolute rule; and Hyacinthin Locks
> Round from his parted forelock manly hung
> Clustring, but not beneath his shoulders broad:
> Shee as a vail down to the slender waste
> Her unadorned golden tresses wore
> Dissheveld, but in wanton ringlets wav'd
> As the Vine curls her tendrils, which impli'd
> Subjection, but requir'd with gentle sway.
>
> (IV, 300–308)

But we note that Eve's tresses are "dissheveld," that is, they indicate her need to be controlled. The next morning her tresses are "discompos'd" (V, 10), and after the Fall they have become "disorder'd" (X, 911). The progression is important: first Eve's hair is loosely hanging in disarray; after her dream which is posited by Satan, it is disturbed through implied emotional stress; and after her fall it has become unruly (with overtones of moral reprehensibleness). For Adam, succumbing to carnal lust, the alteration which this symbol undergoes is expressed by a simile with Samson.

> So rose the *Danite* strong
> *Herculean Samson* from the Harlot-lap
> Of *Philistean Dalilah,* and wak'd
> Shorn of his strength. They destitute and bare
> Of all thir vertue. . . .
>
> (IX, 1059–1063)

Mankind has lost the eternal life, male-female unity, and God-like power innate at the creation.

Whereas things consecrated to God are expressed by hair imagery—for example, the Heavenly Host (III, 360–362), Uriel (III, 625–628), Eden (IV, 131–137)[13]—there is mirrored, infernal appropriation of the imagery for Satan, first as a comet (II, 706–711), and then as a cherub (III, 636–641), both after the fall of the rebellious angels, and finally as serpent (X, 559–560), after the Fall of Adam and Eve. This latter appropriation has been prepared for at the creation (VII, 494–498), to be assumed when Satan in the serpent seduces Eve. The infernal use of the image makes clear the false concept of eternality which Satan offers, the lewd delight, rather than true love and regeneration, now associated with sex, and the specious power which evil holds out to those who consecrate themselves to Satan. Signalizing the change in the symbol after the Fall is the advent of the seasons, "Shattering the graceful locks / Of the fair spreading Trees" (X, 1066–1067). There are no further references to hair in the poem, probably because Milton does not recount those like Samuel or Samson who were of the Nazirite sect, and because the contrast between the sons of Cain and the patriarchs like Noah is starker thereby. Imagery of hair would at least allow that the power of God (as in Samson's case) was potentially to return in the repentant. It is only polarities of good action and evil in the sons of Adam that Milton wishes to stress.

Related to hair in the first description of Eve is the vine, and likewise we note that the Nazirite took a vow to avoid drinking wine. But the vine and its produce are, before the Fall, imbued with the good of God, as are all things of nature. In the description of Eden we read,

> Another side, umbrageous Grots and Caves
> Of cool recess, o're which the mantling vine
> Layes forth her purple Grape, and gently creeps
> Luxuriant.
>
> (IV, 257-260)

This description is soon followed by a clearly commendatory reference to wine.[14]

> And *Eve* within, due at her hour prepar'd
> For dinner savourie fruits, of taste to please
> True appetite, and not disrelish thirst
> Of nectarous draughts between, from milkie stream,
> Berrie or Grape.
>
> (V, 303-307)

But after the Fall all is changed, and the symbol, rather than one of eternal life (nectar), becomes the sign of intemperance, greed, folly, and susceptibility to Evil.

> Greedily she ingorg'd without restraint,
> And knew not eating Death: Satiate at length,
> And hight'n'd as with Wine, jocond and boon,
> Thus to her self she pleasingly began,
>
> (IX, 791-794)

and

> while *Adam* took no thought,
> Eating his fill, nor *Eve* to iterate
> Her former trespass fear'd, the more to soothe
> Him with her lov'd societie, that now
> As with new Wine intoxicated both
> They swim in mirth, and fansie that they feel
> Divinitie within them breeding wings
> Wherewith to scorn the Earth.
>
> (IX, 1004-1011)

In contrast with the approbation which the vine and wine connote in the first half of the poem, before the Fall, is the early reference in I, 500–502:

> And when Night
> Darkens the Streets, then wander forth the Sons
> Of *Belial,* flown with insolence and wine.

We have purposely been informed of the symbol's affinity for unnaturalness, and not only in reference to the sons of Belial but also in the ensuing citation of Sodom and Gomorrah, in order to alert us to what has been lost through the Fall by the removal of vine and wine from the natural order. In alternating contrast, Books IV and V employ the symbol as good, Book IX relates its devaluation to symbol of greed and folly, and Book XII (ll. 19 and 21) shows that those who follow Noah, the "second sours of Men," "With some regard to what is just and right" may partake of wine and still "spend thir dayes in joy unblam'd." The balance of reference between the first and the last books of the epic is worthy of note.

Only the recognition of such use of metaphor, imagery, and symbols *throughout* the poem will enable the reader to view the total structure which it is. There is so much in the poem which resists fragmentation, not only in terms of its literary artistry but the message as well. Here, for instance, we do not discern a basic thought which these two specific symbols relate until we examine those symbols and their opposed meanings. Milton urges upon all of us the vow of the Nazirite to do God's work. The vows to avoid the vine and cutting one's hair are symbolic of obeying God and having faith in him; the vows which we as Nazirites might take would equate these vows in pursuing true love, belief in self and in God's presence, and temperance. A third vow of the Nazirite involved avoidance of the corpse. And though there can be no death in Adam's present world in *Paradise Lost,* we observe that Michael's vision allows Adam to see death. His knowledge that Death will be the Gate of Life for the faithful is to be supplemented, Michael advises, by Faith, Vertue, Patience, Temperance, Love ("By name to come call'd Charitie"). These are qualities intended by the two previous vows. Adam will thus replace Death, sought in X, 720ff. (Thanatos), with Love (Eros), which is Life. The vow of the Nazirite represents his dedication to life. Signif-

icantly, the one occurrence of "corpse" in *Paradise Lost* is used by
Death to describe himself.

> To mee, who with eternal Famin pine,
> Alike is Hell, or Paradise, or Heaven,
> There best, where most with ravin I may meet;
> Which here, though plenteous, all too little seems
> To stuff this Maw, this unhide-bound Corps.
>
> (X, 597–601)

Paradise Lost deserves the kind of literary examination which I
have suggested, and it is my hope that this book assists in some significant way the approach to the poem which the following remark calls
for: "We have not generally brought to Milton's epic the kind of dignity and serious attention that modern criticism has long accorded
fiction, drama, or lyric."[15]

· APPENDIX ·

The Dates of Composition

AS IS WELL known, Milton planned a drama—something like a
morality—on the subject of "Paradise Lost" not long after returning
from his continental sojourn and settling on Aldersgate Street. Spelling analysis suggests that the three lists of characters were put down
on p. 35 of the Trinity MS around the latter half of 1640. The third
draft is divided into five acts and entitled "Paradise Lost," and it is
augmented by some descriptive notes. The title seems to have been
added when Milton wrote these notes, probably soon after listing the
persons of the drama. Another draft appears on p. 40 as a prose outline of "Adams Banishment." This is altered by four brief additions,
one of which is on p. 41, opposite, along with a change in title to
"Adam unparadis'd." Spelling analysis suggests that this draft with
its alterations was set down in the middle of 1641.[1] Milton's nephew
Edward Phillips told John Aubrey that he had read what is now IV,
32-41, around 1642.[2] Phillips, in his life of his uncle prefixed to his
translation of the *Letters of State* (1694), quoted the passage with
one verbal difference.[3] Thomas Ellwood reported that Milton gave
him the manuscript to read at Chalfont St. Giles, which thus dates
the completion of the poem by the latter half of 1665.[4] The agreement with Samuel Simmons for the first edition of *Paradise Lost* is
dated April 27, 1667, and it was registered for sale on August 27.
These are the only facts we have for the date of *Paradise Lost*.

The manuscript of the first book, now in the Morgan Library,
New York City, was the copy for the first edition and is in the hand of
an amanuensis called "D" by James Holly Hanford;[5] this same scribe
wrote two entries in Milton's Commonplace Book on pp. 197 and
248. The dating of the entries by Ruth Mohl[6] is questionable and un-
explained. The first, from Dante's *Purgatorio*, is given as 1650-1667

(?); the second from Nicetas Acominate's *Imperii Graeci Historia,* ca. 1665. Hanford dates the entries simply after ca. 1650 (p. 102), like all other entries by amanuenses. Mohl's dating of the second entry seems to be a conclusion drawn from the fact that the amanuensis was the same one who penned the manuscript of *Paradise Lost.* The edition of Nicetas used by Milton was apparently that published in 1647 and was owned by him before 1658.[7] The terminal dating of the first entry seems conditioned also by the scribe's major work for Milton. It appears to have been added between two entries on p. 197 by Edward Phillips (Amanuensis B), dated 1651-1652 (?). Other entries from Dante (none from the *Purgatorio*) are placed in 1638 or earlier. Perhaps Miss Mohl has suggested the earlier limit because an entry from Dante around 1665 or so seems oddly late (though possible) and because there seems to be a relationship between a sentence (idea) in *A Treatise of Civil Power* (1659) and the Dante quotation. In any case, about all one can conclude is that the manuscript of Book I of *Paradise Lost* and these two entries in the Commonplace Book may have been made around the same time, unless some other possibility—such as Amanuensis D's having been a former student of Milton—prove correct. But that could have been any time after around 1658 or so and before 1667 (I do not imply that it was much before the latter date), or before 1665 if the manuscript Ellwood saw was the same that we now have. The seeming two-year delay in publication probably should be explained by the plague and fire of 1665-1666, and thus we might conclude that the manuscript which Ellwood saw was the same one we have today. The fact that various hands appear in the manuscript making corrections logically suggests that the basic transcription occurred some while (a year or more?) before it was considered "finished."

Intermittent composition seems probable from 1640 through around 1655, with more undivided attention paid to the poem from around 1655-1658 and 1661 through 1665.[8] When Milton decided upon epic form is unclear, although I believe that the decision did not take place before 1652 and it had taken place before 1661. The period of 1655-1658 would be my guess for decision.[9] Allan H. Gilbert has explored the development of *Paradise Lost* from early tragedies to reorganized chronological order to epic revision.[10] He points out the discrepancies between the arguments added with the second issue of 1668 and the final poem. The two major conclusions which should be drawn from Gilbert's study, and which so many people fail to acknowledge, are the very logical realization that the poem was not written as we have it from first to last and, second, the development of the poem was extended over some time. The first conclusion implies that books of the epic or parts of books were written at different times; e.g., most of Book VIII was composed before most of Books V and VI.[11] It would seem, from Gilbert's evidence, that the time spent in development fell into three general periods: one devoted to tragedy or tragedies; one devoted to reorganization and consolidation with movement toward epic form; and one devoted to completion of the epic. Thus, the second conclusion may be viewed in terms of footnote 8 above: the writing and continued development of tragedies may have occurred during the seventy-four months (six years and two months) of 1641–1648; the middle period, during the eighty months (six years and eight months) of 1652–1658; the final period during the five years of 1661–1665.

To try to establish the chronology of Milton's three major poems, Ants Oras examined various prosodic techniques statistically and concluded that *Paradise Lost, Paradise Regain'd,* and *Samson Agonistes* were indeed composed in that order.[12] His use of statistics, however, was patently fallacious, for statistics must be used without predecision and prearrangement. Since, for example, *Samson Agonistes* is seen in just about every category to be closer statistically to *Comus* than any of the other works reported, the traditional order of the major poems should fall under high suspicion. A poet does not develop a poetic technique and then gradually discard it, moving backward to a position not employing that technique.[13] An example is the development away from end-stopped lines to run-on lines. Even if we look at rhymed verse, which has a greater affinity for end-stoppage than blank verse, we see this development.

We can compare the three English odes (*On Time, Upon the Circumcision,* and *At a Solemn Music*), written in rhyme but not in definite patterns or line lengths, with Sonnets 8–15, and these with Sonnets 16–23, and all with Psalms 1–8. The odes, written somewhere between 1633 and 1637 (although I would urge a time closer to the latter) total 78 lines, of which 32 are run-on,[14] or a percentage of 41.0. Sonnets 8–15, written between 1642 and 1648, total 112 lines, of which 42 are run-on, or a percentage of 37.5. Sonnets 16–23, written between 1652 and 1658, total 112 lines, of which 54 are run-on, or a percentage of 48.2. Psalms 1-8 were paraphased in various kinds of metric patterns in August, 1653; they contain 262 lines, of which 153 are run-on,[15] or a percentage of 58.4. The sonnet form makes the incidence of run-on lines less frequent than in blank verse or non-stanzaic forms.[16] The low percentage of run-on lines in Sonnets 8-15 may thus owe that statistic to the influence of the sonnet form, which Milton in his later sonnets was to alter by changing the position of the *volta* (the turn) and, I think all critics will agree, by a purposeful increase in enjambment. At least, if we separate Sonnets 8-15 into two groups, Nos. 8-11 (that is, "I did but prompt"), dated 1642-1645/6, and Nos. 12-15, dated 1646-1648, we find that the first group (56 lines) has 18 run-on lines, or 32.1 percent, and the second group (56 lines) has 24 run-on lines, or 42.9 percent. Arranged in ascending order with Oras's statistics for *Comus* and the three major poems, we have: Sonnets 8-11, 32.1; *Comus,* 39.9; Odes, 41.0; *SA,* 42.1; Sonnets 12-15, 42.9; *PR,* 45.2; Sonnets 16-23, 48.2; Psalms 1-8, 58.4; *PL,* 58.8. Recognizing the lesser frequency of run-on lines in rhymed verse and even lesser frequency than that in such forms as the sonnet, we should be struck at the increase in run-on lines as we move from *Comus* (1634 through apparently 1637) to the Odes (ca. 1637?), to Sonnets 12-15 (1646-1648), to Sonnets 16-23 (1652-1658?), to Psalms 1-8 (1653), to *Paradise Lost* (written 1640-1665?). (Individual books and parts of books of *Paradise Lost* evidence differences, as one would expect of composition over a period of time.)

The preceding should strongly document for all students of Milton that he did increase his use of run-on lines as time went by and his versification became more experienced and more experimental. Acknowledging this development of technique even for just this one prosodic test,[17] but one that is extremely significant,[18] we should be able to deduce that the traditional chronology of the three major poems is open to question and that all three should be examined for strata of composition. My criticism of Oras's method has previously been published.[19] *Paradise Lost* was treated there only in terms of complete books, for a full examination fell beyond the scope of a single article. The problem with that kind of treatment is obvious when one compares Gilbert's discussion and when one observes, for instance, that these prosodic statistics place total Book IV late in time of composition, despite Phillips's statement and Gilbert's catalogue of various sections that seem to derive from the earliest writing. The test of run-on lines, if we call a percentage of 60.1 and above late (the average for *Paradise Lost* being 58.8), confirms, for example, Gilbert's placement of the two sections of Book I (1–669, 670–798) and three sections of Book II (1–520, 629–884, 884–1055) in Groups V (the independent epic) and VI (the epic complete). The fourth section of Book II, lines 521–628, "Hell as a universe," falls squarely in the midst of the percentages for run-on lines. Gilbert had placed this section in Group VI, though the fewer run-on lines suggest composition perhaps in the late 1650s rather than after 1660. It seems foolhardy, however, to proceed through the whole of the poem in this way because of the uncertainties that prosodic statistics manifest for an ordering of composition of parts: (1) parts may reflect their date of composition directly, but (2) early parts were altered at a later time after Milton had decided upon epic form, (3) such alteration may have been slight, thus an earlier prosodic practice may be reflected, or (4) such alteration may have been extensive, thus a later prosodic practice may obscure earlier writing, (5) statistics will be dependent upon which lines are considered for any specific section and upon the reliability of text, (6) brief sections (such as Gilbert frequently lists) allow little substance for conclusion on the basis of prosody, and (7) matters of style may condition the prosody. In any case, what we should admit from these statistics is that the poem was not composed consistently in its present arrangement, that parts of books are later than other parts, and that composition took place over a long period of time.

Notes

CHAPTER ONE

1. *The Reason of Church-Government* (London, 1641 [i.e., 1642]), pp. 39-40.

2. All quotations from the poetry are taken from *The Complete Poetry of John Milton*, ed. John T. Shawcross, rev. ed. (Garden City, N.Y.: Anchor, 1971).

3. Man is treated as male and female, since this discussion is concerned with mankind. But a careful study of Milton's view of male and female is needed. I discount as inadequate, prejudiced, apologetic, or not explicitly attentive to this problem the various discussions of the divorce tracts or Milton's Eve which have been published, for while many published items make very important and valid points, none has come to grips with the received mythic notions of female inferiority and of sexual characteristics of worthiness and unworthiness that lie in the collective unconscious, or with Milton's own sexual orientation. These are matters too complex for investigation here, although they help us understand the human medium through which the literary artifact has been pressed.

4. *Steppenwolf and Everyman*, trans. Jack D. Zipes (New York: Thomas Crowell, 1971); see pp. 1-13 and 300-325.

5. See my essay on *The Tenure of Kings and Magistrates* in *Achievements of the Left Hand* (Amherst: Univ. of Massachusetts Press, 1974), ed. Michael Lieb and John T. Shawcross, pp. 142-159.

CHAPTER TWO

1. Though the Father is male force, this embodiment sees God as the Great Mother, his sons returning to the womb. Both the circle of perfection which God represents (although Heaven is square) and the eternal garden, as Heaven is described, are symbols of the mother archetype, according to Jung. But we should remember that the father is seen as energy; the mother, as form. This, I believe, explains the sexual ambivalence within the poem. See also Joseph Summers's excellent discussion of "The Two Great Sexes" in *The Muse's Method* (London: Chatto & Windus, 1963), pp. 87-111.

2. See Merritt Y. Hughes's full survey of the matter in *Studies in English Literature* 4 (1964) 1-33; the argument of William B. Hunter, Jr., immediately following on pp. 35-42; and Nathaniel H. Henry, "The Mystery of Milton's Muse," *Renaissance Papers 1967* (1968), pp. 69-83.

3. As noted before, God gave Moses a rod by which to show His divinity through miracle, and the rod becomes a serpent when dashed to the ground. As we read *Paradise Lost*, we should remember the serpent as phallic symbol, the earth as female sym-

bol, and chaste engagement in sex as productive of the miracle of life. Only through the sexual perversion of Satan as serpent seducing Eve in the Garden (a womb symbol, the *hortus conclusus* of Song of Songs 4:12) does this beast of the field become the evil symbol. The positive virtues of sex in this poem (as seen, for example, in Book IV) have too often been overlooked.

4. Compare Jesus's last admonition: "A new commandment I give unto you, That ye love one another; as I have loved you, that ye also love one another" (John 13:34).

5. Compare Michael Lieb's discussion of the creation myth in *The Dialectics of Creation* (Amherst: Univ. of Massachusetts Press, 1970).

6. Water is a symbol both of spirituality and of birth. As rain, water is male; as standing water, such as an ocean, it is female. That Milton refers to an aqueous abyss in I, 21, is evident from its echo in VII, 233-237 ("Darkness profound / Cover'd th' Abyss: but on the watrie calm / His brooding wings the Spirit of God outspread, / And vital vertue infus'd, and vital warmth / Throughout the fluid Mass") and from its early version in the *Nativity Ode*, l. 68 ("While Birds of Calm sit brooding on the charmed wave"). This latter reference to the halcyons' breeding in December and around the time of the nativity of the Son as man is of course most significant as another indication of the constant presence of the Son in *Paradise Lost*. Those who follow the Son, who is imbued at his baptism with the Spirit of God, will be dovelike creatures and saved; surely a main point of the poem is to counsel men to follow the example of the Son in his love and obedience. Lines 9-13 of Book III also reprise ll. 20-22 of Book I: "and at the voice / Of God, as with a Mantle didst invest / The rising world of waters dark and deep, / Won from the void and formless infinite." The meaning of "moved" in Gen. 1:2 ("And the Spirit of God moved upon the face of the waters") has this same generative meaning; see David Daiches, "The Opening of *Paradise Lost*," *The Living Milton: Essays by Various Hands*, ed. Frank Kermode (London: Routledge & Kegan Paul, 1960), p. 66.

7. The poet as bird has been explored by Anne Davidson Ferry in *Reason and Imagination* (New York: Columbia Univ. Press, 1962), pp. 183-200, and in *Milton's Epic Voice* (Cambridge, Mass.: Harvard Univ. Press, 1963).

8. Hearing the nightingale in early spring ("Thus with the Year / Seasons return," Milton continues in ll. 40-41) portends success in love; thus will Milton "voluntarie move [that is, create] / Harmonious numbers" (III, 37-38).

9. The ear is a symbol of the womb, a most appropriate touch here.

10. Dreams reduce antitheses to uniformity or at least represent them as one and the same thing. The polarities of God and Satan in *Paradise Lost*, which have often been pointed out, organize into mirror surfaces of each other, becoming another factor in the dream-vision nature of the poem.

11. The reference to Calliope's son Orpheus, the archetypal poet, who was beheaded by drunken Bacchantes, has two functions. It primarily notices that the accommodation of heavenly truth in such popular myths as this of the resurrection of Christ are ineffectual (as opposed to what Milton hopes to achieve by his more direct and unaccommodated use of myth); and it intimates the emasculation of heavenly truth delivered by "Harp and Voice" which lustfulness can bring. Calliope's rejection as "empty dream" — since she is the muse of heroic poetry — is a first statement of the substance of the proem to Book IX.

CHAPTER THREE

1. For the fullest discussion, see George A. Wilkes, *The Thesis of Paradise Lost* (Melbourne: Melbourne Univ. Press, n.d.). Compare John S. Diekhoff, *Milton's*

"Paradise Lost": A Commentary on the Argument (New York: Humanities Press, 1958), p. 115.

2. Rosalie L. Colie has remarked in "Time and Eternity: Paradox and Structure in *Paradise Lost," Journal of the Warburg and Courtald Institute* 23, (1960) 134, "In his self-appointed task as poet and moralist, the maker of a poem to teach a nation, Milton shared some of the problems of the creative Deity." Milton's purpose and lesson may be considered alongside the parable of the angel with an open book who was heard by St. John when he came "down from heaven, clothed with a cloud: and a rainbow was upon his head, and his face was as it were the sun, and his feet as pillars of fire"; and in a voice like a lion, "he said unto me, Take it and eat it up; and it shall make thy belly bitter, but it shall be in thy mouth sweet as honey" (Rev. 10:1, 9).

3. "The Conclusion of Book VI of *Paradise Lost," Studies in English Literature* 3 (1963) 115. William B. Hunter, Jr., in "Milton on the Exaltation of the Son: The War in Heaven in *Paradise Lost," ELH* 36 (1969) 215-231, argues most cogently that in the War in Heaven Milton "is simultaneously narrating . . . three events from three very different points in time: first, the surface narrative of the fall of the angels, which took place before the foundation of the world; second, the defeat of Satan and his fellow devils described in the book of Revelation, which will take place at the end of time; and third and most important, the exaltation of the Son of God, which took place concomitantly with his resurrection as the incarnate god-man." Such a view underscores God's providence as advanced in this chapter.

4. "Milton and the Descent to Light," *Journal of English and Germanic Philology* 60 (1961) 614-630.

5. Perhaps we should remark that, aside from the mystic properties which the number three connotes, the antithesis between the Son and Satan which is enhanced by the Son's defeat of Satan on the third day of battle, and the meaning that Hunter adduces in the article above, the faithful angels can not defeat the rebellious angels since they are only equal in strength and numbers. On the first day, the faithful "win"; on the second, the unfaithful; on the third, the Son, whose single being is superior to the whole force of rebel angels. See Everett Emerson, "Milton's War in Heaven: Some Problems," *Modern Language Notes* 69 (1954) 399-402.

6. "The Crisis of *Paradise Lost," Studies in Milton* (New York: Macmillan, 1951), pp. 13ff.

7. Harris F. Fletcher, ed., *John Milton's Complete Poetical Works* (Urbana: Univ. of Illinois Press, 1948), IV, 10.

8. "The Crisis of *Paradise Lost* Reconsidered," *Philological Quarterly* 36 (1957) 1-19; reprinted in *Milton: Modern Essays in Criticism*, ed. Arthur Barker (New York: Oxford Univ. Press, 1965).

9. "Satan's Journey: Direction in *Paradise Lost," Journal of English and Germanic Philology* 60 (1961) 699-711. The concept of unity which I find basic to the poem is developed by Roy Daniells in *Milton: Mannerism and Baroque* (Toronto: Univ. of Toronto Press, 1963), pp. 64-75. Daniells concludes, "Milton is concerned with the eternal desire of Christendom, the union of man with God, and true to the spirit of his age he conceives of its achievement as through the will of God and of man" (p. 74).

10. "Noon-Midnight and the Temporal Structure of *Paradise Lost," ELH* 29 (1962) 372-395.

11. "The Battle in Heaven in *Paradise Lost," Tulane Studies in English* 3 (1952) 69-70, 92.

12. "The Dramatic Center of *Paradise Lost," South Atlantic Quarterly* 63 (1964) 52.

CHAPTER FOUR

1. See Frank S. Kastor, "Milton's Tempter: A Genesis of a Subportrait in *Paradise Lost*," *Huntington Library Quarterly* 33 (1970) 373-385, and the full study reprinting this article, *Milton and the Literary Satan* (Amsterdam: Rodopi, 1974).

2. Perhaps this begs the question of Milton's alleged anti-Trinitarianism. There is nothing in *Paradise Lost* that denies divinity to the Son. He does not exhibit omnipresence (except as agent for the Father), omniscience, or omnipotence (except again as agent for the Father), but this does not state a so-called Arian position; rather, it indicates Milton's adherence to a common nonheretical doctrine known as subordinationism. In *De doctrina christiana*, Milton differentiates between *substantia* and *essentia* and thereby indirectly explains the concept of three persons indivisible, for the *substantia* of the godhead (that is, the material of being of God) is the source of being of all three persons (thus indivisibility as there is but one *substantia*), but each person has his own *essentia* (that is, personality, individualized self). The terms have been misunderstood and thus have become a source of the contention that Milton was anti-Trinitarian.

3. *The Short Novels of Dostoevsky*, trans. Constance Garnett (New York: Dial, 1951), pp. 149-52, 167.

4. We should note that Satan's appearances are also not in every book; he is prominent in Books I, II, III, IV, V, VI (the first half of the poem in which Milton is elaborating the "cause" for the losing of Paradise), IX, and X. Adam and Eve are prominent only in IV, V, VII, VIII, IX, X, XI, and XII (these latter books being the last half of the poem in which the "effect" is laid bare).

5. See Peter Hägin's *The Epic Hero and the Decline of Heroic Poetry: A Study of the Neoclassical English Epic with Special Reference to Milton's Paradise Lost* (Bern: Francke, 1964), Chap. 5, pp. 146-169, for a discussion of Adam and Eve as hero. Hägin's view and mine are complementary, although I feel he does not push far enough in defining the hero of the poem. The thesis of the study—that the nature of the hero of *Paradise Lost* was a major cause for the decline of the epic—is, I believe, well founded.

CHAPTER FIVE

1. *Milton's Epic Voice*. See particularly chap. 6, "Vision as Structure," pp. 147-178.

2. Ibid., p. 166.

3. Ibid., pp. 149, 155.

4. Ibid., p. 150.

5. See Gunnar Qvarnström's discussion in *The Enchanted Palace: Some Structural Aspects of Paradise Lost* (Stockholm: Almqvist and Wiksell, 1967), and the analysis by William B. Hunter, Jr., of the question for the second edition of 1674 in "The Center of *Paradise Lost*," *English Language Notes* 7 (1969) 32-34.

6. In his examination of Peter Ramus's philosophy, Milton defined a cause as "that by the force of which a thing exists" (*Art of Logic*, Columbia Edition, XI, 29).

7. William H. Marshall ("*Paradise Lost: Felix Culpa* and the Problem of Structure," *Modern Language Notes* 76 [1961] 15-20) sees the ironic action of the first eight and one-half books (or nine and one-half, using the 1674 edition) leading to the Fall as anticipatory of the destruction of Satan. Satan dominates the first half, but man the second half.

8. Rosalie Colie, "Time and Eternity: Paradox and Structure in *Paradise Lost*,"

p. 135, writes: "The irony that the Devil's act of destruction is God's act of re-creation solves, for poetic purposes at the very least, the problem of evil."

9. See XII, 402-404: "The Law of God exact he shall fulfill / Both by obedience and by love, though love / Alone fulfill the Law."

10. See William B. Hunter, Jr., "Milton's Urania," *Studies in English Literature* 4 (1964) 5-12.

11. In "Divine Providence and the Structure of *Paradise Lost*," *Essays in Criticism* 14 (1964) 148-155, J.R. Watson relates Books I and XII (using the revised second edition) in their concepts of providence and redemption, parallels III with X and IV with IX, and discusses VI and VII as the center of a symmetrical pattern, showing that good (including the Creation) comes out of evil. Book IX is thus rejected as climax.

12. Greek dramatic structure was built usually on a prologue, a parados (choric ode), episodes and stasima (three to five), and an exodos/kommos. Elizabethan dramatic structure generally involved five acts, in this arrangement: I, exposition (protasis); II, rising action (epitasis); III, climax; IV, falling action (catastasis); V, catastrophe. See p. 64 for further discussion.

13. See *Paradise Lost as "Myth"* (Cambridge: Harvard Univ. Press, 1959).

14. See "The Harassed Reader in *Paradise Lost*," *Critical Quarterly* 7 (1965) 162-182; "Further Thoughts on Milton's Christian Reader," *Critical Quarterly* 7 (1965) 279-284; *Surprised By Sin* (London: Macmillan, 1967); "Discovery as Form in *Paradise Lost*," *New Essays on Paradise Lost*, ed. Thomas Kranidas (Berkeley: Univ. of California Press, 1969), pp. 1-14.

15. See Mark Schorer, "Technique as Discovery," reprinted in *Critiques and Essays on Modern Fiction*, ed. John Aldridge (New York: John Wiley, 1952), pp. 75-77.

16. As noted before, compare *PL* III, 339-341, and VI, 730-732.

CHAPTER SIX

1. See James Whaler, *Counterpoint and Symbol* (Copenhagen: Rosenkilde and Bagger, 1956).

2. Ibid., pp. 53, 56.

3. See studies by Vincent Hopper, *Medieval Number Symbolism* (New York: Columbia Univ. Press, 1938); Maren-Sofie Røstvig, *The Hidden Sense and Other Essays* (Oslo: Universitetsforlaget, 1963); Maren-Sofie Røstvig, "Ars Aeterna: Renaissance Poetics and Theories of Divine Creation," *Mosaic* 3, no. 2 (1970) 40-61; and Alastair Fowler, *Triumphal Forms: Structural Patterns in Elizabethan Poetry* (Cambridge: Cambridge Univ. Press, 1970). Applications to *Paradise Lost* will be found in Qvarnström's *Enchanted Palace*; by Alastair Fowler in *The Poems of John Milton*, ed. John Carey and Alastair Fowler (London: Longman, 1968); in *Silent Poetry: Essays in Numerological Analysis*, ed. Alastair Fowler (London: Routledge & Kegan Paul, 1970); and in Christopher Butler's *Number Symbolism* (London: Routledge & Kegan Paul, 1970), esp. pp. 140-158. The fullest treatment is Galbraith M. Crump's *The Mystical Design* of Paradise Lost (Lewisburg, Pa.: Bucknell Univ. Press, 1975).

4. *Touches of Sweet Harmony: Pythagorean Cosmology and Renaissance Poetics* (San Marino, Cal.: Huntington Library, 1974), p. 321, n. 32. Heninger is specifically objecting to Fowler's emphasis on iconographic and spatial organization in numerical composition. He quotes William Enfield on p. 142: "The most probable explanation of the Pythagorean doctrine of numbers is, that they were used as symbolical or emblematic representations of the first principles and forms of nature, and particularly of those eternal and immutable essences, to which Plato afterwards gave the appellation of Ideas. . . . Pythagoras seems to have made use of numbers, as geome-

tricians make use of diagrams, to assist the conceptions of scholars" (*History of Philosophy* [London, 1791], I, 384).

5. Compare the similar address of Satan to the Pope in *In quintum Novembris*, ll. 90-92: "But clothed in such garb, the cunning serpent, deceitful, separated his accursed lips with these words: 'Are you sleeping, my son? Does slumber overpower your limbs?' " For the tradition identifying Beelzebub and Satan as one, see Joseph A. Wittreich, "Beelzebub," *A Milton Encyclopedia*, ed. William B. Hunter (Lewisburg, Pa.: Bucknell Univ. Press, 1978), I, 133-138, as well as Satan's remark (V, 678): "Both waking we were one."

6. Fowler's unhappiness with my conviction that "this kind of witcraft offers a phenomenalistic criterion for aesthetic evaluation" apparently arises from a misunderstanding of the word "offers." Of course, some "poetry with complex, ingenious, even subtle numerology may have little poetic merit" and "Good poets have been known to neglect . . . these elements successfully"; but when used metaphorically and well, rather than for mere contrivance, numerological composition can offer a criterion for evaluation of the artistry involved: it becomes another kind of phenomenalistic lexis. Reference here is to Fowler's *Triumphal Forms,* p. 99, and my "Some Literary Uses of Numerology," *Hartford Studies in Literature* 1 (1969) 50-62.

7. "The Center of *Paradise Lost.*"

8. *Counterpoint and Symbol,* pp. 158-166.

9. "Divine Providence and the Structure of *Paradise Lost.*" Fowler, in his edition of the poems, and Butler in *Number Symbolism* also subscribe to these symmetries and to the belief that a twelve-book division was planned from the start.

10. "Structural Pattern in *Paradise Lost,*" *Philological Quarterly* 28 (1949) 17-30.

11. Louis L. Martz, *Poet of Exile, A Study of Milton's Poetry* (New Haven: Yale University Press, 1980), chapter 9, pp. 155-168.

12. See Rymer's comments on the verse in *The Tragedies of the Last Age* (1678) and Dryden's in the preface to the translations from Juvenal (1693); *Milton: The Critical Heritage,* ed. John T. Shawcross (London: Routledge & Kegan Paul, 1970) [Vol. I], pp. 23 and 101-102.

13. Discussion of this crux in Miltonic scholarship with Joseph A. Wittreich has been most helpful and informative.

14. See my "Orthography and the Text of *Paradise Lost*" in *Language and Style in Milton,* ed. Ronald David Emma and John T. Shawcross (New York: Frederick Ungar, 1967), pp. 120-153.

CHAPTER SEVEN

1. One criticism that has been leveled against the Variorum Commentary of the Latin poems has been the listing of numerous references to classical literature, but the fault does not lie in the citation of such "sources," nor in the editor's, Douglas Bush's, not elaborating upon such citations. The fault, it seems to me, lies in the lack of attention that has generally been paid to such citations by those who have made them; an editor of a variorum volume should not be expected to supply discussion that does not already exist in print. Rather, most commentators have simply cited a source because of a language similarity, or at least they do not generally go beyond simple citation. I should have urged not omission of these citations in the Variorum but added information concerning the commentator(s) referencing the citation, for I put great weight in the fact that, say, John Upton or Merritt Y. Hughes has referred to a line or passage from Shakespeare but not that Edmund Malone or Alwin Thaler has. The Variorum citations should suggest to someone the need to study all these citations as meaningful

sources, for example, in a full and much-needed study of Milton and Homer, or of Milton and Vergil. An excellent study of this kind of indebtedness and meaningfulness in classical sources is Davis P. Harding's *The Club of Hercules* (Urbana: Univ. of Illinois Press, 1961).

2. Hume cited Rev. 20:3 for l. 966 ("And Seal thee so"), but further notation of the significance of the passage seems not to have been made. Most biblical parallels are cited by James H. Sims in *The Bible in Milton's Epics* (Gainesville, Fla.: Univ. of Florida Press, 1962).

3. A careful reader will have remembered the Angelic Chorus's references to the event in its account of the War in Heaven in III, 390-396, which in turn is coupled with the Son's future action as man. See also J.H. Adamson, "The War in Heaven: The Merkabah," in William B. Hunter, C.A. Patrides, and J.H. Adamson, *Bright Essence: Studies in Milton's Theology* (Salt Lake City: Univ. of Utah Press, 1971), pp. 103-114.

4. Isa. 40:12; Job 28:25, 37:16; 1 Sam. 2:3; Prov. 16:2; Dan. 5:26, 27, for ll. 997-999. Other cited biblical texts omitted here as language analogues primarily are Gen. 3:24 for l. 971; John 4:35b, Luke 22:31, Amos 9:13 for ll. 980-985; Job 26:7 for l. 1000; and Isa. 10:6 for l. 1010. It should be noted that ll. 999-1001 are a paraphrase of Gen. 1 conditioned by such texts as Job 26:7-8 and Isa. 40:12, God at the Creation weighing equal amounts of earth and air (cf. *PL*. VII, 233-242).

5. The Geneva Bible, like Milton, reads "[is] founde to light."

6. Other verbal citations have been Vergil's *Georgics* I, 226 (Keightley), for l. 984; *Aeneid* IV, 24-49 (Hughes), for l. 987; *Iliad* IV, 443, and *Aeneid* IV, 177 (Addison), for l. 988; *Aeneid* VII, 785 (Newton), for l. 989; and *Iliad* XV, 224 (Newton), for ll. 991-992. Douglas Bush (in *Complete Poetical Works* [Boston: Houghton, Mifflin, 1965]) referred to *Aeneid* XII, 661-952, for the full passage, and ll. 951-952 again specifically for Milton's ll. 1014-1015. He also compared *Aeneid* IX, 661-664, with ll. 980ff.

7. Sources from more recent literature, all merely verbal commonplaces, include Tasso, *Gerusalemme Liberata* XIX, 12 (Thyer), for l. 986; ibid. IV, 6, for l. 987; ser, *The Faerie Queene* II, vii, 23 (1-2) (Masson), for ll. 988-989; and three from Shakespeare, which are typical of these kinds of citations. Thomas Keightley's analogues for l. 989 show a similarity of language and attest to the commonplaceness of much of the language of any Renaissance poet. (See his edition *The Poems of John Milton with Notes* [London: Chapman and Hall, 1859], two vols.) I doubt that Milton had Shakespeare in mind in this line. Yet it is interesting to note that the situations out of which the lines from Shakespeare's *1 Henry IV* III, ii, 142; *Henry V* IV, v, 4-5; and *Richard III* V, iii, 351 come do have a kind of relationship. I assume that this is so because the language was commonly used for narratives of battle, actual or potential, prognosticating the outcome accurately or with ironic error. In *Paradise Lost*, the line indicates Satan's appearance as a potentially mighty and victorious opponent to the Angelic Squadron. The continuation of the episode, in terms of the scales, shows that this is only appearance rather than an accurate prognostication of victory (for his victory over Adam and Eve later is, for man, only an apparent victory in the full run of man's life). In the first instance from Shakespeare, Prince Hal is assuring his father that he will rise to the challenge that Hotspur presents and will appropriate to himself all those honors that now sit on Hotspur's helm when he is victor over the rebel. There seems little parallel with the situation here in Book IV; rather, this kind of consideration of Shakespeare's lines suggests that Prince Hal has affinities with the Son, Henry IV with God the Father, and Hotspur with Satan the rebellious. The second citation is spoken by the Dauphin as his forces are being routed, suggesting the way in which

one's war trappings take on symbolic meaning and attitude. For Satan, his appearance as an armed warrior symbolizes the horror which will succeed should he be victorious. The third reference is drawn from Richard III's false boast in the midst of being defeated: "Victory sits on our helms"; it leads him to pray, "Inspire us with the spleen of fiery dragons." In each of the Shakespeare language analogues, the lines are applied to those exhibiting wrong reason.

8. Gen. 3:15, for ll. 1031-1032; Gen. 3:16, John 16:21, Luke 1:42, for ll. 1050-1053; Gen. 3:19, for ll. 1054-1055; Gen. 3:21, for ll. 1058-1059; Ps. 34:5, 1 Pet. 3:12, Ps. 119:36, 112, for ll. 1060-1061; James 5:16a, 1 John 1:9, for ll. 1088-1089; Isa. 16:9, for ll. 1089-1090; Ps. 51:17, for l. 1091; Joel 2:13-14, Neh. 9:17, for ll. 1093-1096.

CHAPTER EIGHT

1. But see Charles T. Samuels, "The Tragic Vision in *Paradise Lost*," *University of Kansas City Review* 27 (1960) 65-78; Thomas Kranidas, "Adam and Eve in the Garden: A Study of *Paradise Lost*, Book V," *Studies in English Literature* 4 (1964) 71-83; and Gregory Ziegelmaier, "The Comedy of *Paradise Lost*," *College English* 26 (1965) 516-522, as well as Arnold Stein's view of "The War in Heaven" in *Answerable Style* (Minneapolis: Univ. of Minnesota Press, 1953), pp. 17-37. The more usual classification is seen in William P. Shaw's recent "Milton's Choice of the Epic for *Paradise Lost*," *English Language Notes* 12 (1974) 15-20, which depends upon the early forms of the poem as being tragedy and upon tragic elements in the finished work.

2. *The Enduring Monument: A Study of the Idea of Praise in Renaissance Literary Theory and Practice* (Chapel Hill: Univ. of North Carolina Press, 1962), pp. 88-92.

3. This suggests that the finished morality play would not have been tragic by generic mode, but comic; indeed, the true morality should not be catalogued into either type.

4. Hardison, *Enduring Monument*, p. 104.

5. See *Laughter: An Essay on the Meaning of the Comic*, trans. Clondesley Brereton and Fred Rothwell (New York: Macmillan, 1937).

6. Michael J. Lieb's examination of the antithetic patterns and reduplications of the poem in *The Dialectics of Creation* makes clear the geometric structures which I am here urging.

7. Allen R. Benham, "Things Unattemped Yet in Prose or Rime," *Modern Language Quarterly* 14 (1953) 341-347, emphasizes the chronological disorder and happiness of the ending that comes with the resurrection of man.

8. Dante, *A Translation of Dante's Eleven Letters*, trans. George R. Carpenter (New York, 1892), "Letter XI to Can Grande," p. 196.

9. Ibid., p. 195.

10. The reference in the invocation to Book IX to changing "Those Notes to Tragic" (l. 6), that is, to the disobedience of Adam and Eve, implies that the prior notes were not tragic. The tragedy lies only in their disobedience, not in the causes which have brought about their creation through the need to replace the fallen angels, nor in the promised incarnation and the Son's subsequent history. The tragedy of the future lies in man's imitating of his Grand Parents.

11. Typical comic effects that generations of readers seem to have missed are the three following: Rationalizing their act against godhead to Beelzebub (or rather to himself), Satan asks, "till then who knew / The force of those dire Arms?" (I, 93-94).

The answer is obviously everybody—everybody who believes in godhead, that is. There is no question at this point of false gods, whose omnipotence might only be mouthed. Or the word "dubious'" a few lines later, when Satan says, "His utmost power with adverse power oppos'd / In dubious Battel on the Plains of Heav'n, / And shook his throne" (I, 103-105). To Satan it means that the outcome of the battle was uncertain, and his "proof" is that God's throne was shaken on the second day when the rebellious angels discovered gunpowder and cannon and routed the faithful angels pitted against them. But we know that the point of this is that only equal forces were discharged against the rebels so that the first day was won by the faithful angels and the second by the unfaithful. Logically, the throne would not have been shaken had God sent a part of His other available forces or had He stepped in Himself as He does on the third day through the Son as agent. However, to God the word "dubious" would mean that the battle was meaningless since there was no doubt of its outcome. Satan's position as antihero in the sense that Dostoevsky's underground man is becomes crystal clear: he does not accept things as they are. Or a third example, which puts Satan's character into full focus, is the word "extort": "That Glory never shall his wrath or might / Extort from me" (I, 110-111). Godhead in any sense can not be viewed as "extorting" anything; it is a word applicable to Satan, who, in such psychologically valid details, sees things in terms of himself and his own motives.

12. "The Pattern at the Centre," *The Muse's Method*, p. 122.

13. I am in full agreement with Joseph A. Wittreich in *Angel of Apocalypse: Blake's Idea of Milton* (Madison: Univ. of Wisconsin Press, 1975), pp. 168-169, who reminds use that the "epic poem, from its very inception, was a mixture of genres," and cogently remarks that "*Paradise Lost* is a reassessment of all the genres it subsumes, and the reassessment involves an alteration, a perfection, of their ideologies, accompanied by a repudiation of their usual structures." The traditions of epic that are broken in *Paradise Lost* include the nature of the mixture of genres and the treatment of each kind.

14. For example, Dennis H. Burden's comments in *The Logical Epic: A Study of the Argument of Paradise Lost* (London: Routledge & Kegan Paul, 1967): "Book IX had dramatized an issue of literary theory: the Christian and satanic modes of tragedy and epic had been juxtaposed and discriminated. The Fall, seen in the proper way, is a model Christian tragedy: God is providential, and poetical justice is established" (pp. 180-181) and "Given Milton's concern with Christ as hero, it would be surprising if he did not make his account of the Redempton contribute to the literary contention of his poem. He develops it so as to achieve a nice paradox about the tragic and the epic. Michael's account to Adam of the coming of the Messiah is in the epic mode . . . and Adam accordingly proceeds to see Christ's fight with Satan in traditional (and hence wrong) epic terms . . ." (p. 197).

15. The term is specially chosen. Satan's aims and abilities are not simply noncreational, meaning that he wills to counter God's creation, but uncreational, meaning that his physical acts return creation to chaos. See II, 981-984, for a typical example of Satan's boast to "reduce" the region that Chaos has lost by God's creation of the Universe "to her original darkness." We should also note that Milton calls Bishop Hall and "the Arch evill one" "anticreator" in *Apology* (Yale Milton, I, 880-881). The Freudian overtones of all this are most important to an understanding of what is going on in the epic; see Michael Lieb's *Dialectics of Creation*.

We should also remark that the collocation of truth, justice, mercy, and peace, drawn from Psalm 85 which Milton translated in April, 1648, and earlier employed in stanza fifteen of "On the Morning of Christs Nativity," just past the central point of the Hymn, refers to the so-called four daughters of God. Allegorically, it was a means of describing the godhead as a unified trinal being: the truth of the Father, the justice of the Holy Spirit, and the mercy of the Son unite into God, who is peace.

16. Milton related the Son to Prometheus in his two-line poem on the inventor of gunpowder, but he made clear the superiority of the Son to his type. A study of the Promethean character in literature is sorely needed, primarily because of the false identification of Prometheus with Satan as rebels against the command of Zeus (God) rather than as the merciful son of God by a mortal woman, deliverer of mankind from travail when his gift is correctly used.

17. See the discussion of Merritt Y. Hughes, "The Christ of *Paradise Regained* and the Renaissance Heroic Tradition," *Ten Perspectives on Milton* (New Haven: Yale Univ. Press, 1965), pp. 35-62.

18. W.P. Ker, ed., *Essays of John Dryden* (Oxford: Clarendon Press, 1900), II, 89.

19. Compare the like conclusion of Stanley E. Fish in "The Harassed Reader in *Paradise Lost,*" p. 162: "Milton's method is to recreate in the mind of the reader (which is, finally, the poem's scene) the drama of the Fall, to make him fall exactly as Adam did, and with Adam's troubled clarity, that is to say, 'not deceived'."

20. These readings have not been totally eschewed today, and they lead to grave strictures on Milton's artistry. For example, analyze the three statements that follow. (1) To affirm his question "If the Fall is the great moral and theological turning-point of the poem, is it likewise the narrative climax?" (p. 316), H.V.S. Ogden remarked in "The Crisis of *Paradise Lost* Reconsidered": "The poem has now reached its great turning-point; the mortal sin has been completed [IX, 1000-1004]. The forward drive of the narrative no longer comes from our dread of a coming event but from our concern with the results of the Fall and from our desire for Adam's and Eve's reconciliation with God" (p. 321). (2) "And now suddenly, at the last moment, just when we might expect the final fall of the curtain, we are switched away to a panorama of scenes and events in which the previous actors do not figure at all, of which even Adam is only a spectator," and again, "This view [Prince's] may not, does not I think, remove the awkwardness in the placing of this long interlude or of our having to attend so belatedly to this crowded pageant of people and events outside the straight story" (B.A. Wright, *Milton's Paradise Lost* [London: Methuen, 1962], pp. 191, 192). In the text immediately preceding that quoted, Wright acknowledged that the matter of Books XI and XII is "essential to the argument" and approvingly quoted F.T. Prince's analysis ("On the Last Two Books of *Paradise Lost,*" *Essays and Studies* 11 [1958] 38-52). Contrary to Wright's conclusion that "in the main there is no falling off in the poetic interest" (p. 193), Louis L. Martz in his introduction to *Milton: A Collection of Critical Essays* (Englewood Cliffs, N.J.: Prentice-Hall, 1966), p. 10, iterates an evaluation he had expressed elsewhere: "But something goes wrong, I believe, in these closing books: the poetry flags, the vision of redemption wanes, a harsh and bitter tone gradually replaces the buoyant voice of the bard who has guided us through most of the poem. . . . Milton sees somehow to have lost touch with the creative center of his design." (3) "Book VI requires much less explication than the five that have preceded it. It is largely straightforward narration, involving almost no philosophical or theological problems," according to Marjorie Hope Nicolson (*John Milton: A Reader's Guide to His Poetry* [New York: Farrar, Straus & Giroux, 1963], p. 255), and she adds, "This does not mean that there are not great passages in Book VI. . . . But the greatness of the passage [VI, 748-773] comes not from Milton's narrative art but from his poetic genius. For the most part, the battles in Heaven seem fought by glorified tin soldiers" (p. 257).

21. Cf. Roger B. Rollin's well-argued conclusion that "*Paradise Lost* is more than a highly dramatic poem; it is an epic built of dramas; an enclyclopedic work composed

of three distinct yet interlocking plots, each of which approximates the theoretic form of a different genre of Renaissance drama" (*Paradise Lost:* 'Tragical-Comical-Historical-Pastoral,' " *Milton Studies* 5 [1973] 3). To these three plots, Rollin adds a fourth dramatic form, the monodrama of Milton the narrator.

CHAPTER NINE

1. *Milton's Grand Style* (Oxford: Clarendon Press, 1963), p. 24.

2. Harold Toliver investigated this range of decorum in "Complicity of Voice in *Paradise Lost,*" *Modern Language Quarterly* 25 (1964) 153-170. He remarked, "Insofar as each level of Milton's hierarchy is distinct, it has its own mode of being and its own rhetoric," but the difference of his concern from mine is evident when he writes: "The difficulty of communicating among levels (in the language of man before and after the Fall, the language of angels, and so forth) is involved in the difficulty of knowing one's unequals. . . . Satan's evil is an undermining of the accuracy of language and as self-willed creation of new places and names. . . . [O]ne of Milton's aims in *Paradise Lost* is to discover a style that can recite in all the tongues the glory of a single word" (p. 154). See also Louis L. Martz, *The Paradise Within* (New Haven: Yale Univ. Press, 1964), pp. 183ff. John M. Steadman, in "Demetrius, Tasso, and Stylistic Variation in *Paradise Lost,*" *English Studies* 47 (1966) 329-341, likewise indicates the varieties of styles Milton used in his poem. Such variation reflects the emphasis that rhetoric and poetics placed on the subject matter as an index of character and meaning.

3. This is a metaphoric statement of the return of all substance to the single substance which is God, who had created all things out of Himself.

4. Compare the conclusion of Peter Berek in " 'Plain' and 'Ornate' Styles and the Structure of *Paradise Lost,*" *PMLA* 85 (1970) 237-246, who shows that the Father speaks in the simple unambiguous voice of truth, that Satan speaks in the superficially attractive but deceiving voice of fine rhetoric, and that Adam and Eve change in their use of language as an expression of truth before the Fall, as a means of questioning the relationship between words and truth after the Fall, and as a reminder of the style of the Son after their reconciliation with God. The Son's speeches in Book III "bridge the gap between nearly unimaginable perfection and human imperfections" (p. 242); his language parodies false heroism, yet he also furnishes the language appropriate to faithful self-sacrifice (p. 243).

5. See Arnold Stein's essay in *Answerable Style* (Minneapolis: Univ. of Minnesota Press, 1953), p. 121.

6. Ibid., pp. 136-137.

7. All but James Whaler's discussion in *Counterpoint and Symbol* of Milton's prosody, it seems to me, have been inadequate because of their reliance on standard English syllabification. As my further remarks imply, I believe that we must also take into account the verse paragraph and its relationship to thought, to stresses, and to shifting patterns of primary, secondary, and tertiary stress. I believe that what Milton has worked out is a prosody that works in two ways, not really dissimilarly to the warping and woofing of structure through balance and parallelism. The prosody works line by line, with contrast between lines, but more importantly, it also works in groups of lines welding the whole together to sustain the complete thought being expressed. All this demands a different kind of oral reading from that which the poem has usually received.

8. *Four Stages of Renaissance Style* (Garden City, N.Y.: Anchor, 1955), passim.

9. "Architectonic Structure in *Paradise Regained*," *Texas Studies in English* 33 (1954) 45.

10. *Milton: Mannerism and Baroque,* passim.

CHAPTER TEN

1. *Paradise Lost as "Myth,"* pp. 41-42.

2. G. van der Leeuw, *Religion in Essence and Manifestation: A Study of Phenomenology* (New York: Harper, 1963), II, 413-414.

3. It can not be too strongly stressed that the Son *is* God. Satan, of course, forgets this when the Son is "begotten" and critics of Milton's God forget this too. The Father and the Son are aspects of God, and Milton differentiates them not only as purveyors of truth and mercy but in character, concern, omniscience, omnipotence, and omnipresence, and stylistically. I do not imply an anti-Trinitarian position for Milton; the differentiation is part of a doctrine called subordinationism. The Son represents those aspects of God which can be assigned to the mother archetype and thus partakes of the standards of male-female relationship.

4. Where the myth has been accommodated to latter-day form rather than offered archetypally, readers seem to have no difficulty. A case in point is Joseph Conrad's adaptation of Sin and Death in Book II in *Heart of Darkness,* where the two knitters sit in the waiting-room of the trading company, whose offices Marlow must enter after signing some document in order to receive his assignment enabling him to look upon darkness bare.

CHAPTER ELEVEN

1. Harold Fisch has recently noted that the story of Adam, Eve, and the serpent "is felt to have reference to the most 'epical' of all biblical stories, the Exodus from Egypt. It is notable that Rashi prefaces his comment on Genesis I:1 with the remark, no doubt strange to Christian readers of *Paradise Lost,* that the justification for beginning the Scriptures with the Creation and the doings of Adam and Eve is that this is the necessary preliminary to the Exodus and the Conquest of Canaan"; see "Hebraic Style and Motifs in *Paradise Lost,*" *Language and Style in Milton,* ed. Ronald David Emma and John T. Shawcross (New York: Frederick Ungar, 1967), p. 38. Implied is a relationship between the expulsion and the Exodus. Mother Mary Christopher Pecheux has pointed out that "the reiterated references to Abraham throughout Michael's prophecy [in Books XI and XII] function as a device to show the symbolic unity of the wanderings of the Chosen People and of the human race. The Exodus from Egypt itself, the greatest of all these journeys, is associated with both the past and the future: first with Abraham . . . (XII, 258-260) and then with the Savior . . . (XII, 313-314)"; see "Abraham, Adam, and the Theme of Exile in *Paradise Lost,*" *PMLA* 80 (1965), 371.

2. Again, compare Satan's address to Chaos in II, 981ff.

3. Compare Milton's argument in *Areopagitica* (London, 1644): "that which purifies us is triall, and triall is by what is contrary" (p. 12).

4. *Order and History,* Vol. I of *Israel and Revelation* (Baton Rouge, La.: Louisiana State Univ. Press, 1956), p. 113.

5. I am greatly indebted to Christine Downing for many theological concepts underlying this thesis. Downing's exacting view of the exodus myth can be found in "How Can We Hope and Not Dream? Exodus as Metaphor: A Study of the Biblical Imagination," *Journal of Religion* 48 (1968), 35-53.

6. *Order and History*, p. 114.

7. Closest to my view for *Paradise Lost* is the discussion of Mother Mary Christopher Pecheux: "the exile motif is harmonized with the concept of the journey of the epic hero. The virtues of Abraham are precisely those which Abraham as Christian hero is called upon to practice, while both Abraham's setting forth to the land of Canaan and Adam's exile from Paradise are types of . . . the Christian wayfarer, moving slowly but always with confidence towards the heavenly Jerusalem which awaits him in the dim future" ("Abraham, Adam, and the Theme of Exile," pp. 365, 371).

8. *Order and History*, p. 113.

9. James H. Sims, *The Bible in Milton's Epics*, pp. 259-273.

10. James Whaler, "The Miltonic Simile," *PMLA* 46 (1931), 1047, has demonstrated the patristic identification of Pharaoh and Satan. John M. Steadman, "The Devil and Pharaoh's Chivalry," *MLN* 75 (1960) 197-201, going beyond Whaler, shows that the destruction of the Egyptian army was equated with the punishment of the rebel angels, that the Red Sea was a type of the fiery lake of Hell, and that the immersion of Pharaoh's army symbolized baptism (and this we can read as a stage in time when a new beginning will again occur) and also the Day of Judgment (implying a relationship that I have here urged). Sims equates Satan and his cohorts in Book VI with Pharaoh and his host (p. 224), and Fisch, "Hebraic Style and Motifs," p. 39, besides noting like identifications, calls the "Chrystal wall of Heav'n, which op'ning wide, / Rowl'd inward, and a spacious Gap disclos'd / Into the wastful Deep" (VI, 860-862) at the expulsion of the rebel angels from Heaven the same as the two crystal walls of the Red Sea in Michael's vision (XII, 197).

11. "The serpent, too, becomes likened with the serpent which Moses miraculously produced before Pharaoh (Exodus 7:9), with Pharaoh himself, and with the fiery serpents which beset the Israelites in the wilderness (Numbers 21: 6-7)," Fisch, "Hebraic Style and Motifs," p. 39.

12. Compare V, 479-500, also with later remarks on the "degrees" or stages by which successive exoduses will achieve purification of heart and lead to reunion with God.

13. *Order and History*, p. 113.

14. "Hebraic Style and Motifs," p. 50.

15. See Fletcher, ed. *Milton's Complete Poetical Works*, IV, 10.

16. Although we cannot explore the mirror activities of Satan in this chapter, we can mention one explicit parody of the theme of exodus. When Satan returns to Hell in Book X to tell of his bad success (and also of the judgment upon the fallen angels), he boasts,

> Thrones, Dominations, Princedoms, Vertues, Powers,
> For in possession such, not onely of right,
> I call ye and declare ye now, returnd
> Successful beyond hope, to lead ye forth
> Triumphant out of this infernal Pit
> Abominable, accurst, the house of woe,
> And Dungeon of our Tyrant: Now possess,
> As Lords, a spacious World, t' our native Heav'n
> Little inferiour, by my adventure hard
> With peril great atchiev'd.
>
> (X, 460-469)

As he ends expansively, "What remains, ye Gods, / But up and enter now into full bliss" (X, 502-503), the devils transform with a hiss of strident sounds into all manner of reptilian beasts.

In like fashion, Milton built his poem on such antithetic concepts as have been discussed. The "paradise within" (XII, 587) is the obverse of Satan's "hell within" (IV, 20). The way in which the hell within is intensified is the reverse of Adam and Eve's story: Satan leaves Hell behind on purpose only to internalize Hell through successive acts of disobedience and fraud. See Michael Lieb's *Dialectics of Creation* for a full discussion of such mirror imagery.

17. Some while ago, Ruth Mohl argued that the theme of *Paradise Lost* is the making of the greater man; see *Studies in Spenser, Milton, and the Theory of Monarchy* (reprinted, New York, 1962). She wrote, "so far as Milton was concerned, the term *the greater Man* was by no means limited to Christ. To him all mankind were 'sons of God,' capable of becoming better, nobler beings" (p. 83); "To him, apparently, the way to produce finer human beings is not to belittle them but rather to insist on their divine origin, their great capacities for intellectual and spiritual development, and, above all, their ability, in the light of knowledge and right reason, to know and love and obey and humbly walk with God. Such men are 'greater men,' well on their way toward 'perfection.' But there are other greater men as well: those who, having fallen, repent and regain right reason and are restored to their oneness with God. . . . Adam at the close of *Paradise Lost,* is such a 'greater man,' for he, too, has 'regained Paradise' and thus restored the possibility of happiness for all mankind (p. 85).

18. George Herbert's "The Altar" is built on the equation of stone and heart, and should be read against the background of the hardened heart.

19. See Lieb, *Dialectics of Creation,* pp. 229-244, for a full exploration of alchemical imagery in the poem.

20. Note, for example, the oxymoronic and infernal parody of the "burning lake," Milton's version of the fire and ice of Hell, and of the river Phlegethon (the Red Sea), too), which winds its way through the Wood of the Suicides.

21. The words are Laurie Zwicky's ("Kairos in *Paradise Regained:* The Divine Plan," *ELH* 31 [1964] 271) for the meaning of cyclic time. See also C.A. Patrides' discussion of "The Phoenix and the Ladder: Gentiles and Jews" in *The Grand Design of God: The Literary Form of the Christian View of History* (London: Routledge & Kegan Paul, 1972), pp. 1-12.

22. References to the final day in Books VI and XII emphasize the cause and effect of judgment; those in Books III and X, the hope for man which the pyramidic structure implies.

CHAPTER TWELVE

1. *Revaluation* (London: Chatto & Windus, 1949), p. 59.

2. I hasten to remark my admiration for both Pound's and Eliot's poetry, but over and over again I find their criticism of various authors uninformed and invalidly prejudiced.

3. *The Romantics on Milton: Formal Essays and Critical Asides* (Cleveland: Press of Case Western Reserve Univ., 1970).

4. *Paradise Lost and Its Critics* (Cambridge: Harvard Univ. Press, 1947), pp. 17-19.

5. "Criticism and the Milton Controversy," *The Living Milton,* ed. Frank Kermode (London: Routledge & Kegan Paul, 1960), p. 174.

6. *Some Graver Subject* (London: Chatto & Windus, 1960), pp. 223-224.

7. *A Critique of Paradise Lost* (New York: Columbia Univ. Press, 1960), p. 22.

8. I refer to Freudian terminology, not to such loose and erroneous language as calling Satan an "egotist."

9. See Georg Lukács, *Die Theorie des Romans* (Berlin: Paul Cassirer, 1920), and Lucien Goldmann, *Pour une sociologie du roman* (Paris: Gallimard, 1964).

CHAPTER THIRTEEN

1. "A Metaphoric Approach to Reading Milton," *Ball State University Forum* 8 (1967), 17-21.

2. This point is made decisively well by Stanley E. Fish in *Surprised By Sin*, pp. 107-130. Full lexical study of *Paradise Lost*, as suggested in the present chapter, will yield further corroborative meaning for the poem and indicate iteratively an author's artistic control.

3. See I, 5, 383, 634; II, 76, 347, 394, 1050; III, 527, 632, 669 (2), 724; IV, 247, 371; V, 756; VI, 27, 226, 273; VII, 141, 329, 623; VIII, 299; IX, 100, 153; X, 85, 614; XI, 82, 148, 343, 575; XII, 457, 642.

4. See also VI, 197, 644; VIII, 42, 557, 590; XI, 418.

5. See Michael J. Lieb's notes in *The Dialectics of Creation*, pp. 108-110, 232.

6. Compare Sin's remark to her father, "henceforth Monarchie with thee divide / Of all things, parted by th' Empyreal bounds, / His Quadrature, from thy Orbicular World" (X, 379-381).

7. See also I, 181, 383, 467, 796, and X, 237, 424. This pejorative usage in ordinary terms occurs in I, 720 (a verb); II, 674, 931; and XI, 386, 388, 407, 408.

8. See, in the first instance, II, 139, 243, 359, 456, 731; III, 57, 315, 376; IV, 829; V, 156; VI, 671, 892; IX, 164; and in the second, II, 54, 56, 164, 329, 377, 803, 907, and X, 235, 421.

9. See IV, 837; V, 807; VI, 489, 592, 593, 801 (2); VII, 23; VIII, 640 (2).

10. See III, 693; IV, 837; VI, 270, 627; VII, 509, 632; and VIII, 260.

11. Theodore H. Banks's nonliterary approach to imagery totally sidesteps any real significance of metaphoric statement; for example, he wrote: "It is worth remarking that mist is not black, nor lightning red, but aside from these inaccuracies his sense of color seems normal" (*Milton's Imagery* [New York: Columbia Univ. Press, 1950], p. 127). Milton uses black in a moral sense, as Banks does note (p. 126); the black mist of IX, 180, a simile for Satan creeping through thickets, tells us that all unclarity of vision is associated with or is a result of evil. Compare the hovering of black clouds in the poem, which otherwise would have been imaged as bringing necessary rain from God, or, that is, mercy, under other circumstances. In the second example of *red* given, note the pun on "arming" God's "hand"; "right hand" by itself implies great strength.

12. We find it thus alluded to in I, 287; II, 1053; III, 459, 726; IV, 606, 648, 655, 723, 798, 978; V, 42, 175, 263, 418, 421; VII, 104, 356, 375; VIII, 142, 149; X, 656; XII, 266.

13. See also IV, 497; V, 56, 131; VII, 323, 466; IX, 841.

14. See also V, 215, 344, 427, 635; VII, 320. The reference in I, 410, is rather bland, though it does concern itself with the fallen world.

15. Mario Di Cesare, "Advent'rous Song: The Texture of Milton's Epic," in *Language and Style in Milton*, ed. Ronald David Emma and John T. Shawcross (New York: Frederick Ungar, 1967), p. 1.

APPENDIX

1. See John T. Shawcross, "One Aspect of Milton's Spelling: Idle Final 'E'," *PMLA* 78 (1963) 501-510, esp. n. 6 on p. 503.

2. John Aubrey, "Minutes of the Life of Mr. John Milton," ed. Helen Darbishire

in *The Early Lives of Milton* (London: Constable, 1932), p. 13. His words are: "In the ~~2d or 3d~~ 4th Booke of Paradise lost, there are about 6 verses of Satan's exclamation to the Sun, wch Mr E. Ph. remembers, about 15 or 16 yeares before ever his Poem was thought of, wch verses were intended for the Beginning of a Tragoedie wch he had designed, but was diverted from it by other businesse." Aubrey thought the poem to have been begun "about 2 yeares before the K. came-in," since he also reported this information from Phillips (p. 13). References to Aubrey and Phillips are to Darbishire's edition.

3. Darbishire, *Early Lives,* pp. 72-73.

4. Thomas Ellwood, *The History of the Life of Thomas Ellwood* (London, 1714), pp. 233-234.

5. See "The Chronology of Milton's Private Studies," *PMLA* 36 (1921) 251-314, reprinted in *John Milton, Poet and Humanist,* ed. John S. Diekhoff (Cleveland: Press of Case Western Reserve Univ., 1966), pp. 75-125. References are to the reprint.

6. See her edition of *A Commonplace Book* in *The Complete Prose Works of John Milton* (New Haven: Yale Univ. Press, 1953), gen. ed. Don M. Wolfe (Vol. I of Yale Prose), pp. 476n. and 507-508n.

7. See Hanford, "Chronology," p. 102.

8. Approximate times when Milton might have devoted himself to what became *Paradise Lost* could have been: 1641, August-December; 1642, May-December; 1643, January-June, September-December; 1644, March-May, September-October, December; 1645, April-December; 1646-1648; 1652-1658, except for around April-May, 1654, and July-August, 1655; 1661-1665. I enumerate these periods to point out that there was extensive time when we do not know all that Milton was working on or doing. I do not say that he was working on *Paradise Lost* during all of these times. Periods omitted are those when he would have been writing works that are datable, although, of course, he might not have devoted all this time during those periods to those datable works. During the periods enumerated Milton faced certain family and personal problems, was tutoring (through 1647 approximately), was writing *The History of Britain* and probably other uncertainly dated prose and poetry (e.g., *A Brief History of Moscovia*), and was engaged in some governmental work (1652-1658). Yet, the 154 months before 1660 (twelve years and ten months), even reduced by the activities, possible writing, and concerns suggested, allow much possible time in long enough continuous periods for a substantial amount of intermittent composition and planning.

9. This, of course, agrees with Phillips's comment (see note 2 above) and with a frequent interpretation of Milton's remarks in the addendum to *Defensio prima* published in October, 1658: "I am earnestly seeking how best I may show not only my own country, to which I devoted all I have, but men of every land and, particularly, all Christian men, that for their sake I am at this time hoping and planning still greater things, if these be possible for me, as with God's help they will" (p. 171; quoted from the Yale Prose, ed. William J. Grace and trans. Donald MacKenzie, IV, i [1966], p. 537).

10. *On the Composition of Paradise Lost.* (Chapel Hill: Univ. of North Carolina Press, 1947).

11. See ibid., pp. 152-155.

12. "Milton's Blank Verse and the Chronology of His Major Poems," in South Atlantic Modern Language Association, *Studies in Milton,* ed. J. Max Patrick (Gainesville: Univ. of Florida Press, 1953), pp. 128-197. His argument suggests fairly steady composition from Book I through Book XII, plus revision.

13. Of course, any technique may be used because desirable for a specific effect or for a specific reason (e.g., the rhymed, end-stopped verse of *Hudibras* or the heroic

couplet). There is no such effect or reason observable, however, for Milton's three major poems, except perhaps for the use of feminine endings in dramatic work like *Samson Agonistes*. However, see my discussion of a possibly different base of scansion for the tragic poem, one which would not include feminine or masculine endings: "The Prosody of Milton's Fifth Ode of Horace," *Tennessee Studies in Literature* 13 (1968) 81–89.

14. I use Oras's criterion: those lines which have no punctuation at the end of the line are considered run-on. I report statistics from the 1673 printing of *Poems*, except for Sonnets 15, 16, 17, and 22, for which I use the copies in the Trinity MS, the first in Milton's hand, the next two in John Phillips's hand, and the last in Cyriack Skinner's hand. Certainly there may be discrepancies between manuscript and print in such matters as punctuation, and Oras's criterion is thus not fully reliable. Involved are the several degrees of juncture which English employs, too complex a matter for detailed consideration here. Nonetheless, the presence or absence of a mark of punctuation may serve as a rough guide for analysis.

15. Omitted are Ps. 3,23; 6,18; 8,8, which show no punctuation but which clearly are strongly stopped. I have also not counted Sonnet 17, ll. 8, 12, 13, which likewise have no punctuation, though they should.

16. The differences between Sonnets 16-23 and Psalms 1-8, and their similar dates, yield evidence for this point.

17. For example, I do not credit the use of the syllabized ending "-ed" as a significant test, for Milton regularly spelled the preteritive form with "-ed" when the root word ends with the sound of [d] or [t], and when it had adjectival force; that is, when it appeared *before* the noun it modified only. (See my unpublished dissertation, "Milton's Spelling: Its Biographical and Critical Implications," New York University [1958], p. 45.) The form appears often in the prose and is not just a prosodic device. Chronologically, its appearance is meaningless; for instance, *The Tenure of Kings and Magistrates* (written in January, 1649) has two examples of the sonant "-ed" with adjectival force and *Eikonoklastes* (written by October, 1649) has thirty-one examples. In percentages, this is one occurrence in 21 pages in *Tenure*, but one occurrence in 7.1 pages in *Eikonoklastes*. Milton never used the "-ed" form on a participle appearing after the noun modified; he regularly used it before the modified noun. This is true of prose (where no syllabification is in question for proper scansion since there is no scansion) as well as poetry, except that in poetry, because of the demands of meter, the ending is sometimes not syllabized on participles placed before the substantive (that is, he used "-d," "-'d," "-t," "-'t," or monosyllabic "-ied" or "-eed"). Its use is clearly not chronological. But compare Oras's discussion of the matter in *Blank Verse and Chronology in Milton* (University of Florida Monographs, Humanities, No. 20, 1966).

18. We need remember only the way in which budding young so-called poets write (when the unit is not simply the line) and the way a more experienced and "truer" poet writes.

19. "The Chronology of Milton's Major Poems," *PMLA* 76 (1961) 345-358.

Index